Tomato, Fig & Pumpkin Jelly

Lisa Rose Wright

Tomato, Fig & Pumpkin Jelly
Copyright © Lisa Rose Wright 2021

The right of Lisa Rose Wright to be identified as the author of this work has been asserted by her in accordance with the Copyright Designs and Patents Act 1988

All rights reserved. No part of this publication may be reproduced, transmitted, or stored in a retrieval system in any form or by any means, without permission in writing of the author.

*Any queries please contact me at
lisarosewright@msn.com*

*Cover design by Maayan Atias at
spacecadetstudio@yahoo.com
All photographs © Lisa Rose Wright*

ISBN: 9798593931610

For S
Consiento, ahora y siempre

Author's note:

Welcome to the second book of our adventures in beautiful green Galicia. All of our adventures in here are true... honest! S often has a slightly different version of the truth to me – in many things. But, this is my memoir and therefore events happened as *I* remember them... most of the time. The letters home are real, though some have been abridged as I'm sure no-one wants to hear about cousin Jane's haemorrhoids. (Not that she has any, nor that I have a cousin Jane but you know what I mean.)

Every person and animal in this book is also real although a few names have been changed or omitted to protect the innocent, the shy, or the guilty: you decide which!

Lisa

I hope you enjoy this second volume of our adventures in Galicia. If you are curious about this place we call home and would like to see more, just download my free photo album which accompanies this book.
https://www.flipsnack.com/65E9E6B9E8C/tomato-fig-pumpkin-jelly-the-album.html

Or follow me on my facebook page: http://www.facebook.com/lisarosewright.author

CONTENTS

CONTENTS 7
PROLOGUE..1
SPRING IN GALICIA...................................5
AUGUST 31
SEPTEMBER..54
OCTOBER 77
NOVEMBER..102
DECEMBER..126
JANUARY 150
FEBRUARY...176
MARCH 200
APRIL...224
MAY 248
JUNE..272
JULY 296
AUGUST 319
THE STORY CONTINUES 345
THE RECIPES 348
A GLOSSARY OF ENGLISH WORDS....366
ACKNOWLEDGEMENTS 370
ABOUT THE AUTHOR: 371

PROLOGUE
February 2009

As I boiled the kettle on the wood-burning range cooker for a wash, I pondered on how different our new life was here in Galicia compared to our old life in England. Some might say primitive, I preferred rustic.

We had first seen our Galician home on a rainswept November morning two years and three months ago. Ever since we moved in we had been battling to renovate the house, keep ourselves fed from the allotment, and untangle ourselves from yards of Spanish red tape. It was an uphill battle at times but strangely fun.

A Casa do Campo is a large granite stone farmhouse, around 200 years old, basically square in plan-view with stout stone internal walls forming a cross. The house is built directly onto the bedrock of the hillside on which it sits. Around the property on three sides are gardens, fruit and nut trees, and vines. Across a sunken track to the east of the house is my 1500m^2 allotment or *huerta.*

The *huerta* itself had now been dug over to approximately half its length. I had had bumper crops the previous year; of courgettes and beans, potatoes and peppers. Growing my crops in Galicia was a sharp learning curve. I had lost virtually all my tomatoes to blight that first year and mice or moles, or 'the beast' or 'the monster' as I variously named my nemesis, had munched their way through fully

PROLOGUE

half of my leeks. The fruit trees luckily cropped well without any outside help, and we had shelves groaning with jams and jellies, chutneys and bottled fruits. My large cool barn below the house was also full – of walnuts, potatoes, and onions. I had many plans for the coming year and ideas for much needed water conservation and storage.

From the village road the house looks like a squat single storey cottage. The kitchen and storeroom are on this level. As the land drops away at the rear, three further storerooms appear on the lower ground floor. Above these, and four steps up from the kitchen level, are the rooms which form our main living and sleeping area.

On that first November morning the house had been a wreck. Everywhere smelt musty and uncared for. The concrete kitchen floor was swimming with water where the rain leaked in through the rotten and blackened beams above. Upstairs, the ceiling had collapsed in one room and the holes in the old chestnut floorboards beneath, mirrored the ones in the roof above. There was a bird's nest in the bedroom and bats roosting throughout the house. The dismal old, tiny bathroom had no running water to it and no sewerage system from the outlet pipe, which emptied alarmingly onto a very healthy looking apple tree below. Our proposed double height 'big barn' was literally that, a cow shed full of 12 year old cow pats (good for the allotment). And the room where I was to have my preserves and winter stores had last housed rabbits.

The allotment was completely overgrown after 12 years of abandonment and the whole place had an air of dereliction, as if it would disappear back into the landscape at any moment. It was love at first sight.

It had taken us a frustrating six months to complete the paperwork to buy *A Casa do Campo.* There had been deaths, taxes, and an enforced change of estate agent along the way. We then had an even more frustrating three months in England before we could leave our jobs as newt-catchers (or correctly titled, ecologists) translocating protected amphibians and instead relocate ourselves to this beautiful green oasis in the far northwest corner of Spain.

Eventually, after what had seemed to be a lifetime of waiting, we were on our way.

Our worldly goods for the first few weeks of living *casa nosotros* were packed into our ageing Ford Escort, and we waddled along the road from the north of England towards Portsmouth. We arrived at *A Casa do Campo* (literally the house of the field, or country house) on a blisteringly hot August morning and immediately set about fixing up an inflatable mattress, gas stove, outdoor washing area, and night bucket for our immediate needs. Using that bathroom was not even a passing consideration.

That had all been 18 months ago, and as I looked around the warm and cosy kitchen I remembered all the hard work we had put in so far and all the tears and laughter the house had seen since we arrived. We had made many new friends in our adopted country, and our Spanish had improved in fits and starts with the help of our wonderful neighbours and friends in our local tiny market town of Taboada (population 3000).

I was proud of the fact that with virtually no outside help the two of us, me and my partner, best friend and blue-eyed prince, S, had begun to create a real home for ourselves.

The first year we had put in a brand new sewerage system and septic tank, connected to a genuine working toilet (an exciting moment); dug what seemed like an endless acreage of weed strewn allotment for our crops; cleared mountains of junk and old x-rays (don't ask) from the upstairs

PROLOGUE

rooms; and begun to renovate the entire 250m^2 pantile roof.

We completed the roof, for which we had a well-deserved celebration, almost a year later in September 2008. By the end of that same year we also had our comfortable bedroom on the west side of the house with a new sweet chestnut wood floor, a renovated, cleaned and polished sweet chestnut boarded ceiling, and a stunning view of the water mill on the river below us through our nice new double glazed window.

We had created a rather large bathroom from one of the upstairs bedrooms, which we had managed to get plumbed in and useable in time for Mum's Christmas visit the previous December when she had stayed at the house with us for the first time. Oddly, although the bathroom was fully functioning we didn't use it all that much.

The big double bath I had loved so much was, frankly, too big to fill. The hot water tank ran cold after around two inches of water, and the room was rather chill most of the year due to the 70 centimetre thick stone walls and a distinct lack of heating in that end of the house. Sitting in a few inches of rapidly cooling water wasn't that appealing. The few times we had used the bath we'd had to boil two kettles on the wood-burning range cooker (or *cocina*) to top it up. Even then it was only half full. It also seemed one heck of a waste of water.

In summer, our outdoor hosepipe shower was wonderful: a hosepipe was attached to our well, filled with water, then left in the sun for 30 minutes. Result, a hosepipe length of scalding water, all for free. In the winter, the kettles were always hot on the *cocina* and the kitchen was always toasty warm.

I had started using the new bathroom in the evenings to do my nightly ablutions, though S still continued to clean his teeth by the light of the stars in the garden. I rather envied him somehow.

SPRING IN GALICIA
Proposals

"D'you think we should just get married then?" asked S, apropos of nothing, over the breakfast table one morning.

"That's romantic darling," I replied, peering over the top of my eggy soldiers. "I thought you were going to adopt me."

"I don't think adopting a 44 year old would work."

I pondered this news for a couple of seconds. Neither of us had considered matrimony before. Then I had a brainwave.

"Do you think we could do it here, in Galicia?" I asked, warming to my theme. "We could have a party in Taboada, invite everyone?"

I was suddenly enthused. Marriage may be an institution, but a party – now there's a thing!

§

This conversation wasn't really out of the blue. And it may not even have gone quite how I've written it. I'm pretty sure S didn't actually propose as such – but a girl needs a little romance.

I had, for some reason, been looking into Spanish wills and the subject of inheritance taxes had come up. In Spain, the exemption threshold for inheritance tax was only 16,000€. Way lower than in Britain, where we wouldn't even have to be thinking

SPRING IN GALICIA

about inheritance taxes. Moreover, that exemption threshold only applied to legal spouses, children, parents, or siblings of the deceased. For non-relatives, including live-in partners, inheritance tax of 10% was due on all of the inheritance from the very first euro. Additionally, if one left one's share of any property to one's spouse or children (but again not common-law partner) then most autonomous communities allowed a 95% reduction in inheritance dues, providing said inheritor continued to live in the property for ten years. Now that was a good reason to get wed! Anyway, I figured it would be simple enough. I would pop into the town hall and sort it out that week.

Diary Monday 2nd March Sunny with a cool breeze Popped into the town hall to find out what we need to get married. Very helpful chap in the Xulgado de Paz, or Justice of the Peace office, called Manuel. He didn't see any problems. Gave us a form explaining what documents are needed, then we have to go to the main registry (of births, marriages and deaths) to complete the paperwork. See, I knew it would be simple.

Email from Wardell's saying probably no UK newt monitoring job this year due to budget restrictions. Ordered the floorboards for the two middle rooms from Imoltasa in Lugo and paid the deposit through the bank. Bought a sack of seed potatoes for planting. S continued cementing the hórreo roof whilst I plastered the archway to the upstairs hall (not terribly well it has to be said).

Tuesday 3rd March. Sunshine. Heavy frost overnight
Dear Mum,
 Typical! Now we have booked our ferry for April, three lots of newt work have fallen

through. Steve told me last week that his client in Suffolk had pulled out, and now the monitoring job at March (the place in Cambridgeshire, not the month haha) has been cancelled. The company say they don't have enough work for their own staff so won't need any freelancers this year. Asked PAA if they needed us at Corby or Stansted but they think not!

Oh well! It means more time to see you which is always good. And more time to visit everyone. And, as we are bringing the car, we can load up with goodies like walnuts and sun dried tomatoes and chorizos and then take home the essentials like real ale and marmite!

Forgot to tell you when I rang, we had a lovely time at the pig bone stew fair (festa do caldo de ósos) in Taboada. We booked a table at Bar Mencia again. There were 8 of us. Cris and Steve came down from Ortigueira and stayed over with us. We moved back into our ex-bedroom, or the sunroom as it is now officially known, so C&S could have the proper bed. It's lovely and warm in there with the morning sun coming through the picture windows. It's so bright we were up by 9am most days! No wonder you were up so early at Christmas (Oh I remember, you weren't haha).

It was so warm and sunny on the Sunday that we all sat outside on my newly mowed back lawn after our meal, drinking tea and

SPRING IN GALICIA

(in Richard and Steve's case) eating cookies. They are both skinny as rakes. Don't know where they put it!

We had a bit of an incident with Steve and Cris' dogs as I had stupidly left brown bunny outside, in the ark, which S made, whilst we were at lunch. It looked like one of the dogs had gone for her. She is fine but was a bit scared and had lost a claw... fighting back no doubt. Both dogs were in trouble of course, though it wasn't their fault. At least it showed S' design for the ark is a good one!

CJ didn't make it to the bone fair but he did call over to help S cut up some huge logs from the old chestnut tree and give him a chainsaw lesson. The huge chainsaw looks like a toy in CJ's blacksmith's hands whereas it makes S look like a Lilliputian!

S has been reroofing the hórreo (grain store) as some of the tiles had slipped on the track side. It's a tricky roof as it is very steep (and a long drop on the far side!) Don't worry he's being careful... I keep reminding him every minute or two as you are not here to do so!!

As the hórreo looked so nice with its newly done roof I decided to paint the cockerel weathervane which sat on the top. He looks very regal in white, gold and red, a bit like our own Buzz Lightyear.

Talking of chickens, Number Two is behaving very oddly, spending hours sitting *on the nest box and clucking madly whenever I go near. I wonder if she has gone broody? I thought hybrid hens are not supposed to.*

We are cracking on with the flooring for the two middle rooms upstairs. José from Xesteira, the construction yard, delivered the chipboard for the sub-floor just before the fiesta and we managed to get a temporary floor in the hallway for Cris and Steve so they didn't have to hop across the beams. S is busy cutting and fixing it down properly now. May even be bat proof soon. Haha.

I have sown all my tomato and aubergine and pepper seeds. Had our last butternut squash for lunch (frittata, with goat's cheese - very tasty). It had kept well.

We went into Lugo last week to get more seeds and other bits and bobs. Unfortunately it was the Tuesday after fiesta. I knew as soon as we turned into the huge and very empty car park at As Termas shopping centre that we had made a mistake (again). Another holiday! We ended up at Jayne and Richard's for a commiseratory cuppa and look round at how they are getting on.

We finally got to Lugo yesterday. Swapped our non-functioning TV/DVD player for a new separate TV and DVD player. The shop assistant said a combined unit never worked well (ours hadn't been right since

SPRING IN GALICIA

we got it back after Christmas, though I think the amount of dust all over it might have added to its swift demise). See if this one is dust-proofed!
Love you tons and tons
xxxxxxxx

Diary Saturday 7th March Drizzly but mild all day
Off to find the main registry office (xulgado) first thing. Realised too late that of course it's Saturday so everywhere council related is closed. Found the town hall anyway so we know where to come next time.
Tried to get fuel on the way home but the fuel cap was stuck. Went to the spares shop in Chantada where he managed to prise it off and then sell us a new one. Had hot chocolate and churros then wandered along the river towards the market.
It's lovely along the river in Chantada. There is a footpath either side with the very fancy new metal bridge at the swimming baths end and an old, low stone bridge next to the old water mill, which I notice has been renovated. Further along still is a narrow road bridge and the market.
It seemed to be a special market for International Women's Day. Lots of freebies! I managed to insert myself into a queue for a free La Voz newspaper with a Galego music CD included. Bought a cute knitted jacket for my new great-nephew and had my vitals checked at a women's health stall. I'm alive and healthy apparently. Received a tiny olive tree as a thank you for participating. It's about six inches tall.
Also ound out about a council health initiative to get people exercising. Free guided walks around the Ribeira Sacra region organised jointly by the local comarca (Taboada, Chantada and Carballiño councils) and the health services. Signed up.

TOMATO, FIG & PUMPKIN JELLY

Back in time for my homemade pork ravioli with lemon cream sauce and coleslaw.
S planted our baby olive tree on the west side in one of the semi-circles Mum and I dug out last Christmas. Also planted some cuttings liberated from an elder tree (for my cordial) and a Japanese quince.
Continued planting potatoes in the trenches, lined with our own compost. 130 spuds planted so far!

Visiting the *xulgado* office was pushed to the back of our minds as we got busy spring planting, weeding and building. There didn't seem to be any hurry.

The sun was hot those middle two weeks of March. I planted 300 potatoes, 167 onions (yes, I counted every one), four rows of carrots, three rows of beetroot and a couple of rows of maincrop peas. My tomato seedlings, the sweet peppers, and the aubergines, grew strongly in the bright sunroom.

S continued playing with his new boy toy, the chainsaw he bought from Richard, cutting logs for the fire and making me a lovely rustic gate for the allotment to stop the cows trampling my newly planted beds. He put my recently painted weathervane back onto the top of the *hórreo* from where it promptly flew away.

We also spent more time relaxing and walking around the locality. There was plenty to discover from our doorstep and we wanted to get to know the area better now the house was at least liveable.

Diary Sunday 15th March Sunny and warm
Watered the onions which are through already. Soaked peas in petrol to prevent 'the beast' deciding to eat them then sowed two further rows with nice rustic pea sticks (pruned branches from the fruit trees) to watch over them. Pricked out the

SPRING IN GALICIA

first lot of tomato seedlings and sowed some patio tomatoes for the big tub outside.
S continued plastering up holes in the bedroom wall. Said he has found a secret cupboard!
Lunch: Belly Pork from Luisa's pig, roasties, purple sprouting broccoli from the garden. Jam tarts and custard.
After lunch, went for a walk (to get into training for this walking group we have signed up to). Found a third water mill on our rio. It is in very good condition with a smart new roof. Well hidden down in the valley, we only spotted the shiny new roof because the trees haven't leafed up yet.
On the way back we noticed mill number one, just below the house, had a key in the door. An open invitation for a nosey. The roof is not good and the floor is rotten in quite a few places but all the old gear is there. The big granite grinding stones, turned by the power of the water coming down the mill race when it was a working mill, are still in place as is the huge metal hoist which was used to change the heavy stone grinding wheel. The hoist looks like a giant pair of scissors. To the left is a large cupboard made of sweet chestnut with a contraption inside which looks like a big tombola wheel. The ground corn would have gone into here via the stone chute which you can still see, then the wheel was turned manually, the finer flour flying out of the turning box into the tray below, the coarser stuff being left inside the wheel. Quite fascinating. Took a bunch of photos. It's all in a bit of a state but I'd love to have a go at doing it up. We could get electricity for the whole village if we got it back up and running... now there's a project! (NO, S)
Back at home S showed me his secret cupboard. From a certain direction, up the ladder in bedroom two, with the sun angled just so, one can make out

TOMATO, FIG & PUMPKIN JELLY

a flat rectangular shape against the wobbly wall at chest height. S reckoned it was hollow and handed me a mallet. Yippee! Two minutes of destruction later we had a stone lined 40 centimetre-cubed hollow in the wall and a small pile of holey bricks by my feet used to seal it up. Oh, and a small brass key!

Diary Wednesday 18th March Hot
Posted Mother's Day card to UK. Bought chicken feed and checked emails. S is making a wooden trellis for the kiwi vines we bought last September. Made two cakes for tea as CJ said he was calling over.
Lunch: Pork croquettes, green salad, avocado, beetroot and orange salad.
Our tiny avocado tree, grown from an avocado stone, is still alive but not yet at fruit bearing age. Not sure if it will survive outdoors.
'Phone call from Imoltasa to say the floorboards for the hallway are coming on Friday, then one from Juan to say he is bringing the plasterboard on, yes... Friday!
Tea and lots of cake in the afternoon as CJ didn't show.
Getting too hot in the kitchen now, will have to think about letting the cocina out if this weather continues.
Chicken number four (Sarah) is hiding her eggs in the bushes. Number Two seems to have given up being broody so maybe it's Sarah's turn now!

Monday 23rd March. Warm but breezy
Dear Mum,
 A sad day. We have had to say goodbye to Number Two (Fatty). She had a prolapsed cloaca. She had always had a laying problem, often giving us shell-less eggs, and

when I thought she was broody a few weeks ago she must've been having problems laying too. Poor girl was a bit scrawny once we had plucked her, but she will make us a chicken casserole.

We have had a busy week. Both the floorboards for the hallway upstairs and the plasterboard for the stud walls arrived on Friday. One in the morning, the other late afternoon thankfully. S has been busy laying the newly arrived rough planking (which also came on Friday) in the loft above the hallway as a floor. It is quite a big space and will be useful storage… for all that stuff we've found we don't need quite yet but can't throw away just in case!

We haven't found what our secret key opens yet! I'm sure it's going to be treasure… probably buried in the allotment somewhere by a pirate! I bet there's a map still to be found. S says I have a vivid imagination (probably got that from you then mother dear!!). Anyway, there had to be a reason for bricking up a key! We think the cupboard, or alcove, was another potty cupboard like the one in the opposite wall… so why hide a key? And why brick it up anyway?

I've been cleaning up the huge brace and ledge door which opens to the upstairs hallway from the lobby downstairs. (Actually it's a ledge minus brace door which means it is slowly distorting out of true.) It is the most gorgeous dark chestnut and so heavy I can't lift it. It was covered in about a half inch of soot and tar on the lobby side, I'm guessing from the lareira (the open fire which was used to smoke chorizos) in my storeroom to be, next to the kitchen. Can you imagine how smoky the house must have been for all that to accumulate?

S has also cut his hair so it must be spring in Galicia! If we hadn't disposed of that wardrobe full of hair from the old wig maker last year, we could have sold it all on for a profit! Ugh!!

On Saturday we were invited to lunch by a couple who live near to Antas. I had offered them some purple sprouting broccoli as I have so much (I think 20 plants was a tad excessive for two people!) and they kindly offered us lunch in return. Kevin and Sally have a modernised old stone house. We ate in the courtyard which is partially covered for some shade. A very pleasant area. They also have a low ceilinged barn, which Kevin is hoping to convert, and a wonderfully preserved aira, the stone-floored threshing area, outside near to the hórreo.

We had an enjoyable walk around the area after lunch. They are on the edge of the village with open views all around and have a large field running down to the river. The village proper is a higgledy piggledy muddle of stone houses across narrow cow-muck covered lanes. It is quite claustrophobic and we got totally disorientated as it all seems to fall in on you.

I am having a lazy evening reading through my cookery books (S calls it my pornography!) trying to find a suitable pudding for the weekend. I think S is writing a letter... or thinking about it anyway haha.

We are off to try our hand at badminton tomorrow. Luisa told us there were classes in town. They are on Mondays, Tuesdays, Thursdays and Fridays. We know this because Luisa took at least half an hour to explain it to us. She repeated the days five times... 'luns, martes, mercores... no, no mercores, xoves y vernes'. Each time through she did the same, counting the days of the week off on her fingers and each time saying not Wednesday and putting her middle finger down. I kept saying 'sí, sí', and repeating it back to her until I was sure I'd missed something important!
Love you tons and tons XXXXXXXXX

Maybe I had missed something important in Luisa's explanation as we never did find the badminton. No matter, the time had come to visit the *Xulgado de Paz* to sort out this wedding.

We trotted off to our main Justice of the Peace (or registry) office the following day, full of the joys of spring. The town hall was not the location of the registry of births, deaths, and marriages, but a helpful chap gave us directions. The registry building was decked out in the bright colourful flags of Spain, Galicia, and the local council, looking festive and gay as we approached on yet another sunny March morning.

The notes Manuel had given us in Taboada seemed fairly straightforward: birth certificates, *empadronamiento* or proof of residence in Taboada, and NIE or national identity number, plus something called a *fe de vida*. I hoped the judge would explain that one to me as the literal translation, faith of life, didn't really give me any clue.

The local policeman on the door nodded us through to a cavernous and totally empty space. Devoid of chairs or any attempt at welcome, the room was dominated by a tall, imposing counter running along the entire length of the back wall. The only colour in the place was afforded by a huge begonia in a pot, leaning towards the light of the frosted glass windows facing the road outside. The opposite wall was decorated by a few torn and faded posters advertising fiestas of many years before and warning visitors to show respect to the staff. Of the said staff, there was no sign.

We stood roughly halfway across the no man's land in front of the counter wondering what to do next when a door opened behind it and a middle-aged woman stepped through. She was short, as are most *Galegos* over 40, with the solid-coloured mousey brown hair that could only have come from a bottle. She wore a neat blouse of an indeterminate browny-orange colour and a very stern expression. As she looked up and caught sight of us hovering, her stare blazed, singeing my eyebrows.

"¡*Digame!*" she ordered.

The stern expression didn't faze me any longer. *Galegos*, whilst generally friendly and kind, have a resting expression that can only be described as grumpy. It is an expression of total incomprehension, as if they have no idea who or what you are or why you are here. It even happens in people who one knows. Our friends told us a story of coming home one day to their tiny village of a dozen houses in their very distinctive car. There were a couple of neighbours outdoors chatting as they passed. Our friends waved but received only the stern uncomprehending face in return. Until that is they exited the car outside their house. At this moment a switch was flicked and the neighbours smiled and shouted greetings as if they had not seen them for weeks instead of the hour they had been away shopping.

The order to 'tell me' also no longer made me want to run away and hide in a dark corner. As English, we are used to expressions such as 'can I help you?' on entering a shop or office. The *Galego* is somewhat more direct. *¡Digame!* or *¡diga!* is literally 'tell me' or 'speak' but would be the equivalent of an Englishman saying 'what do you want?' As I say, I am more inured to it now but the combination of the very dour face and the barked order made me quake in my wellies.

I put on my brightest smile and approached the counter.

"*Buenos dias,*" I announced in my best *Castillano*. "We are English but wish to get married here, in Galicia."

Before I had even got the sentence out, the mouth turned downwards and the woman grunted "*¡No!*"

To say I was taken aback is to understate my surprise twenty-fold. Still, maybe she thought we were tourists or something. I ploughed on, explaining that we lived in the province and trying desperately to convey some of my enthusiasm for the reasons we wanted to wed here in our beloved adopted country.

TOMATO, FIG & PUMPKIN JELLY

I obviously failed miserably as her reply was, "no, it is not possible."

"But, Manuel in Taboada..." I started.

The fire-breathing dragon in front of me lifted her head and glared at this slight to her authority.

"Documents!" she hissed thrusting her hand at me.

I flinched but took a deep breath and laid out our birth certificates, NIEs and *empadronamientos* on the desk.

My birth certificate she threw back at me. It was the short form of the UK document. For some reason it was all I had ever had and I had stupidly thought it would do.

"*Fe de vida*," she announced, pushing the rest of our documents back across the space as if they were contagious.

"Ah, yes," I stuttered. "I wanted to ask about that, what is it please, erm, thank you?"

We English use please and thank you far more often than the Spanish and neither were needed, but I felt a bit of begging would not go amiss here.

The dragon's head shot up and I swear her lip curled into a sneer of triumph.

"It is the *fe de vida* which everyone has."

"Ah, we don't. What is it for please?"

"You have to have one! It is the *fe de vida*, the book!"

This wasn't becoming any clearer but I gathered it was the Spanish equivalent of a birth certificate, so I went with that idea...

"Ah, yes, sorry, I see, but in England we only have these." I pointed to our flimsy birth certificates. "We don't have a book I'm afraid."

I was reverting to increasingly polite begging terms now, but I could tell I was losing the battle. Her next words confirmed my fears.

SPRING IN GALICIA

"Then, it is not possible." She slapped a hand on the desk to punctuate the finality of her remark. We were dismissed.

We staggered into the sunshine outside. I was crying tears halfway between rage and impotence.

"What an evil woman," I sobbed.

"Don't worry," comforted S. "Let's see what we can see on the internet while we are here."

Ever the practical realist my S.

The internet didn't seem to clarify much at all but I had had a message from the British consulate, which I had emailed back at the beginning of the month to ask about the document legalisation process. A chap called Graham Cunningham was responsible, it seemed, for intercepting all email received to the Foreign and Commonwealth Office – a mighty job I would have thought, and probably the reason for the tardy reply. He gave me a name and email for the new Vigo honorary consul, a Mr Devani. I wrote and waited for his reply. That seemed to be all we could do for the moment. I decided I would get my full birth certificate in a couple of weeks when we went to the UK. In the meantime we had plenty to keep us busy.

Monday 6th I think of April. Must be, as we have April showers today!

Dear Mum,

I have been busy clearing up and baking for our trip! We noticed last time on the ferry that quite a few people were carrying cool boxes. Clever, I thought! So I've organised bowls and cutlery, muesli and milk for breakfast, cookies, butties for lunch, and pasta salad (not made yet) for dinner on board. Plus our trusty kettle for those all-important cups of tea!

TOMATO, FIG & PUMPKIN JELLY

We've had an interesting few days. There was a new couple at the market get together who have just moved to the Sarria area. Their furniture was arriving on Friday so Jayne and Richard, and ourselves, offered to help (anything for a nosey haha). Of course by the time the huge lorry had managed to back itself down the narrow track, all the neighbours were out peering into the van and asking the usual questions... 'How many are they, do they have children, are they moving over too, what does this do?' The latter whilst picking up some random item of their belongings and poking it.

Anyway, it was as S was carrying in, I think, the fourth or fifth box of cookery books that I decided Dawn and I would get on really rather well! She had even cooked us all a full roast chicken dinner in some amazing electric roaster thing. Pretty impressive on moving day! Do you remember all the times you have helped me to move? Fish and chips, and fizzy wine were our usual feast eh?

Dawn and Steve have one of the most impressive houses I've seen here. It's honey coloured stone with a vast slate roof. There is a courtyard hiding behind huge, slightly forbidding gates, with a small barn or smoke room to the right and the main house to the left. The house has an external stone stairway to a first floor balcony with views way over the valley and a large room behind with a chestnut ceiling like ours in bedroom one (except it looks like ours did before we cleaned it up of course). The entrance hall has a huge wobbly stone flagged floor and there are so many rooms I lost count. There is loads of work to do of course but they seem to have some great ideas.

We went back to Sarria on Saturday as it was the big antiques fair there. Sarria is known as the antiques capital of Galicia. One entire street is full of antique shops, brilliant for mooching around though way out of my league moneywise. On Saturday there were stalls set up all the way along the road too. It was an eclectic mixture of eye-wateringly expensive renovated chestnut furniture and equally expensive junk, like old chipped crockery and 'antique' beer bottles circa 2004. I spotted some non-renovated chestnut furniture through a large curtained off part of one shop, which I'd inadvertently managed to slip behind totally missing the three foot high notice saying 'no entry'. Unsurprisingly none of that stuff was for sale. Still, it was a thoroughly enjoyable day – though I wish I could've got my hands on some of the old stuff to play with: our potty cupboards, the bed frames, and even the doors look so wonderful cleaned. As do our kneelers now some clever person has re-covered them for me! May have another job for you next time you visit - we have a lovely old blanket box which needs a new seat cushion…

While we were in Lugo the other day we had a look at stoves for the upstairs hallway. We figure a wood burner in there would take the chill off in winter and even warm the bedrooms up a bit. Even a tiny pot-bellied stove was a bit pricey. Rich suggested the UK may be cheaper so that's another thing for our list.

Today Kevin and Sally (who we visited for lunch a couple of weeks ago) popped in for tea and a look around. Sally brought me some natural soap and hair rinse which she makes, plus a long order list for the UK. The car will be full for its return!

It has been rather windy and wild here this week. Not as bad as the 90KmH (65MpH) winds we had back in January, but windy enough for the polystyrene insulation to bang up and down all night. Unfortunately it's above bedroom one where we are sleeping so not ideal. Will have to sort that before it becomes your room!

Still, the April showers and winds are better than the snow, hail and frost with which we started the month. It had been so warm and sunny in March that all the fruit trees were leafing up - then wham! Heavy frost last Wednesday and all the new leaves on our little kiwis are blackened, as are the emerging walnut leaves. I bought some *fleece at the market and have covered what I can but stable door and horse comes to mind!*

My veg are being well watered, the onions are growing tall and I think I see a carrot top. The tomatoes, peppers and aubergines are doing well in the sunroom and of course they were protected from the frosts in there… as well as the dust we are making in the centre part of the house putting up the ceiling in bedroom two and sanding the newly exposed beams.

See you in a week's time. We dock at around 2.30pm so should be with you by tea time depending on the traffic and weather. I'll ring when we are on our way.
Love you loads
xxxxxxxxxxxxxxxx Just to keep you going 'til next Tuesday!!!

We were off to England, taking the ferry from Santander on 13th April. CJ was to be in charge of the rabbits and chickens, and watering my tomato plants, with a bribe of cake and all the eggs he could find. We put white bunny to Carmen's buck, tidied the garden as much as we could and continued working on the house.

Diary Thursday 9th April – April showers continue. Collected white bunny from Carmen's, after initially choosing the wrong one! Swapped to give brown bunny a go with the beleaguered buck.
S is getting on well with the ceiling in bedroom two. He's having great fun cutting each sheet of plasterboard to fit the wobbly spaces between the

beams. He is probably wishing we hadn't gone with the vaulted ceiling now... but it does look amazing. CJ came over for tea and instructions. He had brought his own notebook... there's dedication!

Bath night! 3 hours to heat the hot water tank with the immersion heater. Ran tap on hot only... 20 minutes to run cold, which due to our amazingly high water pressure meant about 3 inches of water. Another 10 minutes of cold water to be usable (for S) plus two kettles got it to halfway. Just sufficient with the water displacement of two not very large bodies. Very warm and steamy in the bathroom if a lot of fuss.

Diary Sunday 12th April Sunshine
Carmen came round to borrow the ladders...Yippee! That's the very first time she has approached us to actually ask for anything. A breakthrough I feel.

Of course she returned them together with a hug and a jar of honey for Mum. As we had already bought Mum a 12 pack of honey from the market (a year's supply, all labelled with the months of the year) Mum will be very very happy!

Had a good clean round the house. S has left one of the plasterboard sheets under pressure to try and bend it around a particularly bumpy bit of the roof beams.

Topped up the fluid levels in the car, packed our cool box, sprayed the chickens for mites, cut bunnies' nails, loaded car and early to bed.

Our ferry journey was calm and peaceful. Despite a detour in the dark due to roadworks on the Fosse Way, we arrived at my childhood home by 6.30pm on 14th April to a rapturous welcome and a hot, home-cooked dinner.

SPRING IN GALICIA

§

We arrived back in Galicia with our UK haul at 7.30pm on Monday 2nd May. The sun welcomed us home like that first time, when we had arrived similarly laden English virgins, almost two years ago. The grass seemed to be in a similar state of overgrownness and the smell of home (fresh sweet country air with a slight essence of eau de cow) was all around.

We'd had an enjoyable and productive trip. We had visited family and friends, and had them visit us. We had caught up with all the news, spent quality time with Mum, and helped her with a few jobs around the house. I had been to my favourite Asian store in Manchester, Wing Yip. S had toured the DIY shops of Burton and sampled some Burton Bridge ale.

We had found a quirky cast iron stove in Burton. It was long and thin and sat on four legs looking like some crazy insect, but it was the right shape for our hallway and the price sold it to us. It also weighed a ton (actually 56kg).

The lad helping to lift it into the car asked if we were flying Ryanair back. I smiled and said the excess baggage charges on said carrier might be more expensive than the stove.

His boss rolled his eyes and, I felt, only with supreme effort managed not to clip the poor lad's ear. "Look, idiot, it's a Spanish car." He gestured to the number plates in a somewhat aggressive manner.

"But it's a right hand drive," pointed out the unbowed and surprisingly observant teenager.

"Yep, that took some sorting out too," I murmured as we left.

Re-registering the car as Spanish had taken us almost a year of bureaucracy and frustration, and for a moment I pondered why we were putting ourselves through yet more of the inevitable same to buy into an institution we didn't even believe in.

We had real ale and marmite in our bulging bags and boxes. We had loose leaf Yorkshire tea and impossible to find spices such as allspice and coriander. We had DIY goodies from Wilkos and B&Q. We had cheap slippers from Gulliver's, the shoe emporium just down the road from Mum's house. We had orders for our friends and I even had a small redcurrant bush I'd spotted in a plant nursery. And, most importantly, I had my full birth certificate in my sweaty palms. It was time to return to the registry office.

§

We returned to the *xulgado* sure, for some reason known only to the eternally optimistic, that the dragon would be more sympathetic this time.

As we walked into the cavernous office (or as I now thought of it… the dragon's lair) once more, I swear I felt the air scorching my scalp. There was a customer. An elderly lady with a jet-black curly bob and a chubby face wreathed in smiles was explaining that her daughter had had twins. I smiled with her as she stood, proud and happy in front of the grim faced guardian of the lair. Instead of celebrating this joyous occasion with the new grandmother, our foe merely pushed a piece of paper across her counter and barked, "names."

My optimism leaked away like a deflated balloon. I almost turned around and left, but I had to try didn't I? Anyway, I had faced worse than her.

At the suggestion of S, I asked if we could speak to the judge directly, feeling maybe that we would have more luck with that august person.

"¡No!" said the dragon. "¿Y dónde está, la fe da vida?"

I tried once more to explain that we didn't possess a *fe da vida*, whatever one was. That was a mistake I feel. My newly obtained birth certificate was thrown back across the desk and the guardian walked out of the door behind her.

We hung about for a while assuming, stupidly, that she had gone to fetch the judge to speak with us. Then I saw her, hat and coat on, leaving the building.

So that was a no then?

Tuesday 5th May. Very hot

Dear Mum,

We are safely home - to a field full of daisies, plantain and knapweed, very pretty! A very productive visit all in all. And a lovely break, thank you for everything xxx

S is now continuing with his wobbly ceiling. The plasterboard he left under pressure whilst we were away has bent enough to fix to the beams so that's impressive. Still looking for a plasterer, though I think we will end up doing it ourselves again.

CJ had looked after the animals and plants well. He kept a record of eggs for me... looks like someone has been hiding them as only two a day most days. We have also been translocating reptiles (slowworms and snakes mainly) - unpaid sadly - they are all basking under the plastic covering the vegetable beds. Everytime I uncover a bed, there they sit! Found a huge lizard with a bright blue head (male in his mating colours) under one piece. We think it was a Schreiber's lizard.

We have dug in the raspberry cuttings you gave us and the little redcurrant bush at the top of the allotment. Look forward to those fruiting. I've sown all my courgette seeds (two types) and the butternut squash and cucumbers. The tomatoes are doing well and the carrots are up. I sowed the courgettes and squash amongst the corn which is apparently the Roman way.

I have also uncovered the runner bean corms we had left in the ground last autumn. The things were already growing underneath the mulch and plastic. They are about five inches long and a bit pale! Will see if they recover.

Carmen sends her love and a hug. She came over with a huge bucketful of spinach and some to plant. I don't really need any to plant as she more than keeps us supplied. She also brought me over a bucketful of tomato plants so if all the ones I transplanted grow too I should have around 60 plants. Our autumn sown broad beans have done well while we were away. We had a boiling for lunch with sausage and mash and yet more purple sprouting broccoli.

Thursday: Hot but breezy again
I've planted all the primulas and auriculas you gave us in the little strip in

front of the terrace and have re-sown two rows of parsnips, as the first lot haven't come through. Oh and I found the eggs today! Five in the bramble patch outside. Very well hidden, no wonder CJ missed them.
Love you tons and tons. Can't wait until summer and your visit
Xxxxxxxx

Time passed quickly as ever. I put weddings to the back of my mind as we carried on with our spring planting and working to create our new master bedroom and living-hallway.

Before I knew it, August was upon us.

AUGUST
Teddy Bear's picnic

It was two whole years since we had moved to Galicia to live full time. In many ways nothing seemed to have changed. The weather was still erratic, the bats still occasionally flew through the house, and Spanish bureaucracy was still, well, Spanish, and would no doubt resolve itself in time.

One of the things which endeared us to *A Casa do Campo* when we first saw it on that rainswept November morning was its quirkiness. The house is built on different half levels with unexpected rooms popping up from seemingly impossible places. This lends it a mischievous jester-like air but also meant we could renovate it in sections without creating too much chaos in the rest of the house.

Our main upstairs living accommodation is split into almost equal thirds by two, 70 centimetre thick, stone walls. To the east, the stone wall would have been the original external wall of the house. The solid wooden door had an equally solid looking wooden cat flap in it, and a large wooden bar across to prevent intruders. Beyond it was the two room extension where we had lived when we first arrived. This housed our temporary living room, complete with toilet behind the sofa, and the grandly named 'sunroom'... for reasons which will become clear later.

The rest of the upstairs formed the original footprint of the building, before the various extensions were added and it was altered beyond recognition. To the west were the bathroom and bedroom we had completed the previous year. This renovated section was separated from the central section by another thick granite stone wall, part of the cross forming the internal structure of the building. In this wall was a low, low archway. At that moment there was a heavy woollen curtain draped across the archway, keeping the dust of this year's works away from our nice clean bedroom and bathroom.

In January 2009, we had started our new project: to turn this central section into a master bedroom and a hallway-living space, the latter where the old, unused and un-mourned bathroom had stood.

The first job had been demolition.

On the first Friday of the new year, we had commenced operations by pulling down the old, and somewhat rotten, lathe and plaster ceiling from that entire five metre square mid-section. We had tidied away six large black buckets' worth of kindling and plaster dust, and then examined the roof space above the master bedroom carefully.

Within the un-plastered area above the removed ceiling we could clearly see the original apex of the roof. I was amazed how much the house must have grown over the years. More importantly, the roof beams were interesting enough, and in a good enough condition, for us to decide to have a full height, vaulted ceiling in our bedroom. With the dark red end wall I had decided on in my mind's eye it would look stunning, and quirky enough to fit right in with the rest of the house.

The second day of demolition saw us remove the puny brick wall between the two rooms. The huge open space we were left with had me pining for a grand boudoir. But it was neither practical nor on my carefully drawn plans. A new wall would be constructed once we had the new chestnut flooring down.

TOMATO, FIG & PUMPKIN JELLY

We were so filthy on that particular 'bathnight' at the local swimming baths that I had to wash my hair three times before I even ventured into the pool.

By August we had a new, clean and painted bedroom. The bedroom was a full height masterpiece with that delicious deep red wall on one short side. There would be floor to ceiling wardrobes opposite, when we found some to fit. The ceiling beams shone from polishing, and the wobbly plasterboard within the even wobblier beams seemed to fit the house perfectly. The new, sweet chestnut floor was completed ready for sanding and our normal three coats of hard wearing varnish.

That had almost been a disaster.

We had ordered the same width sweet chestnut floorboards, from the same company, as we had for our previous project. S started in the bedroom, laying boards as he went. On one particular day, he opened one of the new packs.

They didn't fit!

We had ordered 20 centimetre wide floorboards but these were 19 centimetres wide. They didn't match the existing boards when laid in a line. In the bedroom it was fine so long as each full row was of the same width floorboards. But in the hallway they had to join the existing floor. Luckily, there were enough of the old 20 centimetre floorboards left to complete that area. It could have been much worse and taught us a valuable lesson – always double check everything very carefully.

For now, the hallway-living area was partially completed. Still awaiting its new chestnut flooring and plasterboard ceiling, one long wall had been stripped of plaster and mortared. Some of the granite stones were huge. As I carefully mortared around them I had wondered how on earth anyone had managed to manoeuvre stones that size into position, some four metres above ground level, in the days before tractors and cranes. S, helpful as

AUGUST

ever, told me of neighbours and oxen, of ramps and Egyptians, but that didn't lessen the wonder I felt. One section of that wall has a stone which has been oddly carved out, as if to fit around something. This is where the original toilet had sat in that dark and dismal bathroom. I liked the touch of strangeness and left the stone exactly as it was.

Tuesday 4th August
Dear Mum,

It has been an odd summer so far. Today is hot and humid. Last week it was cloudy and overcast, and on market day on the first it rained heavily. Nowhere near as hot as last year in July. Luisa told us back in June it was a poor summer this year and I laughed! I remember Jen's dad telling us that the year we arrived had been dreadful up until the middle week of August (the very day we landed in fact.) They called S the Sun God for weeks. Of course you were the Snow Queen after your arrival at Christmas in that blizzard, and CJ's friend Pete always brings the rain with him when he visits. He has only ever been once… summer or winter… and had good weather. That was the time he had to change his flight at the last minute. Needless to say it rained the week he should have come over.

There was a big crowd at the meet up on the first, despite the rain. Stefan and gang (nearest English neighbours, tattoos) came over in the afternoon to see what we have been doing. I love showing people round but he really does wind me up, criticising everything and questioning why we have done something a particular way... Like why did we bother exposing the beams? And the windows are set wrong. And why is there a glass panel above the door? I wouldn't mind but his work isn't exactly top quality. His idea was to renovate quickly, sell, and move onto the next one. Of course that's much easier said than done in rural Galicia where there are far more derelict houses than there are people. He may be waiting a long time to sell. It was nice to see Annie and the boys though. The youngest is doing so well at school and is so enthusiastic about everything he learns. He soaks it up like a little sponge. I showed Annie my allotment. She tells me the neighbours have given them a plot of land to use (they can't buy or rent it because a Galego will not sell you something easily... if ever). I think the neighbours are up to something. They gave Annie the potatoes to plant, the lettuces and the cabbages. Stefan said his back was killing him from planting so many spuds and Annie said they would never eat all the lettuce. And that, I think, might be the point... an elderly village population with a plot of land no one has time to cultivate. A young family with energy and too many vegetables to eat... a match made in Galicia!! Maybe I'm becoming Galego in my thinking.

AUGUST

My tomatoes are ripening now. I have pruned all the side shoots off as you suggested, and tied them to canes, keeping a good air space around after the disaster of the blight last year. I think it's the high humidity here even in the summer, with the morning mists. I read somewhere that the average humidity here in August is 78%. Anyway, if I hold off the blight we should have enough tomatoes to preserve for the whole year, as I have around 65 plants in now. I'm planning to try sun drying some more as they worked well last year. And making more sauce.

The runner bean corms which survived over winter, have produced the tallest runner bean plants I've ever seen! And of course we had beans much earlier so that is something I'll try again!

Looks like the plums are going to give a good show again. Red, yellow, green, purple and blush all starting to drop off. Must start picking before the hens get to them!

Wednesday. Thank you for your letter and parcel. The postie woke us up banging at the door. The seeds and knickers are very welcome, but I wish he would wait until <u>after</u> 10 o'clock to deliver haha.

Steve and Dawn came over this afternoon to pick some plums... I'd put out a general call for anyone who wanted some to come and help themselves. A sort of free pick-your-own farm. Anyway Steve and Dawn have *invited us over for lunch while you are here. We can visit Sarria. You will love their house... and Dawn's cooking!*

I've been carrying on with my ten-year mission to remortar all the external stone walls of the casa. By the time I've finished I reckon I will know what I am doing! It's a lot of wall. I've calculated it's about 270m² and I do about a square metre (a square yard) at a time. As I say it could take a while.

See you very soon Xxxxxxxx
Love you tons and tons

The re-mortaring of the whole house really was a long job. I had to knock off the old 'decorative' plaster, some of which had been replaced by solid concrete, by hand, using a cold chisel and hammer, then jetwash the section I had done to remove the lingering bits of plaster and expose any bits I'd missed. After the stones were exposed, I laboriously re-mortared between each one using a knife and, mainly, my fingers. I got through dozens of pairs of rubber gloves as the granite shredded them mercilessly. But, I improved and on the 11th of May 2018 I mortared the very last section in the top southwest corner, some twenty feet in the air, on a surprisingly blustery day. It had taken me, off and on, eleven years but I had done every bit myself. Except for a teeny tiny section called Iris's stone, which Mum had helped with. (She got bored after around five minutes). All I have to do now is re-mortar some of the early bits which are lacking in the professionalism of the later work.

Mortaring 270 square metres of granite wall was simple compared to trying to persuade our less than

AUGUST

friendly dragon receptionist at the *xulgado* that it was fine for foreigners to get married in Galicia. In one final attempt to see the judge personally, we returned to the dragon's lair. To say that I failed would be to state the blindingly obvious at this stage. But I did manage to prise a list of what documents *she* felt were needed from her.

I had also had an email reply from the honorary consul for Galicia, Aruni Devani. There was no consulate in Galicia at that moment but one would be up and running in Vigo before the end of the year. He explained that the *fe de vida* was the Spanish equivalent of our birth certificates, called a certificate of life. It was in the form of a book which one received on marriage. All the couple's subsequent children are registered in this book and a copy kept by the local registrar. We didn't need this in order to get married in Galicia but we would need to sign an affidavit at the British consulate to swear we were free to marry. The consulate would then issue a certificate of no impediment and would also publish the banns for us. He asked when we were planning on getting married. That at least made me smile.

> Dear Aruni,
> Thank you for your continued help. We have not yet set a date for the wedding as we have been here long enough to realise that it is rarely a wise move to organise anything too far in advance when Spanish bureaucracy is involved.
> If the Vigo consulate is likely to be up and running by the end of the year we will happily wait for that rather than making the 1000km round trip to Madrid to sign the affidavit. Maybe we will be your first customers!
> In the meantime can you confirm with me exactly what documents are needed for the registrar here please? We have visited both our local town hall and the *xulgado* office and have two (only slightly different) lists of requirements. The lady at the *xulgado* tells me the consulate has to translate our birth certificates…

although there is little to translate other than father's occupation. And that they, the consulate, then need to stamp the documents. Your letter suggested we need a *traducción jurado* here and then a stamp from the UK legalisation department. I would appreciate clarification over this.
Best wishes
Lisa

This done, we carried on working and enjoying our *vida dulce* here in Galicia.

Wednesday 12th August. Very very hot
Dear Mum,
Well I was right to predict a weather change. It started getting hotter on Sunday... exactly two years to the day since we arrived here to live. Since then the mercury has risen every day. It is now 31 degrees on the terrace in the shade!

I have been staining the new ceiling boards we got from Xesteira, the builder's merchants, for the kitchen ceiling. We seem to be getting on well with this year's main project and one of the other things we want to do this summer is to sort out the kitchen ceiling. We want to get it done before we relight the cocina in autumn. The ceiling has to come down as it is mouldy and rotten but I like the smoke-stained colour so decided to give it a head start by staining the replacement pine boards. It will be nice not to have to cover all the food in case any woodworm dust falls into it!

S has fixed the plasterboard for the last bit of the wall between the bedroom and

AUGUST

hallway (on the hallway side). If you remember his brother helped him with some of that last month when they visited for S' birthday. I've been plastering some of the intricate bits around the archway. I wanted to expose most of that end wall but keep the archway itself nice and bright. As it is so low (other than for us Galician sized people) it might stop people bashing their heads too!

Had no eggs again today. I think that since I found their last hidey hole they have gone off to lay in another one!

I made a lovely hot water crust pork and ham pie this morning. Slightly cheating as I did it in a loaf tin then turned it out to brown the sides. Would love to do a proper Melton Mowbray raised pie one day.

It has been Taboada festival this week again. On Monday there was supposed to be a folk festival on, but when we arrived at around 9pm there was no sign of anything. Of course the posters didn't give a time or place so no idea if we missed it, if it was hidden indoors somewhere, or happened at a different place entirely!! I'll learn one day haha... Or maybe not, as last night was supposed to be the 'sorteo'. We have been given free raffle tickets with every purchase around town for weeks now and last night was the draw... except we couldn't find that either! Not a bad evening though as the local Priest, Don Pepe, bought one round, José's dad the second and Martin and

Linda, who are housesitting for Stefan, the third!

We didn't even know Stefan and family had left! We were going through the village one evening when we saw smoke from their chimney. Of course we called to say hello, but it wasn't Stefan who answered the door but an older chap. As soon as I spoke in English he dragged us indoors for tea and chat. I think he was so delighted to meet some Brits (Stefan hadn't bothered to tell them we lived nearby) that it wouldn't have mattered who we were!!

Thursday. Even hotter!

I found the eggs! They were in an old rusty oil drum which had been put round one of the fruit trees probably 15 years ago. The tree has grown of course but there is a nice hen sized space inside the drum. Took me half an hour of searching with the chickens all laughing at me and giving no hints at all! I was covered in leaves and dirt. Little devils they are!

Olive, our new black hen, is laying soft-shelled eggs. I hope she doesn't have the same problem poor Fatty had. Seems happy for now anyway. I will increase her share of the ground egg shells to see if that helps.

We went to the fiesta again last night. Someone had told us the band were good. They are called Orchestra Panorama. What an amazing show! They had the biggest stage-wagon I have ever seen which opened

AUGUST

out into a vast stage a good 30ft long. Must have been 20 performers on stage. One guy had a great operatic voice but it was far more than the usual salsa. They did one song where the band 'played' using angle grinders on the metal framework of the stage, complete with sparks! They ended with all the kids on stage for Michael Jackson's 'We are the World'. Everyone was mesmerised and I have never seen such a crowd in town. To explain the numbers... you know the main street, about what, 500 yards long? It was full of people from end to end and from side to side when the band finished. You literally could have walked on heads!

That's our excitement for a while!

Got the very last of the plums off today. I have made some more wine and dried the rest. Now it is hot and sunny they only take a couple of days to dry under the fly net on the table outside.

We are off to CJ's tomorrow to help him put his new garage roof on. Hope it's slightly cooler as we will be pretty exposed up there! Will need our sunhats for sure.

Love you tons and tons and see you in just a week. Hope the sun stays for you

Xxxxxxxxxx

It was another *dia 'escorchio'* on the Friday, with the temperature topping 32 degrees in the shade. The roof on the other hand was in full sun, the corrugated cement board hot enough to fry eggs on.

TOMATO, FIG & PUMPKIN JELLY

But the three of us made a good team and we had CJ's roof on and sealed by lunchtime. After a delicious workers' lunch we made our way home to finish cleaning in anticipation of Mum's impending visit.

Mum arrived for her visit a week later on a perfect cloudless day. At least it was in the Lugo hills when we left home. As we neared Santiago it began to rain, and rain.

Only in the capital of Galicia can it rain with such glorious abandon and vigour. I have been to that most beautiful of Galician cities in summer and lost my umbrella to the vicious winds which swirl joyously through the narrow cobbled streets, snatching at hat, coat or an umbrella unfurled inadvisably. And I have been drenched from head to the tips of my non-waterproof shoes for daring to step away from my temporary shelter beneath a stone archway, along with a few dozen other beleaguered souls.

This time we weren't going into the city. By the time we had met Mum at the airport, checked she had the correct passport, and made our way to Melide, the sun was shining and we were able to have our picnic by the river there watching the birds and the locals enjoying their summer.

This was the second time that Mum was to stay with us, *casa nosotros*, rather than at the hotel in town. The first time had been last Christmas and that visit had begun with far worse weather than a drop of rain...

§

Diary Sunday 14th December 2008
Woke to sleet! Perfect for collecting Mum from the airport then. Boiled eggs and soldiers as is now traditional on a Sunday then off to Santiago. By the time we reached the tops at San Martiño it was

AUGUST

snowing heavily. Luckily the flight was on time but the flurries became a blizzard as we came up to the 600m mark on the way home. At San Martiño, the windscreen wipers were flapping madly and achieving little. S was driving and Mum sitting serenely in the back, oblivious to danger, or supremely confident in her chauffeur. The car in front braked hard, inadvisably, due to another car sitting in the ditch, occupants outside and uninjured, looking miserable and embarrassed, waiting for rescue. S changed down gear as the car in front began to spin across the road. There followed an elegant dance whereby at one heart stopping moment I saw the whites of our dance partners' eyes as they swirled inches from our door. S, calm as ever, regained control of the car and we continued safely home to where the cocina awaited us, blazing a warm welcome to the snow people.
Mum is now officially the Snow Queen!!

§

On that previous visit Mum had reupholstered the two *pries dieu* that had been left in the house when we bought it. Along with a myriad of old chestnut bed frames, wooden potty cupboards and even a, now working, grandmother wall clock, these prayer stools looked fabulous restored to their former glory. Thanks to *Galegos'* dislike of 'old' things, we were getting a nicely furnished house for free. I had more work for her this time but first we had some visiting to do.

August is party season here in Galicia. Pretty much every season is an excuse for some kind of party but August, when those who live, work or study in the big cities flock home to their rural roots to spend time with family, catch up with friends, and generally enjoy the long summer holidays, is peak fiesta time. We'd had our Taboada festival this year but the day after Mum arrived was the *Empanada* Festival in nearby Chantada.

Empanadas are the large, discus shaped, meat or seafood pies which are a staple of every *menú del dia* in Galicia. Most bakeries (*panaderias*) pride themselves on their *empanadas* and the recipes are a closely guarded secret. Traditional fillings include tuna with onions, peppers and tomato; *lacón* (pork shoulder); *pulpo* (octopus); or *zamburiñas* (scallops) but almost anything is possible. I recently saw a recipe online which Google had kindly translated to 'octopus with nipples', sadly I got side-tracked so never did check what the original had been. Pity, as the mind truly boggles!

The lady at the swimming pool had been raving about the *empanada* festival for weeks. I imagined stalls selling tasters of their very best recipes or better still, giving free samples with which to tempt customers to buy a whole pie to take away. The idea of trying different foods is always a winner for me and Mum loved the idea of visiting anywhere, so we set off the 15 kilometres to Chantada and a lonely stretch of woodland on the outskirts of town where the event was to take place.

Our first inkling that my fertile imagination was maybe not going to bear edible fruit was the sight of hundreds of people emerging from the already packed field being used as a temporary car park, walking along the road clutching greasy flat brown paper packages. The scent from these packages was of meat, fish, onions and lardy pastry. *Empanadas*! These folk also carried cool boxes, blankets and folding chairs. That we seemed to be in a minority of three not similarly burdened was slightly disconcerting.

We arrived in an area of scattered trees, and scattered families eating, drinking, and laughing below them. Beyond this group of picnickers were longer tables decked in snowy cloths below flapping, gaily coloured awnings. Along the centre of each table were platters of *empanada* slices and jugs of wine. Obviously the folk carrying their own *empanadas* were the ones picnicking below the trees. These must be the official *empanada* lunch tables. People were beginning to take their places along the benches either side of the feast tables so I hurried over to a young chap wearing a Day-Glo green T-shirt bearing the name of a local bar.

He looked puzzled at my polite enquiry as to where I could buy a ticket for the lunch. Then again, most *Galegos* who don't know me tend to look puzzled at my mangling of their language and my rather bizarre accent. In Taboada most folk are used to me now, a bit like that friend you have with the really strong accent: after a few years, the strange sounds all start to make some kind of sense. This chap did not know me, but that wasn't the reason for his confusion.

"It's a private party," he explained, pointing to his logo. He then pointed to the other awnings which I now noticed all bore different logos: some bars or restaurants, others workshops, garages or shops.

"All private", he continued helpfully in broken English. "Company buys a table."

I looked at the laughing groups as my heart sank. There were no stalls selling *empanadas*, it was a great big teddy bears' picnic in the woods, and we had no ticket and no food. The lad looked sympathetically at me but before I could ask anything more a friend grabbed his arm and they were away, laughing and drinking wine from a huge plastic cup, my dilemma forgotten.

Deflated I walked back to S and Mum, who was sitting on a nearby erratic. These granite lumps, which vary in size from table to small car to house, are found all around this area. Erratic rocks were left behind after the glaciers retreated some 18 000 years ago at the end of the last ice age. I have seen houses in the Galician hills with erratics forming one of their walls.

I digress. Mum looked unfazed by my revelation that we could not have *empanada* and walked determinedly toward the lone *parillada* concession near the roadway. These pop-up grill restaurants are at every single festival anywhere in Galicia. We installed ourselves at a long table after ordering a platter of octopus for us and a mixed grill for Mum. It wasn't *empanada* but at least it was food. The day was hot and there was a pleasant breeze under the awning. I relaxed.

Just then the waiter came over with our food. He stopped as he reached the table. We were the only occupants of a mile of whiteness stretching away behind us. I smiled. The waiter pointed to a tiny label, discretely pinned to the cloth. 'Vazquez 15' it read.

"Reserved," he said.

Sighing I stood and headed to the next door table, also clothed in white, also empty. On it was another label... 'Rodriguez 12'. The next was 'Gomez 22'. They were ALL reserved? I looked at the waiter, more in disbelief than hope. He shrugged eloquently, both hands full of our meal, as a jostling crowd began to descend on the previously empty tables, shouting out names, joking and generally enjoying themselves.

"*¿Para llevar?*" asked the waiter. 'To take away?'

And that is how we ended up at a teddy bears' picnic, which was billed as an *empanada* festival, with a platter of octopus and grilled ribs, sitting on a granite rock which had been there for millennia and failing totally to eat any pastry based delight whatsoever.

§

AUGUST

Many years later we had an *empanada* festival of our own when a friend invited us round to watch how they were made.

Susana inherited an old stone farmhouse from her father and had had it restored immaculately and tastefully. In the covered courtyard was the restored *horno* or bread oven. It was made of granite stones, was fully five feet in diameter and, unlike ours, had been fitted with a very smart chimney. We had been talking about Galician food and the fact that we had never successfully used our *horno.* Susana suggested that her cousins would be happy to fire up the oven and give us a demonstration.

The cousins, all country folk, arrived en masse on the morning in question. They carried sacks of *masa*, the dough with which to make the *empanadas*, and buckets of meat based fillings, pre-made and ready to go. Susana, a city lass at heart, had laid out tables upstairs, with napkins, glasses, and plates ready to receive the food.

First the fire had to be lit. The cousins had brought along piles of dry gorse. They explained that the oven had to get not just warm but white hot. When the granite blocks at the doorway glowed white then the oven was ready. The thin pieces of gorse brush would be just the thing to get the temperature up.

A table was required to knead the dough. Just around the corner was an old door, waiting to be disposed of. With the aid of two upturned wheelbarrows, the cousins soon had a workbench fashioned. The head cousin then proceeded to batter the dough into submission before rolling it out into a rectangle half the length of the door. The filling ingredients were laid over one side of the dough, the unfilled side folded over and the whole roughly stuck together. Using a *pala,* the old wooden long handled spatula, the bread pie was thrust into the glowing coals.

TOMATO, FIG & PUMPKIN JELLY

There was a whiff of burning hair as the *jefe* pulled his arm away, the hairs already crinkling from the ferocious heat. Within minutes the *empanada* was ready. The cousins once more braved the heat, launching the newly baked pie onto the makeshift table from whence everyone dived in, ripping and cutting chunks of hot pie, juggling it in burnt fingers and washing it down with local red wine. We stood around that old wooden door, eating with our fingers, laughing, and talking. Rolls of kitchen paper were found and distributed. The upstairs tables were forgotten, the need for decorum dismissed. It was one of the best parties I have been to.

§

Luckily Mum's stay picked up after the non-*empanada* event. Which, I might add, she found hilarious and most enjoyable. Then again, Mum just loved being here in Galicia. Rain, snow, 'empanadaless' picnics, she loved it all.

We visited Lugo, our local, Roman-walled city, and I showed Mum some new shops we had found, one selling huge fresh cheeses, another, hard to find spices. She helped me to pod mountains of borlotti beans for drying and to sort the spuds we dug up for storing. We had a reasonable haul of potatoes but many of them had holes in them from mice, or whatever it was that was still eating my underground crops of carrots, parsley, leeks and onions. Each one would start to disappear into the ground, the bulb end being nibbled away until only a limp green top remained. I had tried everything from cats to land mines to get rid of the pests but had failed spectacularly.

Mum also made potfuls of tomato sauce which she froze. These were delicious but I soon realised that the freezer would be full well before the

AUGUST

tomatoes ran out. I decided to try making jars of thick cooked tomato sauce, or passata, instead.

Mum also got through my pile of sewing jobs (which I can always put off indefinitely) and upholstered the top of our blanket box. This was in a matching fabric to the two *pries dieu* and would also be in our newly completed bedroom.

Diary Friday 28th August Hot during day
Made pasta salad for tomorrow's picnic lunch in Monforte whilst S finished putting the glass panel back in above the bedroom doorway. Mum continued working through my sewing pile in between playing with the hens and chicks and going for long walks down the track to 'her' field. I'm pretty sure we could persuade her to move over eventually. It just needs to be her idea!
Swimming/bathnight in Chantada. Saw an advert for a jazz concert by the river so decided to go along after our swim.

The concert was advertised as starting at 10pm. We made our way along the river to where chairs had been set out on the grass next to the recently restored water mill. The chairs faced away from the river toward a small makeshift stage. Of course we were the only people there at the designated hour, and by the time the seats were filled at 11pm we were frozen.

The day had been hot, the thermometer rising to 31°C, but the evening brought a chill wind and by the time darkness fell the temperature had dropped to 7°C. Mum had on her summer dress. S popped back to the car to fetch my spare fleece, gloves and woolly hat (be prepared, said my guide leader, and never is it more appropriate than in rural Galicia). Once suitably attired the concert was excellent.

TOMATO, FIG & PUMPKIN JELLY

Diary Saturday 29th August Hot
Visit to Monforte de Lemos. Had our picnic lunch down by the river then drove up to the parador on the hill above the town for coffees.

Monforte de Lemos is the second, and only other, city in Lugo province. It sits in the centre of a flat plain, encircled by hills. The old tourist information centre used to have a large contour map on its wall: from above, the town and surrounds resemble nothing so much as a Spanish *roscón* tin for making those ring shaped cakes with a hole in the middle. The roads running across the flatlands to the town are arrow straight as they pass through a patchwork of green fields dotted with villages. In the very centre of this plain, rises a tall protrusion like a wizard's hat. And on the very top of the mount (or *mont*) is a large stone building, the *parador* (Spanish government owned luxury hotels).

As one descends into the flatlands from our direction, you catch tantalising glimpses of the *parador*, the old monastery of San Vicente, often seeming to float above a lake of mist. This is the *Estación de niebla*, according to the newspaper *La Voz de Galicia*. In summer we can leave home in T-shirts under a blazing sun to be met, 40 minutes later, by a blanket of white arising from the river Cabe which winds through the city of Monforte de Lemos. The Monforte basin acts to trap moisture from the river and cause a temperature inversion, producing mists at low level. It also produces spectacular thunderstorms.

When we stayed in Monforte for a week looking at houses five years earlier, there was an electrical storm every single night, starting at around 7.30pm as we left the *hostal*. Thunder would echo around the hills and lightning would fork down to earth for an hour, as we valiantly bar hopped under Galician umbrellas.

AUGUST

The city of Monforte is widely believed to have begun on the hill as a Celtic village which the Romans called Castro Dactonio. The Lemavi tribe and the *castro* were destroyed in the 8th century by invading Moors intent on creating a commercial centre here.

The name 'Monti Forti' is first mentioned in a document by Alfonso IX in 1190 AD, and in 1456 the land was given to the Counts of Lemos in perpetuity. Monforte de Lemos remained the seat of the Conde de Lemos until the 18th century when the 11th, and final, count died without issue whereupon it passed to the Dukes of Alba.

In 1888, the railway came to Monforte bringing commercial prosperity and social growth as a way point on the Madrid to A Coruña line. The line was inaugurated by the then king, Alfonso XII (there were a lot of Alfonsos in Spain). The train he and his extensive entourage travelled in can be seen in all its ornate and eye-wateringly lavish grandeur at the excellent Museo Ferrocarril near the railway station.

We ate our picnic lunch on benches in the *parque dos condes* overlooking the ducks on the river Cabe and the spectacular façade of the *Escolapios*, the huge school which sits next to the main car park. Afterwards we drove up to the *parador*, winding around the hillside of San Vicente.

A quicker way to the top is to take the steps from the Plaza de España towards the medieval town, which itself hugs that wizard's hat hillside, and to keep heading uphill until the *parador* and the square tower next to it become visible.

I have often made this steep but short climb with visitors and, even allowing for stops to admire the remnants of the old city walls and the last remaining archway into the old town, I usually beat the car to the top.

The roadway through the old town is cobbled and uneven. The houses are in varying degrees of renovation or abandonment. Some have wooden balconies on the first floor so low that any tall person (that is, over five foot six tall) would hit their chin on them. The *parador* at the top makes a perfect coffee stop. The café is open to the public and offers an opportunity to look at the old *cupola* in the internal courtyard and enjoy a sit down in the luxurious high backed settles.

Next door is the Torre de Homenaje (or *homenaxe* in *Galego*), a solid four-storey square castle keep with six foot thick walls, a vast underground rainwater storage facility for those long sieges, suits of armour dotted around the rooms and a chimney large enough to send six children to clean. Oh, and the best view of Monforte and its surrounds from the roof.

All of this costs, at the time of writing, an alarming 1.55€.

Mum managed the third floor of the tower, with its ancient wooden table and ornately carved cupboard but declined the open roof area with its magnificent views and spectacular drop.

We arrived home in time to put the chickens, and count the chicks, to bed. All was well *casa nosotros*.

SEPTEMBER
Naming the hens

I had been right about our little Wyandotte. Back in March, Sarah Bernhardt had gone broody. She had begun to hide her eggs, and each time we found them she would go off elsewhere. Eventually, as the weather improved, we decided to let her have a go at being a mother hen.

Throughout July, Sarah had sat patiently on her nest of nine eggs outdoors under a bramble bush. She had sat through sun and through rain. I was as anxious as a surrogate expectant mother could be. Despite the fact that Sarah had so far sorted everything out for herself, I worried. To S' delight and amusement I had even put an umbrella over the nest when it began to rain heavily. It looked quite bizarre poking out of the brambles. Each time Sarah got off the nest for a run round and a squawk, which she did daily, we would remove any new eggs and make sure the existing ones (each marked with a dot) were not cracked or damaged.

The other hens seemed to much prefer to lay their eggs in Sarah's nest amongst the brambles, and to run the gauntlet of her complaining when they sat on her, than to lay in a nice warm nestbox indoors. If we hadn't collected the extra eggs our tiny Wyandotte would have been sitting on eggs six deep after the three weeks.

Our efforts paid off, or maybe we were just entirely non-instrumental in any success, but on the

TOMATO, FIG & PUMPKIN JELLY

1st of August the eggs began to pip. By the end of August the eight chicks (one egg had been infertile) were all over the garden: small balls of fluff in my flower beds, falling into plant pots, eating anything they could find, and generally causing mischief.

At four weeks old, the chicks were still being taught to scratch about and feed themselves by Sarah. They were still tucking themselves under her wings, from where I would sometimes see a tiny head pop out when they were supposed to be having their afternoon nap. For the rest of the day though they loved to explore.

Our chicken wire fence was designed to keep in adult chickens and keep out predators. The holes were far too large to keep in baby fluff balls so, once they got brave enough, they simply wandered through and roamed freely around the garden. Sarah would squeak and call and get quite strident but they took no notice at all.

Until we lost one.

Diary Tuesday 1st September
Only 7 chicks. Hunted everywhere but nothing. Can only assume one of the village cats or a buzzard has had one. Locked the rest safely in the inside pen.
Off to Monterroso market. Quite a crowd. New people: John & Fiona from Palas, Ana & James and their sons, also from Palas, plus all the regulars.
This afternoon S cut a hole in the chicken wire to the 'downstairs' pen. Decided we would put the adults down there, open to the outside run, and leave Sarah and the babies enclosed in the top, secure run until they are too big to squeeze through the wire mesh. It's all we can do.

Diary Wednesday 2nd September Sunshine but dark clouds in the evening. No rain.
We have been helping Carmen next door today. I

SEPTEMBER

think after lending her the ladders she has decided we are not going to bite after all! She asked us yesterday if we would help move her chickens and rabbits, as the area in the garden where they are now is going to be a new utility room. Each time we start a new job it seems that builders immediately materialise elsewhere.
Anyway, we spent the morning clearing a space in Carmen's barn for the rabbit cages and to make a chicken enclosure. We got some new wire mesh from Taboada and dismantled the old to partially reuse... being the Wombles that we are.
Mum kindly made lunch whilst we were busy shed building. Very tasty too. Roast rabbit legs with courgettes, onion, tomatoes and french beans.
This afternoon we carried the rabbit cages over, me sneezing away... looks like I'm allergic to rabbit fur as well as cat, dog and horse! There goes my idea for a new fur jacket.
Both needed showers before tomorrow's trip to the coast.

We had been invited to stay with our friends, Cris and Steve, in Ortigueira again whilst Mum was here. We'd had a fabulous time at Christmas visiting them and the stunning (and empty) beaches around that wild northwest coast, so were looking forward to a rerun.

Diary Thursday 3rd September Sunshine... even on the coast!
Left early to get to Ortigueira for lunch. Beautiful trip in the sunshine. We stopped by the little zoo/park in As Pontes de Garcia Rodriquez and showed Mum the deer and llamas. Then stopped for our morning cake (minus tea) right on the tops next to one of the huge wind turbines. Amazing views. Had a good look round the bases for dead birds but couldn't find any. I'm wondering how

much of the English complaining about wind farms is to do with 'nimbyism'... not in my back yard. I remember the turbines in March, when I worked there, having to be stopped at night because the noise disturbed the prisoners in the high security prison nearby at Whitemoor. I also remember a story in the newspapers here about wind turbines. It was not long after we arrived. I thought it was locals complaining as in the UK: it was... that they hadn't yet got the promised wind turbines nearby! Arrived in Ortigueira in plenty of time to help Steve level his new driveway, have lunch in town, and visit yet another beach they have found in their travels (still deserted).

The following day Cris and Steve took us to a local ethnographic museum. It was run by an elderly couple who had collected all the items themselves and created the exhibit rooms. It was amazing. There were various rooms set up in outbuildings with more than 3000 exhibits; an old *Galego* kitchen with an open fireplace or *lareira*, a room set up as a dental surgery complete with an old dentist's chair and some scary looking equipment, an old school house, a pharmacy or apothecaries shop, an old forge with vast leather and wood bellows. (I took some photos of the latter for our resident blacksmith CJ.)

The proprietor also had the biggest kiwi vines I'd ever seen. They were held up on concrete pillars and loaded with fruit, though he told me it was a bad year. I was more than a little concerned about our flimsy looking wooden framework holding those monsters up in years to come.

Cris and Steve also took us to a special village, Espasante, which for many years had a pig (or rather successive pigs) called Antón, or Toñito to its friends.

SEPTEMBER

The origins are lost in the memories of the village elders but, on the festival of San Antón on 13th June, four men were traditionally crowned as members of the festival committee. One of their most important tasks was to buy a young pig. This pig would live in the village, being pampered by the villagers and roaming free in the town, on the beaches, or wherever it pleased, until, on 5th January the following year, it would be raffled off to one of the villagers to no doubt meet its end as *chorizos.*

St. Anthony is the patron saint of pigs, in addition to that of skin diseases and amputees (who on earth makes these up?), but the tradition of Antón the pig freely wandering the streets of Espasante ended in 2005. He began to cause problems, eating his way through garlic crops (I bet the pork was especially tasty that year) or famously falling off a cliff from where he had to be rescued (alive!). Still, the legend that was Antón the pig lives on and his statue sits in the centre of the village.

That last morning, it was drizzling in Ortigueira but, as we often found, it hadn't rained a drop when we arrived home that evening. Over the weekend, we carried on building Carmen's chickens their new home. As a thank you we were invited for tea on the Saturday. It was a lovely gesture and, as Carmen's cousin was there who spoke English, thankfully all the translating was not left to me. Carmen had made a tortilla and platters of *Jamón Serrano*, *chorizos* and local cheese. All washed down by local red wine, it was a most enjoyable evening.

S finished Carmen's chicken shed on the Monday and brought back some unwanted floor tiles and the promise of a second wooden wine barrel to match the one from *A Casa do Campo*, which we had already cut in half and planted up.

TOMATO, FIG & PUMPKIN JELLY

On the Tuesday there was another big fiesta. This one was at the Ermida da Nosa Señora do Faro.

We had visited the tiny chapel at the very top of the Monte do Faro before. Then it had been a quiet, windswept place of rare beauty and peace. On Tuesday 8th September, it was hell on Earth!

There were cars chugging slowly up the hillside, looking for increasingly sparse parking spaces: too slowly for our old Escort which began to overheat long before we reached the car park. We spotted a space at the side of the road, too low down the mountain to be of interest to the hordes, and abandoned the car. It was a long uphill slog in the stifling heat. There was no breeze on that side of the hill, and the day was sticky as only Galicia can be on the hottest of summer days.

On the very top of the mountain was an overflowing car parking area and stalls selling plastic tat, *churros* (doughnut sticks), and hotdogs. There were bouncy castles in the shape of Sponge Bob Squarepants (*Bob Esponja*), air tennis tables, and children's carousels. All were jostling for space and shouting their wares. In the tiny chapel a priest was giving a service, vying with the rabble and noise beyond. The brightly coloured balloon figures of My Little Unicorn competed with the cries of stallholders vying to get attention. The whole, sorry scene reminded me forcibly of the Biblical story of Jesus casting out the merchants from the temple. I'm sure the original festival didn't include bouncy castles. Still, there was a slight air movement up here and a welcome ice-cream in the shade of a large oak tree.

Deciding to forgo the embarrassment of trying to get a table at the *parillada* after our disastrous attempt at the *empanada* festival, we returned down the mountain to the wonderfully cool interior of Bar Mencia in Taboada. We even spent an enjoyable half hour chatting about possible menus

SEPTEMBER

for the wedding to be, and totally failing to pin Luisa down to a price.

> *Diary 11th September So hot…31°C on the terrace. Up early to take Mum back to the airport. She has had a great time, she says. She has certainly been helpful processing my thousands of tomatoes, podding beans, and covering the blanket box (with the help of S again and hindrance of yours truly, who doesn't know one end of a needle from the other).*
>
> *Back home for lunch of pasta with fresh tomato sauce and basil.*
>
> *S is back on the roof, cementing behind the kitchen chimney in an attempt to stop the leaks when it rains heavily. Of course we won't know if he's been successful until it rains heavily!*

After two and a half weeks of 'holidaying' with our visitor, we returned to this year's primary project. I spent the weekend varnishing the floor in our new master bedroom while S tried, with only partial success we found out later, to stop those leaks through our kitchen chimney. We also put on the final pieces of plasterboard for the new hallway-living room ceiling. We were finally bat proof!

Tuesday 15th September. Actual drizzle - for 30 minutes…

Dear Mum,

…And dry again by lunchtime haha.

I am missing my sous chef here! Made another huge jar of tomato sauce this morning. Certainly a better year than last. No sign of blight so far so I'm hoping tying them up to the sticks and letting the air circulate worked. I've also taken off most of the lower leaves as you suggested. Can't say it's a drier year, though we haven't had any rain since the day you arrived in August, and September so far has been much hotter than the 'summer' months this year. Pity the outdoor pool closed at the end of August, would've been just right now for a dip!

Yesterday, S finished the second chicken shed for Carmen (this one for the pollos... the big fat white chickens for eating rather than eggs), then we rolled the barrel she had given us across the road. S is going to cut it in half for me. I think I will put the two halves in front of the Long Barn in the sunshine and use them for parsley and carrots. The monster is loose in the allotment again, so I can't plant them there.

Mike and John, who you met at the market, have invited us to a party next week. Their friend Helen is having a birthday bash. I think she is 85. If Mike is cooking it should be good.

I used up the last of that Balinese rabbit dish to make meatballs today. They were delicious with noodles and coconut sauce. Have to use up the evidence before my niece comes on the 23rd!

Wednesday cooler and drizzly. CJ's friend Pete has arrived so we knew the weather was about to change! It will improve when Belle arrives, I don't think she has ever had a bad weekend here. Who needs a barometer when we have weather inducing friends and relatives haha!

I have finished varnishing the floor in our bedroom (to be) and have been plastering around the doorway to the sunroom (to be) whilst S carries on filling all the tiny gaps in the plasterboard. I have also had a go polishing the ceiling in our current bedroom again. (Well, yours really, once we finish the 'master' bedroom.) I had done it before we started to use it last year but the wood has just soaked up the polish so I have given it another go with my liquid polish, I can hear it sighing in pleasure!

Thursday. I thought I had a paella lesson with José Manuel at the Anduriña today. He had promised to show me how he makes his paella as it is my favourite. As usual I must have mistranslated something because I got the time wrong. We have re-organised it for next week instead.

I did fillet pork and prunes, in a cream sauce for lunch. Our prunes, or sun dried plums, were very tasty but they haven't kept well so I need to dry them longer I think before putting them in jars. I'll get the hang of it eventually.

S has put the skirting board on in the middle bedroom while I've been podding beans... where are you? Haha. I also sowed some fresh celery seeds on the pea patch. It grew well last year and one plant had gone to seed. Worth a go.

TOMATO, FIG & PUMPKIN JELLY

The chicks are missing you feeding them and playing with them. They are causing all sorts of trouble! Hunting them all down in the evening to shut them in seems to take twice as long without you!
Love you tons and tons, hurry back
xxxxxxxx

The remaining seven chicks were thriving. We now only let them out to play in the garden whilst we could keep an eye on them. One day Sarah was squawking more than normal. I went to see what was amiss. She was strutting in front of the fence to the sunken lane and calling loudly. One of the chicks had managed to fall, or jump, or flutter, off the six foot high wall and was wandering up and down the track in unison with its mother above. Of course it was unable to get back up to her. We spent a delightful afternoon with butterfly nets trying to catch it while Sarah continued to squawk and chunter with alarm from above. Just two days later a different chick performed the same trick. This time we were organised and managed to corral it before it headed into the bramble patch next to the stone wall.

I would be pleased when they were too big to escape the wire fencing.

Why I had worried about the other hens harming the babies I have no idea. Tiny Sarah, from the day the first egg hatched, turned into an aggressive whirlwind whenever a hen made the mistake of passing within a few feet. She would fluff up her feathers until she looked like a huge round white ball, flap her wings, and hiss most alarmingly. The other hens soon learned to take a different route even if it meant a huge detour to get to the food bowl.

SEPTEMBER

The only one Sarah allowed near to her precious brood was our handsome cockerel, Buzz Lightyear. Ever the gentleman, Buzz would find titbits and cluck for the chicks to come and eat. He was never once aggressive to the babies and clearly adored Sarah.

Diary Friday 18th September Drizzle
Still no significant rain but a distinct change in the temperature overnight. Feels quite autumnal and the living room is quite cool in the evenings with its single glazed window. Plastered the last bit of the doorway to the sunroom-to-be and S finished sanding off the filler in the plasterboard in the hallway. We are ready for painting!
Made four pots of grape jelly.
Called at a glass place CJ recommended, on the way to the swimming baths. Asked for a quote for a glass door to the sunroom. S thinks it will let more light into the hallway, and the old wooden door is a bit tatty, although a number of people have called it rustic... and I do like the wooden cat flap! Watched the baby chicks being taught how to have a dust bath by Sarah. I think the white one is an Angel, and the big cockerel will have to be Ginger...

People often think I am strange naming the hens. At one point we had 15 and I knew the names and lineage of every single one. Although they are not the brightest creatures in the animal world, chickens nevertheless all have distinct personalities and ours were no exception.

Our babies were at last starting to get their proper feathers and adult colouring. Angel was pure white and obviously from one of Sarah's eggs. She sported a flat top comb and her father's gentle nature. Her wings were especially long, making her look even more like an Angel when she stretched them out. Blondie was blonde and energetic. The group's mischief making ringleader, she was always looking for the next fun thing to do. Baby (whose real name was Frances, after one of my favourite film characters) was the smallest and youngest of our brood, and the last to come into lay. She grew into her proper name over the years and was never left in a corner.

There seemed to be two cockerels amongst the group. We had promised Jayne and Richard one, along with two females, in exchange for a (plucked and oven ready) duck. They chose a handsome chap of dark brown and ginger colouring and a cheeky nature, called, unsurprisingly, Ginger. The other cockerel would end up being dinner as we couldn't keep two.

Then on the 19th September, disaster struck.

We were enjoying our morning cuppa on the terrace when S gave a shout. As I looked up I caught sight of a shape near the chicken run. A cat? It took off. Not a cat then. I screamed as the shape manifested itself into a deadly buzzard, and I ran down the path waving my arms frantically.

"Did it get one, did it get one?" I burbled.

S thought so, and a quick head count confirmed we were another chick down. Too late we herded the remaining babies inside and closed the pop hole.

I was upset about the chick and felt it was somehow my fault for not keeping them safer. S pointed out that battery hens are kept perfectly safe but have a terrible life. I knew he was right but it didn't make me feel any better. Neither did the fact that it was the second cockerel who was, in any case, going to be dinner. It just wasn't the point. I wondered if he had felt anything and hoped not.

Diary Sunday 20th September
Late boiled eggs and toast soldiers. Spent the morning in the kitchen making lunch and choux

SEPTEMBER

buns, and thinking about our poor little chick. S fixed the last bit of skirting on and prepped the middle room for painting.
Lunch: Rabbit and ham stew with green beans. Choux buns with cream, figs and toasted walnuts.
Went on an apple hunt after lunch. One box of cookers to save and one to use up. Two bags of eaters to save from the good tree (no idea what variety but delicious apples, red and crunchy. They store well too). Made two pots of apple butter and cracked a small pile of walnuts. Then we both started painting the last wall in bedroom two. S cutting in (he's neatest), me rollering (and making the most mess!).

That evening we had a miracle.

I was egg collecting in the outside run when a chick limped from under the bramble bushes. It couldn't be, could it? I asked S for a head count but my instincts were right, it was our missing cockerel chick.

The chick was cold and shivering, and rather dishevelled having spent the night under the bushes, but very much alive. S offered it some corn which it gobbled down in record time.

We pieced together events as best we could.

The buzzard, I still maintain due to my screaming (I can scream really rather well) and arm windmilling, must have dropped his prize as he flew away and Lucky, as the chick inevitably became known, would have hidden in the bramble patch, alone and abandoned, until hunger won out over fear.

We think his leg was either damaged in the fall or through being gripped by his attacker. However his injury came about, he needed help getting into the chicken pen for a few days but had no lasting problems... other than a tendency to boast about his fight with a monster to anyone who would listen!

TOMATO, FIG & PUMPKIN JELLY

Lucky actually lived up to his name a second time. But that was still in the future...

Diary Tuesday 22nd September Hot by 11am
Up late. Collected our first melon and first aubergine. S scraped the pan clean after I burnt it again (oops!) with the tomato sauce. I made muffins, and a pork and cucumber stew for tomorrow.
Rich and Jayne collected us to drive to Helen's birthday party at Mike and John's.
Mike had made a great lunch for around 18 of us and there were lots of new people to chat to. One lady runs a Casa Rural nearby and offered us a look round. Lots of building and design ideas.
Home 9pm, tea and bed. Need to be up early for Belle.

My niece, Belle, arrived with no surprise whatsoever to sunshine. Pete left the same day. They were like the weathervanes in a clock. One in, one out. It was even mild overnight as we walked back from Bar Mencia in the dark, along our quiet road enjoying the silence... other than the snuffles and squawks from our resident wildlife and our giggles from trying not to wander off the blacktop into a ditch.

Diary Thursday 24th September Sunshine...of course
Belle helped me pick grapes and start another batch of wine while S strimmed the grass in the orchard, then we all helped to rake the grass into piles before lunch at the Anduriña. Postponed my paella lesson until next month but enjoyed José Manuel's deliciously unctuous paella for lunch. (Starter of course! Galegos never have paella as a main course.)
Visited the river beach at Da Cova after lunch. Sunbathed and read. A young chap with his kids

SEPTEMBER

was fishing from the pier. We wandered over to have a look in his pink plastic bucket which was full of crayfish. They were throwing in a piece of string baited with toucino (pig fat) and pulling them out by the dozens. For a river paella, he told me. Slightly concerned that the crayfish were all congregating by what looks like a sewage outlet pipe.

Grape picking has started along the Miño. The steep terraces are filled with shouting people carrying huge plastic tubs full of blood red grapes or virginal white ones to waiting flatbed trucks and vans. I'm wondering if it's easier to haul the empty crates uphill then carry the laden ones down to the road... if you are topside of the roadway, or take the empty ones downhill then drag the heavy crates back up to the road... if you are on the downside. I think that on balance I'd prefer to allow others to pick and just drink the resulting produce.

A number of years later we were persuaded to help in the grape harvest by our local *Cura*. Don Pepe has a vineyard in one of the most stunning settings I have ever seen. It sits high above the mighty river Miño, benefitting from long sunny days. His bodega is a cosy one roomed affair with a huge open fireplace in one corner and the biggest glass topped table that could possibly fit into the stone built space. In fact I couldn't help but wonder if the bodega was built around the table. Don Pepe told us that a team of helpers had carried the table down the hillside for him and installed it into the bodega. Such is the power of prayer. Sadly the magnificent glass top, fully ten foot by five foot was cracked in the process. It still feeds more than the last supper though.

We first met Don Pepe in our local bar, Scala, where he was engaged in a very vocal game of cards with some other patrons. We had no idea he was a priest at the time. Don Pepe is nothing like my idea of a priest. He reminds me of a naughty schoolboy, like Just William: one who is always into mischief but never quite gets into trouble because of that cheeky smile. On that first meeting, one of his friends was accusing Don Pepe of cheating at cards.

Don Pepe also, by his own admission, makes some of the best wine in the region. He even has a wonderful little ditty to remind people... *'Si no gusto el vino Pardal, preparar para su funeral'*. Roughly translated... 'if you don't enjoy the Pardal wine, you must already be dead'.

The *Cura* had mentioned his harvest previously but had failed to tell us where the vineyard was. There are miles of winding lanes along the Miño, each branching constantly to different vineyards, dead ends, or lethal drops. Then one day, Don Pepe found mum and I in Bar Scala having a coffee and using the internet. Seizing his opportunity he decided to kidnap us and show us his bodega. By the time we reached the vineyard – a scant but terrifying distance away (Don Pepe's driving seems to owe more to the good Lord than to road safety) we were exhausted.

As we parked, far too near the edge of a terrifying drop, I stared at the view. The tiny, one way track we were on was around three quarters of the way up the hillside. Below us marched rows of neatly trimmed vines all the way down to the Miño some hundred feet below. Above us were more vines, a set of narrow stone steps and, nestled into the hillside, sheltering below the roadway, a modest stone building – the bodega. A bodega (or *adega* in *Galego*) is literally a wine cellar but they appear all along the Miño as buildings for viticulture. The law states that one may not sleep in a bodega but they are used for pretty much any other daily activity.

SEPTEMBER

First we had to inspect the throne room. In an adjacent shed-like building was a fully flushing toilet, complete with a redstart and its nest perched above the sink. There is no sewerage system on that steep hillside. I didn't ask where the toilet flushed *to*.

Inside the bodega we were seated at the magnificent glass topped table. Stubby glasses were found, rinsed off, and filled with a glowing golden wine. A cupboard at the far end of the single roomed building yielded a thick length of *chorizo* and an ancient chunk of cheese. These were sliced and offered up together with a second glass of wine, this time one of Don Pepe's famous (at least in Taboada) young reds. The sharp strong cheese and chewy salty *chorizo* were perfect accompaniments to the fresh acidic wine. However I was aware that it was now 1pm. I hadn't yet started lunch and S would wonder where we had got to. Also I was starting to feel a little tipsy... it was early for me to start drinking!

Don Pepe dropped us back at the bar clutching a bottle of completely clear liquid, his homemade *augardente*, a treat for first time visitors to his bodega, and a promise to help with the harvest the following week.

On the day we finally helped Don Pepe with his harvest there was a cold, all-consuming mist along the Miño as we drove up. I was bundled in four layers of clothing and wondering why we had agreed to this early start to the day.

By noon I was down to my T-shirt as the mists lifted to reveal that stunning view in all its glory. The temperature had been just 3°C when we arrived and I could see little puffs as I breathed out. By the time we finished that afternoon it would be 33°C and I would feel drops of sweat rolling into my eyes as I puffed along the rows.

TOMATO, FIG & PUMPKIN JELLY

There were around 12 of us grape picking. Each was assigned a row and handed a pair of secateurs and a plastic crate to fill with fat bunches of grapes. Don Pepe had white and red grapes to pick but that day we were concentrating on the reds. The purple Garnacha, which give the wines their deep colour, and the prized local Mencia grapes needed to be kept separate. Don Pepe showed us how to differentiate. The Garnacha are red inside whereas the Mencia grape has a red skin but white flesh. It soon became obvious which was which but I spent a good while at first squeezing grapes to check which variety I had, and my gloves were soon sticky and reddened from the Garnacha juice.

Picking involved crawling down the narrow row between low growing grape vines pushing the crate ahead and snipping the hanging bunches. In our area, the Ribeira Sacra, grapes are generally grown as short three foot high cordons, the rows separated by a space just wide enough to fit a fairly narrow body. The heavy mists over the Miño are said to improve the flavour of the wine as the natural yeasts go to work on the grape skins. Too much mist or rain sends the grapes mouldy though. This is why the timing of the harvest is always so important. Too early and the grapes are not sufficiently ripe for a good flavour, too late and they start to rot. That year we were just in time. The grapes were bursting with flavour and juice. As each crate filled it had to be dragged to the end of the row where a railway line awaited. Don Pepe had a rare narrow gauge funicular railway running from the bottom of his vineyard to the track, where a truck waited. The collectors stacked our filled crates onto the little wagons and the electric railway climbed its way upwards. Much easier than having to carry loaded crates up the hill.

By 1.30pm we were sweating, sticky with juice, and wasp magnets. It was time for lunch.

SEPTEMBER

Mum had been roped in to help with the catering. Being Galicia, lunch can never be a snackette or a sandwich but always a full three course meal, heavy on protein and carbohydrates. Galicians may not be the most svelte race on this earth but they are, by and large, healthy and long-lived. On this day, Mum had peeled the potatoes for our *carne ó caldeiro*, literally boiled beef in a cauldron. This is a very typical *Galego* dish which benefits from being left bubbling away for hours. Today, the cauldron had been set up outside on a huge gas burner such as used for the *pulpo* on market day.

We started though with the *torremos,* thick slices of salty home-cured bacon speared onto a pitch fork (which had probably been cleaned since forking up cow-muck infested straw, though one never knows) and thrust into the glowing fire. This has to be one of the simplest yet tastiest ways of cooking bacon I know. As the bacon cooks it is unceremoniously plonked onto a waiting tray of sliced, local bread. Galician bread has to be the best in the world. Slow risen using only natural yeasts and baked in wood-fired bread ovens it has a solid, almost impenetrable crust and a soft spongy interior that resists degradation by liquids. Sit a lump of *Galego* bread in your soup and you are guaranteed it will not have fallen to pieces by the time your soup bowl is empty, unlike most quickly risen commercial breads. In this instance it is perfect for soaking up all that bacon fat, making probably the best bacon butty in the world.

After the showmanship of the bacon, we settled down inside the wonderfully cool interior of the bodega to a banquet of fresh *empanada*, mussels, cheese, *chorizo*, and salad (made by Mum and the only 'vegetable' course generally accepted by a *Galego* male), followed by our *carne ó caldeiro*: the meat silky soft from long cooking, the Galician potatoes sweet and earthy. Galicians also have wonderful potatoes. They are yellow and floury with a rich taste and some of the only potatoes I can eat with no accompaniment. These potatoes though were covered in sweet paprika and olive oil with more chunks of fresh bread to dip the juices.

Dessert was a delicious chestnut cake made by one of Don Pepe's army of lady helpers. Everything was washed down by the priest's own red wine, and coffee was accompanied by *augardente* and, for Mum alone, a specially found glass of brandy.

After lunch we somehow managed to waddle back to the upper terraces to finish the day's picking. Over-full of delicious food and even more delicious wine, the last couple of hours were exhausting. It had been fun. But hot, dehydrated, and tired we were pleased to finish for the day.

Tuesday 29th September Hot and sunny
Dear Mum,

We have had a lovely long (and sunny) weekend with your granddaughter. She has helped me to shuck all the corn for the chickens (3 big tubs full), pick grapes and rake grass. We nearly missed her flight though! We had been into Santiago to look around as it was an early evening flight. We had a lovely lunch at Dezaseis where I went with our English students 2 years ago, then we saw a notice for a 3D exhibition near the cathedral. It was fabulous. They had a virtual (pretend) botafumeiro, the big swinging incense bottle, which we had to operate by pulling on ropes. Our 'team' nearly sent it through the roof! Good job they didn't let us loose on the real thing. There was a car race, careering through the

SEPTEMBER

streets of Santiago (all on a big TV screen with us driving). S was very good at that. Then we sat in a cinema bit and had a sort of big dipper ride over the roof tops of Santiago. Very effective as the seats move from side to side as you go. Makes your tummy drop as you go down... through the roof of the cathedral, through the floor and the crypt and... into the fires of hell!!

It was so good we didn't check the time and it was getting rather late by the time we left. Of course it was a bit of a walk to where we had left the car (you know we won't pay haha) and it was parked on a very steep hill. Unsurprisingly, someone had blocked us in. S had to hold the handbrake while I manoeuvred us out as I couldn't pull it up enough to hold on the hill (really must get a new cable, it is so stretched you almost have to pull it level with the top of the seat to achieve anything!) There was quite a smell of burning by the time we got the car out and even less time to reach the airport. We had 35 minutes 'til the flight... and the gate closes 30 minutes before the flight time! Belle and I jumped out while S parked the car and we ran, rather quickly and inelegantly! Luckily she only had hand luggage and was straight through customs as everyone else had gone. The beauty of a small airport! I think Belle was a little stressed as her text said 'I love you Aunty Lisa but please don't do that to me again'. I thought 5 minutes to spare was pretty good, we try to leave much less time than that if possible!!

We called into the window place at Agolada on the way home to try and get a quote for an internal glass door (for between the hall-living room and sunroom). S thought it would let more light into the hallway and the chap we asked in Chantada still hasn't got back to us. Of course!

Still no proper rain, despite Pete's damp visit.

The washing machine won't do a full cycle now. The water pump from the well comes on and won't click off by the time we get to 'rinse'. That means it's hunting for water down there so the sump isn't filling quickly enough. We are having to rinse by hand then spin. I read about some 'magic' washing balls that don't use soap… can you check Lakeland next time you get a catalogue to see what they have? We could miss out the rinse cycle then, which would save water.

My tomatoes and peppers have enjoyed the long summer anyway. I pulled probably the last ones off today and even a couple of aubergines. We have 18 jars of sauce and I think about a dozen tubs in the freezer which you did for me plus some dried tomatoes and peppers and some frozen fried aubergines and courgettes.

SEPTEMBER

Wednesday. Had an amazingly loud thunderstorm this afternoon. Sounded like the thunder was right overhead and there were some spectacular lightning flashes and... not even a half inch of water in my bucket outside!

Monterroso market tomorrow. I'll post this on our way there. Anne and Simon are bringing us another 1000L water collection tub for the allotment.

Love you tons and tons

XXXXXX

PS The chicks send their love. They are growing daily and like jumping on our shoulders when we go in the pen.

I was fascinated by our teenage chickens and loved to watch them learn to peck, to flap, and to somehow fly into the highest branches of the trees. And, although we have had many hatchings since, that first brood of our very own chicks, with their losses and rescues, long wings and lucky escapes, will always remain special.

OCTOBER
Fungi foray

A warm and pleasant September moved into a warm and pleasant October. The 'expats' meet up, held at the market in Monterroso on the first of every month, was buzzing and someone had the bright idea to hold an indoor picnic, at the hotel where we met, the following month on *Todos Santos*. Yours truly was left to organise it.

Diary Friday 2ⁿᵈ October Sunshine
CJ arrived at 10am to help concrete the storeroom floor. Shuttered and poured half the floor. All finished by tea (and cake) break.
Rang round to see who is willing to bring stuff for the picnic lunch next month. Mike offered to make one of his excellent paellas on the spot if he can use the kitchens. Suggested he speak to the hotel directly.
Sorted apples for storage and eating, and checked the spuds for any rotten ones. They seem to be keeping okay in the big wooden box in the downstairs barn.
S had a trip out to order more sand and gravel for our next concreting day then sorted out his electrics, tidying up the mass of spaghetti-like wires.
Cleared out the Long Barn to fit the new cube Anne and Simon brought over. It will be attached to guttering draining the roof and hopefully fill up.

OCTOBER

The idea is to then deliver the water across to the allotment where it is most needed.

Diary Saturday 3rd October Sunshine
Hoed asparagus bed while S finished clearing a space for the cube. This one must have contained some kind of juice. S has tipped it over to drain.
Pushed Eusebio's rock (which he told us to take, honest!) off the track and into our growing wall on the west side. That area is looking more garden-like by the day.
Made a jar of cucumber pickle and picked a load of damsons for jam. S levelled the second half of the storeroom floor ready for CJ tomorrow, moving the small freezer out of the way and removing the wooden shuttering.

Our next project was the kitchen ceiling and my longed for storeroom. We needed the ceiling completed before the winter so the *cocina* could be relit. And we needed a proper floor in the storeroom first so we could move a temporary kitchen into there whilst the old ceiling came down. Our friend CJ had promised to help concrete the floor, and provide the cement mixer. We just needed a few more nice days to get the floor finished – that's all.

The Galician weather had other ideas.

The rain, when it came, came as only Galician rain can – heavy and persistent. And just in time for our second lot of concreting.

Tuesday 6th October. Plenty of rain
Dear Mum,
It has now rained constantly for three days. Started Sunday when CJ came to help concrete the rest of the storeroom floor. Luckily they set the cement mixer up in the horno bit so only S got soggy, barrowing it

down to CJ inside. It looks very nice and level. I shall tile it eventually then I can get all my preserves out of the kitchen. I shall have shelves round the walls full of all my stuff!

It carried on raining on Monday all day. The new water cube in the Long Barn has already filled up from the short piece of guttering S put up along the Long Barn roof as an experiment and we have filled the water butt on the allotment. (Using a hosepipe to connect the two.) So it seems to be working! Eventually we will extend the guttering along the whole roof area and try to make a more permanent connection across the track. We even got some nice thunder and lightning displays to go with the downpour!

I spent most of Monday running about anyway.

I needed some more sugar for my jams (damson this week) so collected Martin (who is staying in Stefan's house) as he needed a new gas bottle. No gas bottles to be had in Taboada, and no sugar, so that was a wasted morning! S meanwhile was painting the ceiling in the hallway upstairs, but he ran out of paint so I said I'd collect Martin again and try Chantada for the gas. At least that was a success. We got the gas bottle and the paint, and Martin bought me a bag of sugar so I got my jam done too.

OCTOBER

I had planned stuffed vegetables and hummus for lunch but I was in a rush by then and forgot to prick my aubergine which exploded all over the oven! Incredibly messy and took way more time to clean it up. Ended up with stuffed peppers... but no aubergine. I did make a nice hot water crust pork pie though and 5 pots of damson jam. And the hallway ceiling looks nice and white!

I've been out today too. Met up with Jayne for lunch and to sort out our seed club. We decided that as you get so many seeds in a pack with things like cabbages, it would make more sense to share. So we spent the day deciding what to order and, it has to be said, mainly chatting!

First two salamanders out tonight on the road. Managed to relocate them. We have to drive really carefully back from the swimming pool when it's mild and damp as the silly things sit in the middle of the road waiting for an insect to land on their nose. The neighbours must think we are daft. I sit as lookout, and every time we spot one I jump out and carefully relocate it off the road. Mind you, the neighbours already think we are daft so it doesn't matter if they see me haha.

Wednesday. Think we have had enough rain now! Certainly the washing machine is going fine, so no rush for those washing balls!

TOMATO, FIG & PUMPKIN JELLY

As it's not outdoors weather I've been in the kitchen. Made 4 tubs of peach (or apricot) puree and more tomato sauce. I also got ahead by making a pork stew with peanuts for Sunday and a pasta salad for Friday. The reason I've got so ahead on the cooking front is that we are planning to pull down the kitchen ceiling on Friday (before going to the swimming baths as I think it might be a slightly mucky job!) so I won't have an oven for a while. We decided we had better get on with it or the new ceiling won't be up before I want the cocina relit for winter. We will get back to finishing flooring the hallway upstairs afterwards!

We emptied most of the foodstuffs out of the kitchen today into the newly concreted storeroom. Will finish clearing the room out tomorrow after my cookery lesson at the Anduriña.

Love you tons and tons
Xxxxxxx

Thursday was my aborted *paella* lesson from the previous month. I did a bit of shopping whilst in town (essentials such as bread, chicken food and the wonderfully useful expanding foam which we call *espuma* and the Spanish use to fix everything) then headed up to the restaurant.

It took a while to make José Manuel hear me, as he was busy in the kitchen when I arrived, but he was very patient and an excellent teacher.

He showed me how to cook the onions slowly in olive oil to create a wonderfully sweet caramelised flavour base. He grated the tomato so none of the

OCTOBER

juice is lost but the skin remains behind to be thrown away, a clever trick.

I asked José Manuel if it was difficult to know how much to make of each dish. He told me they can have from three to 33 covers over a lunchtime. He usually does *paella* on a Thursday (hence the lesson) and does 12 portions. Once it has gone, it has gone. Any shortfall is made up with the regular starters like Russian salad or soup.

Once the *paella* was ready José covered it with tinfoil until lunchtime. He kindly offered me a portion for lunch. As S was still at home emptying the rest of the kitchen, I opted to buy a second portion and took them both home. Dinner sorted!

Diary Friday 9th October Probably dull but in the kitchen all day so not sure.
Set forth to pull down the ceiling in the kitchen. S decided it was better to knock it off from above and clear the rubble as we go. I got to bucket the rubble onto the track and into the cheese store near the gate. Quite successful as it goes. The largest lumps of brick missed my head by inches, but they did miss! And a piece of ceiling board, which wasn't as rotten as it should have been, was deflected off the cocina, did a somersault, and landed smack on the new chest freezer (which we hadn't moved because it's full) putting a nice dent in the top. Otherwise, as I say, quite successful and all out in time for lunch, which was the tuna pasta salad I made on Wednesday.
Afterwards we both moved six wheelbarrowfuls of dust, rotten wood, and various animal remains plus stacks of useable firewood and more rubble. Swept and tidied the kitchen. Nicely dusty and filthy for our bathnight. I wonder what they think of us at the swimming pool?
Stopped for tasty scones and chat with CJ on the way home but my lungs have so much dust in them today I couldn't breathe, so didn't stay late.

TOMATO, FIG & PUMPKIN JELLY

By Saturday evening we had got rid of all the rubbish. S had removed dozens of nails from the roof timbers and cemented the gaps between the roof and the top of the stone wall to stop more mice entering the roof space. We live in hope. The kitchen was not however useable as there was rather a lot of dust still floating down onto the worktops from the open roof space. Our little two ring gas burner which came with the house, and which had caused all sorts of fun when we had initially tried to get a gas bottle to use with it, was called back into service for our meals.

Saturday was egg and chips day, easy, and Sunday's casserole was already prepared. I even managed poached pears and ice cream for Sunday pudding.

We'd had such a fun time demolishing the kitchen ceiling that by the Monday we decided to treat ourselves to a day off. I'd heard that there was a rather special festival going on in O Grove on the wild, west coast of Galicia – the exaltation of seafood (*Fiesta de Exaltación del Marisco*). It would also solve the problem of Monday's dinner.

Our friend and builder extraordinaire, Les, and his family, had camped nearby the previous year and recommended the area. My old guidebook meanwhile described O Grove as 'the Blackpool of Galicia'. That in itself was intriguing enough without the thought of fresh oysters.

So it was that with visions of kiss me quick hats and candyfloss under a tower, we set off for the coast. In that respect, O Grove was a complete wash out with not a silly hat in sight. In every other respect, it was perfect.

The west coast of Galicia is full of inlets, rias or fjords, like a childish drawing of a coastline. O Grove is on a peninsula, a bulge of land above a long, narrow spit joined to the mainland near Vilalonga. The causeway is the width of two lanes of blacktop

OCTOBER

with golden sandy beaches either side. At the top the land bulges like a balloon with two horns. The westernmost horn is San Vicente do Grove, beyond which is the wild Atlantic sea all the way to the Americas. O Grove is at the northeast tip of the isthmus. Facing back towards the mainland, it is sheltered from the worst of the Atlantic fury and only a rather wet hop, skip and jump away from the seaside town of Cambados.

O Grove town is a small fishing port. The shallow waters of the ria are perfect for artificial mussel beds, which line the harbour reaches as far as the eye can see. It also makes O Grove the perfect spot for a seafood festival.

We arrived on a beautiful sunny morning and set to exploring the area. We wandered the harbourside, gazing at the granite sculptures lined up for a competition in progress. I watched competitors making last minute adjustments with angle grinders. I couldn't help thinking, one slip and the statue would be the next Venus de Milo.

There was a large marquee set up by the harbour but we were saving the main attraction until later so wandered off to find lunch.

Many of the restaurants in O Grove, unsurprisingly, excel in seafood. Specifically a seafood platter made for sharing. As we would hopefully be indulging in a surfeit of seafood that evening, we opted for a restaurant serving a more eclectic *menú del dia*.

The *Mesón*, called imaginatively, *Mesón del Mar*, had a reasonably priced *menú del dia* in addition to the ubiquitous platters of seafood. As we entered the restaurant, a black clad waiter appeared and escorted us to a round table in the middle of the room from where I could happily observe other diners and, more importantly, other meals as they were carried to and fro. He handed us a printed menu (brownie points there) and left us to peruse.

TOMATO, FIG & PUMPKIN JELLY

At the next table a couple tucked into a platter of seafood for two. It was enormous. But as they waded through the crab, lobster, langoustines, oysters, and the rest, the pile of shells rose in proportion. By the time they had finished, the platter looked as full as it had when they began.

The *menú*, was interesting: in addition to the usual suspects were a *fideuá*, a sort of *paella* made with pasta, a rack of pork ribs, and fresh grilled baby squid (*chipirones*). S was considering his main course choice when the waiter reappeared with some freshly made *empanadillas* (small fried pies) filled with fresh mussels – a very welcome but highly unusual touch here in Galicia.

My *fideuá* was delicious, full of the flavours of the sea and only dripping down my chin on relatively rare occasions as I slurped. S had opted for the *chipirones* which he said were equally tasty.

We had already chosen our desserts. There were a number of offerings in a large refrigerated cabinet behind us but one stood out. It was a large glass coupe of chocolate mousse topped with mini Oreo biscuits. Two please!

After paying our measly 12 euros a head for a rather filling lunch, we opted for a walk over the bridge into A Toxa.

Although O Grove is at the end of the peninsula, it isn't the end of the road. To the east of the town, nestled into the small gap between it and the Galician west coast mainland, is a small island called La Toja (or A Toxa in *Galego*). A Toxa means 'the muddy place'. Named for its health giving muds and thermal waters, legend has it that a man had a very sick donkey which, rather than kill, he left on A Toxa island to fend for itself. A week later, possibly feeling guilty for abandoning the poor creature… who knows… he returned to find a healthy animal, rolling in the muddy pools. Thus was born the beginnings of the island as it is today.

OCTOBER

La Illa da Toxa is now a luxury wooded private living complex of executive homes, spa hotels, a casino, golf courses and tennis courts, and a shell adorned church. It is reached via a short road bridge built in the 1800s and has sentry boxes positioned on the island side, presumably to deter undesirables from invading this rather exclusive place. Luckily for us the sentry boxes were unmanned on this sunny weekday lunchtime so we were allowed in.

The small chapel on A Toxa is known colloquially as the shell church (*capilla de las conchas*) but is in reality a chapel dedicated to La Virgin de Carmen del Mar, patron saint of the sea. It is a small building entirely covered in scallop shells – the symbol of St. James, and of the pilgrims walking the Camino de Santiago, and shone a blinding white in the afternoon sunshine. The streets around the *capilla* were lined with stalls selling tatty miniature reproductions of the shell church, nicely made lace, and holy water. Not for the first time I mused at the incredible commercialism of many religions and the ability of others to take money from those who can least afford it.

Although the shell church is famous for its cladding, it was by no means the only building to be covered in this way. In years past, large shells were often used near to the sea, where they were abundant, as a practical insulation against the salt water and high humidity of the area.

It was warm in the October sun so we wandered the streets for a while before stopping for a siesta on one of the shaded tree-backed beaches facing back towards the harbour of O Grove.

In the evening we returned to the harbour front eager to sample some fresh seafood.

The harbour area was covered by a large marquee. Quiet that morning, there was now pandemonium inside in the cool of a Galician October evening. People were rushing hither and thither carrying brown ceramic platters and bowls of fresh seafood (how much fresher can you get than a few metres from where it was landed?), baskets of bread and bottles of wine, slabs of Santiago tart and folding chairs.

After a few minutes staring in awe at the sights, we figured out the system: potential diners had to go to a large raised dais in the centre of the marquee, which accommodated a desk and four smiling ladies, to choose their delights from the three page menu provided (in *Galego* obviously).

Once our dishes had been chosen and paid for we were issued with cloakroom type tickets, to hand in at the relevant stalls. As the 'walls' of the marquee were lined with said stalls, each one specializing in one particular dish – maybe tiger mussels or raw oysters or the famous *centollo* (spider crabs), the reason for the chaos soon became clear.

There were large trestle tables filling the space between the stalls and the central platform, with people jostling for elbow space on them and shouting to friends and family as they tried to secure a meagre part of a table. There were no chairs, hence the folding ones brought by knowledgeable folk.

I decided we had better be organized about this (what me?) so I sent S off to procure bread, wine, and a table whilst I traipsed the stalls, hunting for the ones we wanted. This was made more difficult by the fact that the name of the dish on my scrap of paper (*ostras en salsa marinara*) did not match the name on the stall, which was that of the company or outfit selling the dish.

Eventually I made it back to a small gap, which S had grabbed at the end of a crowded trestle table, with my haul: oysters, both raw and in a seafood sauce; huge langoustines; razor clams; a seafood *paella* and oven baked scallops in their shell. But I had missed out on the *percebes* (goose barnacles) – a

OCTOBER

Galician delicacy which are both outrageously expensive and outrageously dangerous to harvest from the slippery, algae covered rocks, as the unpredictable seas swell and crash over the collectors.

Our supper, including the wine, bread, and a slice of *Tarta de Santiago* each came to under 20 euros - a ridiculously small amount for the freshest of seafood, even if we did have to stand up to eat it. We even got to keep the commemorative ceramic dishes, each labelled with the *Exaltación del Marisco* logo and the year.

O Grove's seafood festival has been held each year since 1963 giving the town the moniker of 'seafood paradise'. Over 200,000 people annually swell the town's population over the course of two weeks from the first Friday in October. That year was particularly busy due to the unusually good early October weather. We'd had a wonderful time. And a pleasant break from our labours.

Tuesday 13th October.
Dear Mum,

We had a lovely day off at the coast yesterday. Will have to take you there although you wouldn't enjoy all the seafood! It was a lovely place and having our meals out made a change from cooking on the little gas ring.

Today I had invited some of our friends over for a fungi foray but I still have no useable kitchen... hadn't thought of that when I organised it all!

Luckily it was bright and sunny again today so at least we could sit outdoors. I went out early to check where and what goodies might be out. Lots of parasols along the lane out towards town and a single wood blewit, looking so beautiful and lilac coloured underneath. I was so engrossed I nearly got myself run over by CJ and Gala arriving for the foray. They kindly gave me a lift home and had brought along one of CJ's delicious victoria sponge cakes for morning tea.

Richard and Jayne arrived soon after, so we had tea and cake whilst I did a talk on fungi and how to identify different groups (and which ones to avoid). I think it went well! We then left the chaps to carry on cementing and I took the girls on a wander. Found some ceps (the only wild mushroom Gala will eat, she doesn't trust me, whatever qualifications I may have haha). One largish puffball, though sadly no giant puffballs such as the one I found once in Stansted - I stuffed that one whole and wrapped it in bacon, scrummy. And a cauliflower or brain fungus (for its shape rather than its taste which is actually fresh and crisp when fried).

As I only had the ring burner set up on the terrace, I decided to make scrambled eggs, which of course we have plenty of, on toast, with fried mushrooms for those who dared! We finished off with more cake and fig sauce, the cake this time provided by Richard. I notice that with the exception of yours truly, cakes seem to be a male domain

OCTOBER

within our group!

Wednesday: The weather continues to be warm and sunny during the day although the early (9.00am) mornings are a bit chilly now. We want to get the kitchen finished off as soon as possible so we can light the cocina for the winter. Now we have finished making a mess knocking off the ceiling (and removing all the junk up there) S has started to fix the new, stained ceiling boards up, so hopefully in another week or so the room will be done. Hoping the nice weather lasts 'til then!

I have been on the allotment sowing clover as a green manure crop. We still have carrots and cabbages growing well and the leeks too. I also still have some tomatoes on though I have brought most indoors now to finish ripening as there is frost forecast this week. It has been a wonderful year and no blight thanks, I'm guessing, to our new method of growing them. I have 18 jars of sauce plus all the tubs you put in the freezer and six jars of sun dried ones. Should last us well into next spring. And so much tastier than tinned tomatoes.

The walnuts are starting to fall off. I thought we wouldn't have many due to a late frost and I was sadly correct. I think we had 56kg last year, don't think we will manage a quarter of that this year.

Had a tomato risotto for dinner with courgettes, peppers, aubergines, and toasted walnuts plus another part of the cauliflower mushroom. It goes lovely and crunchy when fried, a nice contrast to the ratatouille mixture.

We had another buzzard attack this afternoon. I saw it flying off. Luckily everyone was okay. Sarah had herded the babies underneath the bramble bush. She seemed very shaken but the babies of course were unconcerned. Not sure what we can do to keep it away now it knows dinner is down there.

I've uncovered my area for the broad beans which I will plant after we have some rains haha. The sunflowers and sweetcorn did reasonably this year so I will try that again and the squash grew well beneath. Clever those Romans eh?

Off to tidy up and light the fire upstairs as it's a bit nippy in the evenings now. S says I'm going soft with all this easy living. After last year I think he might be right... thankfully, haha.
Love you tons and tons
XXXXXXXxx

The late sun, rains, then continued sunshine meant it was a good autumn for fungi. I spent every spare minute hunting for specimens. I don't really care if they are edible or not. I just love to identify the things. Did you know that there are over two million species of fungi worldwide? And of those, only around 150,000 are described. I remember when I chose fungi over grasses for my identification module at university, the lecturer, Paul Lunt, saying,

OCTOBER

"most people choose a genus, you choose a whole kingdom to go at!" That was one of the hardest modules I did. Identifying fresh fungi is one thing, but all the specimens for my exam were dried and leathery, and looked exactly the same. The ergot on an ear of wheat was a dead giveaway though!

Around our house, here in Galicia, we have a raft of fungi. Some are edible, some delicious, and others deadly poisonous. I am fascinated by them all.

My go to fungi book is a 30 year old copy of the photographer Roger Phillips' *Mushrooms and other Fungi of Great Britain and Europe.* Although not as comprehensive as some field guides, the photographs are stunning and so much better for identification purposes than a drawing. The photographs help when deciding between two very similar but possibly deadly specimens, but the text is my favourite part of the book. Phillips talks about some species with a wry humour I love. For instance, talking of the aptly named Death Cap (*Amanita phalloides)* he says: ...

Sorry, I had this quote all lined up to use here but MacMillan, the large printing house which owns the copyright on that particular tome wished me to pay an amount I considered totally unreasonable for 60 completely referenced words. I shall therefore paraphrase...

The Death Cap is deadly and despite years of research into the toxins it contains, there is still no antidote. Symptoms include prolonged vomiting and diarrhoea lasting some time. Typically, this is followed by an apparent recovery. Within a few days death results from liver and kidney failure.

Makes you think doesn't it? (And I have to admit that Mr Phillips said it better.)

Here's some interesting trivia about fungi: The largest living thing on the planet is a single honey fungus (*Armillaria ostoyae)* which extends some 2385 acres or almost four miles underground. It's in the Malheur National Forest in Oregon if you want to check it out. Fungi are an entire kingdom of organisms the same as plants (flora) or animals (fauna). Unlike most green plants, which build up complex nutrients from the simple ones of water and sunlight, fungi break down complex substances into simple ones which they can digest.

Fungi have some of the most complex toxins known and, unlike the toxins produced from say a venomous cobra, there are no antidotes. The common fly agaric fungus (*Amanita muscaria)* is probably the cause of those rumours about Santa's flying reindeer. It is a strong (and unpredictable) hallucinogenic known to be irresistible to reindeer. The toxins work on the central nervous system causing the intoxicated person (or reindeer) to make exaggerated movements such as leaping high into the air to avoid a tiny obstacle. Thus a reindeer under the influence of the toxin could be seen to be flying.

Finally, the liberty cap (*Psilocybe semilanceata)* is a well-known hallucinogenic which grows frequently in lawns and pastures. When I worked at Friern Barnet psychiatric hospital it grew all over the grounds, and of course our patients knew exactly where to find the choicest specimens. Nature, and human nature, is interesting isn't it?

Friday 16th October Frost overnight, some courgette leaves blackened.
Hung up a load of tinsel around the chicken pen as that buzzard was flying around yet again. Don't think it can get to them but better to be sure. Dug a trench for my over-wintering broad beans while S continued putting up the wooden ceiling in the kitchen.
Found a polypore (chicken of the woods) mushroom on Mr Grumpy's tree. Not sure if he noticed me cutting it off but no one seems to eat

OCTOBER

them here. Carmen brings me all the parasol mushrooms she finds. She knows they are edible but says she isn't keen on them. I don't mind. The parasols dry well and the polypore looks spectacular.
Pasta with chicken of the woods mushroom, walnuts and cheese.
S was sick later. Shouldn't be any problem with the mushroom and I am fine but he tells me (now) that he had a bad reaction to mushrooms once as a child too!
Cut and dried 2 more trays of apricots outside as sunny and warm during the day.

Chicken of the woods, or sulphur polypore (*Polyporus sulphureus*) is one of the most distinctive looking mushrooms there are. I first saw one in a park in Stafford during a fungi hunt for my university module. It was growing out of the trunk of a chestnut tree, looking like a huge yellow and orange jelly bean. I could not believe it was actually edible, but taken young it has a pleasantly lemony sour taste. There are no known cases of poisoning from a chicken of the woods and it is a delicacy in some regions, including here in Galicia. Still, there is a first time for everything. (Note to reader. Please check any fungi you find before eating. Many fungi can be poisonous. Here in Spain pharmacies will identify fungi for you. Even common looking mushrooms can be deadly.)

Monday 19th October. Another lovely start to the week - sunshine though it is a bit breezy. Good drying weather.
Dear Mum,
Our new kitchen ceiling is almost complete. It would have been finished but we were 2 boards short (that's my measuring... oops)

so we had to pop into town for extras. It was a productive trip anyway as S checked his fuel allowance from the British Government... now he is 60! It will pay for one load of firewood so worth having (and they can't say it's too hot here in winter). I also checked my emails, and on the way back we found 2 parasol mushrooms for tea. I left the lad to carry on with the ceiling boards while I went on a further mushroom hunt. Found two more parasols to dry and a huge beefsteak mushroom on the old oak tree. Did you know that these were prized in the past as they give the wood a lovely dark hue? Taste good fried too. I had made some lovely rabbit meatballs (Thai style with coconut and lemon grass but no chilli of course!) for lunch. I had our parasol mushrooms on toast with goat's cheese for tea but S had eggs due to his adverse reaction last time... just to be on the safe side! I even picked a few chestnuts to dry. I want to try making some chestnut flour this year so will have to make an effort to pick a few more.

Tuesday: A bit breezy and cloudy today but no rain yet - which is just as well as now we have a nice clean kitchen, S has decided to grind out the disgusting old cement that had been plastered onto the old granite sink under the window. We had thought of replacing the old sink or, as it is so low even for me, putting another modern sink in over

OCTOBER

it. Firstly though it is part of the actual wall so knocking it out is not really an option. Putting another sink over the top would be complicated as there is no U-bend or trap to the sink or any way to easily fit one. The old sinks literally had a hole in the wall with a small stone trough on the outside to guide water away from the wall. I'm told that when they were at upper floor level, walking below after lunchtime was never wise! It's also part of the heritage of the place - the same as the cocina, with its odd arrangement of seating behind. I would prefer to keep it intact.

Unfortunately it can't be cleaned without some... very considerable... mess! The lad has started to grind out the old cement. The corners are particularly awkward but it will be worth the effort. The black and white granite underneath matches our worktops. I bet it could tell a story or two!

I made S take a shower outside this evening before he was let back into the house - he was grey from head to toes!

Wednesday: I have been planting my broad beans for spring as it drizzled a little today and yesterday evening. I remember Dad used to plant them in autumn. I will fleece them if it gets really frosty. S made me a very fancy cloche for the allotment, which I can move around to cover things, using some spare wood and poly-plumbing tubing. I just have to throw a fleece over it! Clever!

We are also picking the walnuts. We have to pick them every evening or the field mice come in and nibble them overnight. I don't mind sharing but they take a bite out of every one. Most annoying when you see a nice looking walnut in the grass then pick it up to find a neat circular hole in the other side! I suppose they are hungry too.

The sink is starting to look good. There was so much plaster on it that the lad's grinding disc has ground itself down so he had to pop into 'Arkwright's' for a new one. Of course Pepe spent the whole time trying to sell him a more expensive disc (and a load of other stuff he didn't need) instead of the one S wanted. All the time he was rubbing his hands together like Ronnie Barker in 'Open all Hours'. Oh that is such a good nickname for poor Pepe.

Thursday: At last the grinding is done. We have spent the morning cleaning up my nice new kitchen. Dust absolutely everywhere! I even got some in my eye, I think, as it was really sore this morning. I went into town to make an appointment for the doc but as I was at the counter I heard a booming voice shouting 'Is that Lisa Rrrose Wrrright?'. It was our doctor. He pronounces my name like no one else, rolling the r's forever. I love the sound of it!! He came to ask what I needed and when I showed him my eye he dragged me off to his office past all the waiting people and while

the poor receptionist was still looking for an appointment for me. He tells me eye problems are serious. That didn't help with the glares from the waiting hordes though as I came out with my prescription! He is the best doctor, always friendly and of course he speaks English!
Love you tons
xxxx

When we first signed up for a doctor here, the receptionist asked if we preferred a male or female doctor. While I was still debating, S, quick as a flash, said 'one who speaks English.' There was only one and Haizam got all us foreigners. Now sadly retired, he was a wonderfully funny doctor, always asking questions unrelated to the particular illnesses and always ready with a hello in the street or a quick diagnosis in the bar.

Within a day my eye was better, though it took longer to shrug off those looks as I walked past the waiting patients in the surgery.

Thursday 22nd October Sun morning and evening, drizzle between
Finished cleaning the kitchen up... took a while... before S lit the cocina. It must be autumn then! As we had made such a mess in the kitchen, moving the dust around, we had lunch out at Bar Mencia for a treat followed by more cleaning and vacuuming of the walls, floor, cupboards, everywhere! I even mopped the floor to dampen down the dust a little.
Carmen called over with a large tub of membrillo (quince preserve) and money for the work S did on her chicken shed. Declined the money but took the membrillo. Lovely with fresh Galego cheese.

TOMATO, FIG & PUMPKIN JELLY

Found a field mushroom in the compost bed. Looks like an Agaricus bisporus *but I will have to check very carefully to make sure. Too many lookalike species in that family.*

The *Agaricus* family contains most of our supermarket mushrooms, but not all of the family are as tasty. The one I found in the compost bed turned out to be a poisonous yellow stainer (*Agaricus xanthodermos*). The cap turned bright yellow when I squeezed it. Things, it appears, are often not what they seem!

Tuesday 27th October. Sunshine.
Dear Mum,
  We have been to Lugo today for supplies, and because we had a message from the telephone company to say we have to register our mobile phones. It is apparently a new thing to ensure terrorists can't use unregistered phones or something. Anyway it meant a trip into Lugo with some proof of ID so we did some shopping. Also called into the new Japanese place for a menu and price list. It looks rather expensive to be honest and very very empty at lunchtime. We, of course, went to Recatelo for lunch!
  We called in to see Richard and Jayne on the way home to pay for our wardrobes which we have ordered from B&Q in England. They will collect them (along with our real ales and marmite) in November. We couldn't get any built in wardrobes here as they are all 8 foot high (made for new flats I suppose) and we only have 6 foot and

OCTOBER

a bit at the lower end of the bedroom. Luckily the UK ones come slightly shorter (no idea why) so by the end of the year I should have somewhere to hang my boxes of clothes... how exciting is that haha. I shall be forgotten half of what I have!

On Saturday it was our third organised walk with the healthy walking group, so of course it rained. Very enjoyable anyway. We walked alongside the river Miño and stopped for snacks and drinks along the way.

S has gone back to laying the remaining floorboards in the hallway upstairs now our kitchen is clean and tidy, with its new ceiling and shiny sink. He was too enthusiastic with his spuma gun though as it broke! Luckily José exchanged it without any problems.

CJ brought us over two lovely metal brackets for the hanging baskets. They are ones he made years ago and he says he has nowhere to put them. I'm going to get the lad to put one near the horno and plant some little violets in it over winter.

I have painted all of the nice new kitchen (after three days of cleaning to get rid of all the dust). I now have the enjoyable job of restocking it. I just need some wall cupboards up and somewhere to put my cookery books! S says they will need far too much space... meanie.

After the rain at the weekend it has gone

back to sunshine again. A very strange but very pleasant October all in all. I found the biggest field mushroom on our local wander on Sunday. One of the fields near to the village up the hill has sheep grazing on it. The mushrooms must have loved the droppings as the field was full of them. One was the size of a dinner plate with dark dark gills and it smells heavenly. At least I know that one is edible, unlike my find last week, sigh!
Love you tons and tons
Xxxxxx

NOVEMBER
Beggars, and footsore walkers

As a child I was lucky to live in a council house backing onto fields and woodland as far as the eye could see. Those fields and woodlands were our playground, and I spent many happy hours wandering far and wide.

Across 'Massey's field' was an old manor house, derelict and fascinating. We were warned to be careful as the ground above the cellars was likely to subside. The cellars though were the best bit to play in. Those and the old swimming pool, still tiled but no longer holding water. The stables were collapsed and the house itself vanished beneath the undergrowth. I imagined it as it used to be: with a rose garden and horses peering over the stable doors. I hankered to return it to its former glory. Maybe buying *A Casa do Campo* finally allowed me to realise my ambitions. Albeit in a different country.

By November we had all but finished this year's 'projects'. The bedroom was painted and awaiting the fitting of the wardrobes. The hallway just needed the floorboards sanding and varnishing and our new stove to be installed. And the kitchen, though still old, had a nice new ceiling and shiny granite sink.

November 1st was All Soul's Day and the big *feira de ganadeiros* at Monterroso. This is the biggest fair of the year for the town, with stalls lining every street and *pulpo* stands threatening to trip up the unwary. There are animals for sale at the huge covered market at the top end of town, and we watched the horses parading down the main street. We 'expats' had a picnic planned at the hotel, though as usual things didn't go quite to plan.

Diary Sunday 1st November Todos Santos. Wet...obviously
Picked Linda and Martin up for the 'picnic' at the hotel. Linda had made one of her delicious apple pies whilst Mart had insisted on making cheese and onion sandwiches as his contribution. We laughed at him as being unimaginative but his sandwiches were one of the first things to go. Serves me right for being a food snob. (They were absolutely delicious... I had three!) The shared meal was excellent and Augusta had let us use the dining room overlooking the hills beyond. Unfortunately there had been a dispute over Mike bringing his gas bottle and paella pan. It seemed it would not meet health and safety regulations. Mike was understandably upset after buying all the ingredients and refused to come at all, so a group of us drove to theirs in the afternoon for a magnificent paella on top of the huge buffet lunch. Managed to somehow drive home despite having gained 10lbs in the day I think.
A&S dropped another 1000 litre plastic cube off for our rainwater collection project.

Diary Monday 2nd November Cool and cloudy but dry
Both manoeuvred the third cube to the top of the allotment. Dug a space out for it to sit level. I'm thinking one huge 10 000 litre tank would be good... and we could use it as a swimming pool in summer... just a thought. (NO! (S))

NOVEMBER

Spent the rest of the day sanding floorboards in the hallway ready for varnishing.
Lit the cocina. It didn't smoke, so left it burning 'til late.

Wednesday 4th November. Rainy and dull
Dear Mum,

We have been varnishing the hall floor. It looks so smart (and so different from when we first saw the house with that poky dark bathroom in there and the mouldy dank corridor to the other end of the house. Because the varnish is 'briliante' the floor is almost a mirror finish. And with the walls and ceiling all painted you wouldn't recognise the place! Once we get our stove set up we will use it as a sitting room in winter. At least until we get the big barn done.

Had our council tax bill yesterday. It was 28.88€ for the year again. You do realise that if you moved here you could live on what you save in bills!

Anne & Simon (cats and dogs) brought us another big plastic water cube on the 1st. It is for the allotment with the other one. The last one had juice or something in it but this one was motor oil. S has emptied out two five litre tubs so far. And, best of all, it is the same oil we use for the car so that's saved a bit haha.

I've been making chawl (or brawn) with the half pig's head CJ gave us when we went for our usual Friday night post swim chat.

CJ won't eat it, though he loves pork. I made two tubs of chawl on Saturday. I've made a couple of pork pies with some of it and have frozen the rest for sandwich pâté.

Had rabbit stew today with chestnuts (good this year) and a Sussex pond pudding for afters. Can't move now! I have also made some chestnut flour. If you remember I said I wanted to have a go. I dried the chestnuts (cut in half) behind the cocina. They fall out of the shells that way. Then I ground them up as fine as I could and left the 'flour' on a tray to dry out a bit more, then ground it again so it's pretty fine. I'm not sure how well it will keep so have been experimenting with using it. It is gluten free so doesn't work the same as ordinary wheat flour. The pancakes sort of fell to pieces (nothing to stick the mixture together without the gluten) but the chocolate sponge pudding was delicious so I made a couple extra for the freezer!

We had a short walk after lunch, and when we got back we found Lucky the cockerel in the garden enjoying the grass. He must've flapped his way out. Maybe off the roof of the well. He has got gradually more and more cheeky since his little adventure in September.

Thursday: Tried to put the cast iron stove together today for the hall-sitting room upstairs. We thought it would be simple… only four legs and the front ash catcher tray to fix. There were no instructions, or rather there were but they were for a different stove! We laid the stove on its side and found some holes where the legs obviously went... except when we stood it up the thing looked like it was kneeling down. The front legs were on too far back so it was at a very odd angle. We eventually found the right place for the legs and it looks very smart. We have ordered a granite slab for it to sit on from the marble place in Chantada. It is black and white local granite and three centimetres thick to take the weight. Then we can sort out the chimney and bingo, a second sitting area.

Anne & Simon were supposed to be coming for lunch today but they rang at 2.30pm to say they were running late. Eventually arrived at 5pm... we'd had our dinner by then. It seems they got lost! Instead of coming their normal route they had followed the new satnav which took them miles out of the way. By that time they had been wandering so long they were running out of fuel. The satnav then sent them back miles in the wrong direction for a petrol station! It eventually announced they had 'arrived' somewhere in the Taboada hills near the Miño!! Good job it's safe around here or anything could have happened to them.

Love you tons

Xxxxx

TOMATO, FIG & PUMPKIN JELLY

The community where I was brought up was safe and rural. As children we were given plenty of freedom to roam, though woe betide anyone who was late for dinner! Me and my friends would walk miles during the long, hot summer holidays.

One of my favourite places was a tiny hamlet called Boothorpe. Although it has a road to it, we would approach across the fields and it always seemed remote and cut off from the modern world. It was peaceful and the fruit trees always seemed to have an abundance of fruit just ripe for scrumping. When I was older I would cycle to Stretton-en-le-Field, another magical village. The name was an immediate draw: a touch of exotic in the heart of middle England. The village itself is hidden from the main road which runs past it, amongst tall trees. To my fertile imagination it was ephemeral and other worldly. I was sure that as soon as I cycled away again it would disappear like Brigadoon.

Although I moved to the 'big smoke' in my teens, some of my favourite places in London were alongside the Grand Union canal, or in Alexandra Palace Gardens when I lived nearby, or later in the less visited spots at Kew Gardens.

I moved back to Leicestershire in my thirties, to a hamlet of a couple of dozen houses and a church. It seems you can take the girl out of the country but you can't take the country out of the girl!

Moving to Galicia was a dream come true for that country bumpkin of a girl. We have chestnut woods all around. Being the last house in our tiny *aldea* of six, we can step into the woods from our garden and walk for miles without seeing another soul.

By that second year, we had explored much of our local area and had established a number of favourite walks. The local walking group we had joined back in March was an ideal opportunity to find favourite walks further afield, and we were excited to explore our piece of paradise.

NOVEMBER

So far we had participated in three walks and missed one due to visitors.

The first one, in June, was along the ridge of the Sierra do Faros – the high hills to the east of us. It was a 15 kilometre hike and designated a generous 'moderate'. The Faros are littered with wind turbines marching along the ridges. It is fascinating to see them, so huge and imposing, and silent, close up. It is also a long haul up to that point.

Upwards of 50 people set off on that hot and still June morning. The ridges between the windmills are bare, offering little shade, and by 10am the sun was beating down. I was pleased we had thought to put sun cream on.

Thankfully the group was well organised, with water and snacks on offer at regular intervals and an emergency vehicle for stragglers or those who could not manage the whole distance, of which there were only three. One of these was a young woman wearing high heeled strappy sandals who had blisters by the second ridge. She complained so much that the emergency vehicle offered her a lift. The look on her face as she was driven away in comfort, chatting animatedly to the two good looking emergency guys, said it all.

At the start of the walk we were given bright orange T-shirts to wear. It was surprisingly hard work to climb a ridge only to have to descend the other side then repeat this endlessly. Strung out as we were, we looked like a bright orange snake winding our way along the tops. Near the end we crested the highest point, the border between Lugo and Pontevedra provinces, the Monte do Faro, at 1180 metres above sea level. Up here there was a gentle breeze and some welcome shade. It was a lovely and peaceful spot. At the very top, looking down over the wind turbines below, was the Ermida da Nosa Señora do Faro. This remote and highest point of A Serra do Faro was probably a place for pagan rites long before a Roman temple was built over the remains of the earlier one. Now the *Ermida* stood on the same spot.

In front of the church was a large cross bearing a depiction of the crucifixion of Christ. From the Monte do Faro it was downhill all the way to the coach waiting below a steep and very slippery shale ridge, down which we half ran, half skied.

The second walk was altogether more pleasant. We rambled along quiet roads and woodland tracks above the river Miño, coming at last down to the great hydroelectric dam at Belesar. Even though July was hotter than June, it was a beautiful and enjoyable walk. We even got chatting to some of the other walkers and made some new friends.

August was holiday month, so of course no one could go walking. In September we missed the walk as Mum was here and we felt a 15 kilometre hike might be a bit much with her dodgy hip, but in October we went on a third walk, alongside the river Miño in the drizzle.

This walk started from near to Os Peares, an interesting place in itself, where the three rivers of the Miño, the Sil, and the Bubal meet. The coach dropped us at a junction above the village. We wandered down a winding road beneath the antiseptic scent of eucalyptus trees before heading along a terrace hugging the side of the steep river valley, tramping through damp pastures and picking mushrooms. I even learnt the *Galego* names of some of the group's favourite fungi. The bright orange and yellow chicken of the woods I loved so much has the same name in Spanish, *gallina de la bosque*. They showed me one of the Galician's favourite fungi, an orange milk cap with a bitter sap and a worrying predisposition to colour dark green on bruising, called *nícalo* or *rebollón* (*Lactarius deliciosus*).

It was an afternoon of eating. We were introduced to the Strawberry tree (*Arbutus unedo*). Called a *madroño* in Spanish, this pretty tree has small red fruit which taste like a rather gritty strawberry. We picked oranges alongside the Miño, next to fertile gardens growing cabbages and giant pumpkins ready to be turned into a carriage for Cinderella. The Miño reflected the vegetation like a mirror as the mist hung low over the hills, and the walking was pleasant through villages and along the terraced vineyards. We chatted to some of the group and found out more about the area.

Clara told us, as we passed the *Fondós* waterfall, that the huge craggy vertical quartzite rock next to the falls was called locally *Penedo do Castelo do Monte do Graúllo* (or *Garabullo*). Legend has it that the rock originally formed part of an old castle. It was certainly arresting, standing some 50 metres high and ever so slightly overhanging the main road which passed it on a nice sharp bend.

Clara, whom we had met on one of the earlier walks, had become a good friend. Her English was excellent, and accentless, and she found our northern pronunciation hilarious.

One day she heard S saying that the summer weather had been erratic. Immediately she pounced.

"Soomer?" she queried.

"No, summer."

We pronounce the word with a short 'u' – at least that's what it sounds like to me. Obviously to Clara it didn't, as she drew out the 'u' sound to ridiculous lengths. Each time set her off into a fit of giggles. Clara had plenty of opportunities to practice her northern English as her grandmother lived in Chantada so she would drop in to see us when she was visiting.

Diary Thursday 12th November Pleasant with some sun
Into Taboada to post Mum's letter and check emails. Just home when Clara rang to say that she

was in the area. Had a cuppa, then back into town to collect her from the bus.
Showed Clara round and sat chatting over English tea. Martin arrived with one of Linda's famous apple pies for us, so more tea and chat. Clara had to get back to her gran's before lunch so we dropped Martin off on the way. Unfortunately the Chantada bus was just leaving as we rounded the corner into town!
CJ arrived in the evening just as I was hoeing the allotment… of course I had to stop for more tea and chat. Tidied up, lit the sunroom fire and that's another tea filled day gone!

Our local bus timetable is somewhat flexible. Although the start and end times are fixed, the route points along the way depend entirely on the number of passengers and the traffic. That day, the driver had obviously had few passengers, or was racing to get home for his dinner, as we arrived to see the bus vanishing down the street.

I gave chase, hoping to overtake it and then pull into a stop further along the road. Not only was there no opportunity to get past, he made not one single stop on the 15 kilometres to Chantada. I dropped Clara off at the depot just behind the bus and told her we would see her at the final walk in ten days' time.

Monday 16th November. Rain all day again!
Dear Mum,
 I'm beginning to think it will rain all November! We were up rather late again as it's so dark in the mornings. I then spent the morning rearranging the attic boxes yet again to create some space. I found the quilt, covers, and some other bits for the new bedroom. It's great fun going through

things after so long as I've forgotten half of what's in there. I redid my inventory list as we have fewer boxes now (well, marginally fewer, it's surprising how many are left!) and I amalgamated some of the partially emptied boxes.

Still a few walnuts falling off, though with this rain it's less fun picking them and I have to make sure they are properly dried before I bag them up or they will go mouldy. Not going to be many this year. I made a walnut, apricot and broad bean pilaf for lunch. Dessert was a chocolate sponge from the freezer, made with the chestnut flour, with chocolate sauce, and a lemon bombe I'd made on Saturday. Two little piggies we are!

We were a bit late finishing lunch so decided to go for a walk in the rain. We went up to San Lorenzo along the track, to look at the church up there and do a circuit round. Some huge field mushrooms still out, though most are sodden now. Collected two to try freezing them.

When we got back I noticed Carmen's builder seemed to have backed his van into the low corner of our roof. There was glass all on the track and he reappeared later today with a new rear window. No damage to our roof tiles thankfully. S has put an old bike reflector on the corner so they can see it, though I doubt it will help as Galegos don't tend to use the rear view mirror!

TOMATO, FIG & PUMPKIN JELLY

Tuesday: Sun…briefly!
We went in to Lugo today. Called into Roca to look at stove pipes (chimney) but they didn't have any to fit our English stove. We wanted the double insulated tubes (for going through the ceiling) to connect to the ordinary ones but they didn't seem to connect up. S asked the plumbing guy for help but he couldn't get them to fit either. We explained what we wanted to do and the guy suggested buying two sizes of ordinary pipe, fitting one inside the other then filling the space with espuma (the expanding foam stuff they use for everything here). S pointed out that the can of foam spray is labelled flammable quite clearly. The guy said that was only for the spray but it was fine once dried.

S of course decided to try this at home. He placed a piece of dried extruded foam on my clean cocina. As expected it caught fire. So glad they employ experts in these places! Will try 'Arkwright's'.

Jayne and Richard came back with us, to drop off the wardrobes we had ordered from B&Q in UK along with our real ale supply, so we treated them to lunch at the Anduriña.

Wednesday: I have been feeding the chickens the prawn heads I peeled for lunch (seafood paella). They are going crazy for them. They look just like a rugby scrum – there are wings outstretched, beaks pecking, feet going. Guess they like them then!

NOVEMBER

We have started on the wardrobe interiors. They come with two shelving units and a good length of railing to cut to size. S has very kindly decided that I can have two thirds of the wardrobe space whilst his measly collection can fit into the other third. Seems fair to me haha. The doors are mirror-fronted which will make the room look really long and we will be able to see ourselves in bed… except I won't 'cos I'd have to leave my contacts in all night. Of course because of the sloped ceiling, fitting them and making a 'lid' to go above will take some thinking about. Still, we are getting there.

Now our shiny varnished floor in the living room area is dry we can put the rugs down. Once the stove is working we can 'move in'… it's a bit nippy to sit without a fire in November as we found out our first year. Mind you, it's a whole lot warmer indoors now we have floors and ceilings, without holes, in all the upstairs areas!
Love you tons
XXXXX

The coming weekend was to be our fourth and final walk with the 'healthy council' group. We had visitors due that weekend. S' daughter was visiting us for the first time so we had invited her and her partner along, together with our friend Mike who loves walking. Or more accurately running. He had recently come first in the 'over 55s group of a local *carreira*, or fun run – though running rarely sounds like fun to me.

TOMATO, FIG & PUMPKIN JELLY

We had also been invited to a party the same evening, and we wanted to do some concreting whilst we had some willing workers here. It was going to be a full weekend.

Diary Friday 20th November Still wet but much milder
Cleaning day ready for our visitors. Me on sunroom and hallway, S bathroom and bedroom one.
Had a quick pasta salad for lunch then back to cleaning. I cleaned bedroom two and made the 'bed' for Emma (mattress on the floor) whilst S swept the terrace and downstairs hall. Getting longer these cleaning days... much quicker when we only had one room to clean ha!
To Chantada swimming baths via the marble place to collect our nice shiny, and exceptionally heavy, piece of granite for the stove to sit on.

Diary Saturday 21st November Wet...of course
Managed to lift the granite slab out of the car between us and upstairs to the hallway. Manoeuvred the stove onto it. Had a quick brunch then off to the airport to collect the girls.

The final walk was a morning affair of 15 kilometres along the opposite bank of the river Miño to the previous one. Once more the coach was to collect us at the bus depot in Chantada, and we were meeting Mike and his workawayer (a voluntary organisation, of which we found out much more in later years) there. This meant getting up a good two hours earlier than normal at 7.30am. It was still dark, and cold, and raining of course. I had to wonder why we were doing this as we trooped out to the car in our waterproofs and walking boots.

By the time we had driven the 15 kilometres to Chantada, the sky had lightened and the sun had

NOVEMBER

started to peek through the clouds. As we trooped off the coach at the start point for the walk, we were each handed a shiny new aluminium walking pole, a waterproof jacket with the 'healthy council' logo on it, more T shirts (which we declined, already having two each), bottles of water, and the promise of snacks en route. It was a promising start to the day.

Black clouds hung menacingly over the hillsides as we set off along the terraces of 'heroic viticulture' clinging to the valley side, but the sun was warm and the rain only gently mizzly for the entire morning. We walked through trees festooned with pale green lichen like an old man's beard. These colourful organisms, a mix of an alga and a moss, are ubiquitous in this area. Lichen only grows well in unpolluted atmospheres and can take many years to accomplish a modest ten centimetres. The valley across from our house remains green all winter in part due to this hanging foliage. Interestingly, we can tell the type of tree we are looking at in winter from the type of lichen on its trunk. The old man's beard has an affinity for chestnut trees whilst the walnut trees are usually coated with plaques of sulphur yellow.

The Ribeira Sacra, or the sacred rivers, is the name given to the area in which we live. It is an area of water and mountains, forests and vineyards. Running through the area are the great rivers of Galicia. The mighty Miño, which arises near to Meira, north of Lugo, joins the deeply cleft valley of the Sil as the latter makes its way westwards from Castilla y León. The whole area is greatly influenced by these two rivers.

The Miño is wider and slower. Its landscape is gentler, clothed in green, and its vineyards picturesque and pleasant. Much of its length has been dammed for hydroelectric purposes, whole villages buried beneath thousands of gallons of fresh water.

TOMATO, FIG & PUMPKIN JELLY

One year, the Belesar reservoir nearby had to be emptied for maintenance work. As the water level shrank, a new and wondrous landscape began to emerge. First came a narrow roadway, etched into the banks of the river, running at a gentle gradient downhill to where a beautiful stone clad bridge appeared. The *Ponte Fortes*, was built in the 1940s as an alternative to the boat service which used to ferry people from one side of the Miño to the other. The bridge was built using cheap local labour (some people recall being paid ten pesetas a day) and political prisoners. But its days were numbered before it was even built, as plans were already in place to dam the valley.

With a capacity of 654.5 hm^3 (hectometres cubed, or 654.5 *million* cubic metres) the Belesar reservoir is the largest in Galicia. The valley, and the bridge, were flooded in 1963. The boats returned to service for a further three years before the great iron bridge, known as the Bridge of Screws due to its construction, was built high above the river.

The old *Ponte Fortes* had a wide central arch with three narrower tall arches on either side. It was built of concrete and stone with glorious ramparts. Set into the mud of the river were dead trees, captured in their final positions as the water swallowed them. Lower down were terraces of vineyards running along the banks of the original river. As the water receded further the roadway was seen to continue on the far side of the river towards a village.

The village of Mourulle was visible for the first time in over 40 years. A landslip meant the road to Mourulle was dangerous and all but impassable, even on foot, but the bridge was in surprisingly pristine condition. Once the mud had dried to a hard, cracked finish it was possible to walk along the edge of the original river and across the stone bridge.

NOVEMBER

It was like walking back in time.

From the opposite bank of the river, it was possible to come down a dirt track to the old village of Mourulle. We returned time and again. It really was the most extraordinary feeling, to stand on a pathway through vineyards. The preserved wood of the vines was still rooted in the ground, gnarled and watchful, propped up on old wooden poles as we picked our way between them. Houses stood, blind without any glass in the windows, the stonework blackened from their years below the waters. Walls, doorways, *hornos*, and chimneys all remained.

Unlike in Portomarín, some 20 kilometres northwards, Mourulle had not been razed to the ground before being flooded. The residents here had packed up their homes, locked their doors for the final time, and left. Even the graveyard, with its silent inhabitants, had been moved to higher ground. The church, with its circular rose window, and the tiny chapel, further along the pathway, remained beneath the waters of the reservoir. Ivy still clambered up the stone walls, frozen in time forever.

Walking along the pathways was a humbling experience. As time went on, vegetation re-clothed the cracked mud pathway and the village sparkled in the sunshine. On one occasion I met an elderly man sitting on a wall looking pensive. I asked if he knew the village.

"Yes, we used to live in that house," he said, pointing to one of the cottages with triangular window apertures beautifully framed in slate.

I tried to get some idea from him of the devastation they must have felt leaving their homes.

"The wine is not so good now," he said after a time. "The vines here made the best wine in the Ribeira Sacra," he added, nodding.

The waters were some 100 metres lower once the reservoir was emptied. The much narrower river

Miño swept lazily through the village. The valley floor was almost flat, the village enjoying its own warm and sunny microclimate. I could almost taste the quality of the wines from this favoured spot.

The same winter, we watched the reservoir slowly being refilled. One by one the houses of Mourulle disappeared again into their watery grave. As the water began to lap at the first house I felt a sadness take hold and as the final roofline disappeared beneath the river some two months later, I actually felt a lump in my throat for the loss of that magical place.

The Canyons of the Sil also boasts vineyards but it has a much more dramatic scenery. The river Sil races through deep narrow gorges, as vineyards cling precipitously to the bare hillsides. The deep canyons make the river seem dark and forbidding, cold and somehow dangerous.

The name, Ribeira Sacra, refers to the huge numbers of Romanesque churches which are in evidence alongside the rivers. These are inevitably grey granite, almost hewn from the surrounding landscape, sitting squat and firm in the face of heresy, indifference, or walkers in bright waterproofs tramping by.

This fourth walk was certainly picturesque, winding as it did down to the river Miño, but by the time we arrived at the little river beach of A Cova I was flagging and in need of sustenance. I thought (wrongly) that the coach would be waiting in the car park behind the café. Instead we had another two kilometres of uphill walking along a narrow and winding road. I'm not sure how I pulled myself up the bus steps, but I did.

As I was searching my backpack for a chewy bar or some peanuts, a lady came along the bus handing out packets of homemade sandwiches and cartons of juice. Never has anything been more welcome. I took a huge bite of the ham and cheese sandwich before almost spitting it out in surprise.

NOVEMBER

The bread was sweet!

Normally we only buy the artisan bread, made in the local *panaderias*, which is substantial with a thick dark crust and a chewy interior. The offering that day was the local *pan de molde*, sliced white bread made in a mould, or 'mouldy bread' as we inevitably had nicknamed it. The main variety of moulded bread is called Bimbo which is off putting in itself for us Brits. Still, beggars, and footsore walkers, can't be choosers, and the thought was most kind, so I gobbled it down.

We had only time to say farewell to Mike, drive home, grab quick showers, and of course change into more suitable clothing, before heading off to CJ's house for our convoy to Maribel's new bodega, and a party.

Maribel was our Spanish estate agent who had been so helpful when we first arrived in Galicia for our winter sojourn three years earlier, and we had kept in contact. She had recently got into renovating old houses to sell, in addition to offering the usual broken down ones the 'foreigners' bought. This one was a bodega sitting above the river Miño, overlooking terraces of vines as far as the eye could see. CJ was the only one who had been before, so he was designated lead vehicle.

It was a winding route through woods and alongside fields. Every so often we would glimpse the Miño. Suddenly the vista opened up to a view often described as Swiss or Austrian: deep wooded valleys dotted with tiny red roofed villages and, many metres below, the winding ribbon of the Miño valley. It was stunning.

As ever in rural Galicia, signposts were few and far between and often positioned (if they exist at all) so they can only be seen when looking in the rear view mirror after you have passed by. It was a slow procession but, in fairness to CJ, he only took one wrong turn and we arrived at the light-filled bodega within acceptable boundaries of Spanish timekeeping.

It seemed that Maribel had invited the whole of the 'foreigner' contingent to her party. The single roomed bodega was full of shouting, chatting people, and the temperature was in the high thirties due to the huge roaring open fire or *lareira* which took up one entire corner.

At this fire was a figure, carefully tending his *churrasco* of ribs, steak and *chorizos*. The smells were divine, and our lunchtime mouldy bread seemed a lifetime ago. In front of the fire were wooden trestle tables set at right angles to each other with benches running along each side. The only spaces left were those nearest to the leaping flames. We stuck Gala next to the fire as she likes to be warm, and CJ opted for the sturdy wooden chair at the far end of the table. The rest of us squashed into the spaces between.

Dinner was loud, delicious, and plentiful. The wine flowed and eventually Maribel and her son got up to sing. They both have amazing voices, Maribel a warm contralto, her son Pablo a tremendous alto. They regaled us with Spanish carols, lending the proceedings a festive atmosphere. The wine had warmed us inside and acted to loosen our inhibitions. We decided to join in from the Brit side to show what we were made of.

Sadly few people there knew the words to even one carol all the way through, and Ian and I ended up working our way through a truly dreadful rendition of *Two Little Boys* instead. What the musically minded Spaniards thought of our efforts I have no idea.

Coffee was served, for some reason that is still not clear, from a ceramic boot which I swear I earlier saw filled with plants, though I could be wrong on that one. At least I'm relatively sure it was cleaned before use…

NOVEMBER

After a fun filled and tiring day we were all ready for bed. And we had another hard day planned for the Monday.

Diary Monday 23rd November
Up early for our boiled eggs as we missed them on Sunday. S got the cement mixer out. He mixed, the girls barrowed and I spread the stuff in the lower chicken pen.

I got the job as cement spreader as the smallest person present. The lower part of our *Galego* two storey chicken shed, like the upper part, is built of stone and brick but, unlike the storey above, it had only an earth floor, not easy for mucking out. The idea was to concrete it for hygiene purposes, and because we thought the chickens would like it.

Unfortunately this lower part is only four feet high. Fine for chickens but a bit low even for my five foot two frame. My back was killing me by lunchtime, but the floor was nicely level and I hung a little plaque on the wall that we had found in the house. It had a picture of a mountain clothed in green and a little ditty in Spanish. I hoped it would make the hens feel at home.

After a busy morning we decided on lunch out and an afternoon siesta. The perfect end to our guests' short break.

Tuesday 24th November. Actual sunshine but rather cool
Dear Mum,
That's three days running we have been up early! Well, for us anyway. You had probably had your lunch by the time we got up today haha. We have been to Santiago to take our visitors back to the airport. The flight wasn't

until 12.30pm but they were anxious to be early. I think they must have heard about Belle's near miss! It meant we had time for a sit in the park at Melide to eat our butties on the way home. The sun was shining and it was very pleasant watching the fish in the river and the squirrels running up the trees. No mosquitos in winter either so that's a bonus!

We popped into Leroy Merlin again on the way back to look for some kitchen wall tiles. Nothing I liked though. I fancy a burgundy red to match the door. Maybe some cookery stuff on them, or perhaps some chickens.

Talking of chickens, the babies were all up on the well this morning. I peeped out of the sunroom windows and there they were. Cheeky lot! One... Angel I think... was halfway up the apple tree. She probably flew there with her long wings!

Had a lovely walk on Sunday, the last of our organised walks. We shall have to find another walking group to join now. We have really enjoyed them though Eusebio thinks we are crazy. He saw us walking up the hill out of the village the other day practising for Sunday. Of course he asked what we were doing.

'Oh, no,' he says 'walking is bad for you.'

This from a man who walks miles with his cows. Still maybe that is the point. It's probably not exactly fun if you have to do it day in day out!

NOVEMBER

I've left S making our dinner while I write this as the stove smoked like crazy when he lit it, and the kitchen is full of smoke. I was coughing like a hyena and wheezing away so the lad kindly volunteered. Stirfry rabbit with pineapple and broccoli. Possibly it will be smoked rabbit.

Wednesday: Had a phone call this morning from Linda and Martin. Their gas had run out so I went over to collect Martin. Bit difficult to carry a gas bottle on your back from town and they don't have a contract so can't use the Repsol delivery man. At least this time we managed to find a gas bottle in Taboada.

Martin asked me about registering with the health service as his prescription is a bit expensive to buy. Their neighbour Maria had offered to get the medication on her prescription but unfortunately this kind act was soon rumbled as one item was for prostrate problems, something 'Maria' couldn't possibly have. The chemist found it amusing!

Luckily for us the registration process was still nice and simple at the health centre. It's good to know something is, in bureaucracy land! And Martin was happy even if he did initially tick the M (for mujer) box as he thought it was M for male. As he said, it seemed obvious. (Male in Spanish is an H... for hombre, of course!).

S is fitting our wardrobes. He had to make

a long beam across the room to fit the top sliding door runner to (and to lay a 'lid' onto eventually). It is a good job that we have so many old chestnut beams lying about. By this afternoon he had fitted the top and bottom runners so we both lifted the sliding doors in place. Guess what? They all ran into the middle. This means that... surprise surprise, our new floor isn't quite level! Anyway he managed to pack the middle of the floor and they now roll along perfectly. Just the top and the wooden fascia to go. Wonderful! I am so looking forward to hanging up my clothes - small things please me eh?

Love you tons and tons
Xxxxxxxxxxxxxx

*Diary Sunday 29*th *November*
Scrummy boiled eggs for breakfast (twice in one week!) then over to the allotment to dig veg for lunch: carrots and the first leek... huge thing it is, nearly as tall as me!
S finishing off the wardrobe 'lid'... getting close.
Made lunch plus jam tarts, cheese pies and mince pies to freeze.
Lunch: twice cooked pork belly with stir-fried leek, peppers, carrots and landcress. Apple and rhubarb crumble and custard.
Afternoon walk along the track to keep in trim (especially after that huge lunch). Started to rain, then at the furthest point (isn't it always?), it began to sleet and snow. Wonderful! Home about 6pm. Dried off, had tea and relaxed.
So much for walking being good for you. Maybe Eusebio is right after all!!

DECEMBER
For want of five letters

After all that walking, we needed a rest! Of course we were unlikely to get one with so much still to do on the house. Nevertheless, this year's main project was all but finished and my birthday was coming up.

Tuesday 1ˢᵗ December. Drizzly all day
Dear Mum,
  Actually managed to get up by 9.30 this morning. Earliest we have been since Emma left! It was the market at Monterroso of course. Ten of us for lunch at Luisa's. Including a new couple called Kath and Jorge. He is a large jolly Spaniard who likes a drink or three. She is tall, willowy and beautiful. She also speaks perfect Spanish having been raised on Tenerife.
  Anne & Simon had brought two helpers with them. The lass was vegetarian. I explained this to Luisa, who thought long and hard before suggesting the fish and chips for a starter. I pointed out that fish wasn't considered vegetarian which bemused her somewhat. She eventually managed a lovely looking tortilla Galego

with chips and salad for the girl so all was well.

Mike and John came well prepared for lunch... in their long johns and with John carrying a hot water bottle! It is icy upstairs in bar Mencia in winter so they had the last laugh.

John had a fish stew for his main course. When Luisa asked if anyone wanted seconds, he said yes, but could he try the lamb this time! Without a word she came with another plate, full of lamb and potatoes so we were all laughing at him. He asked Luisa how much he owed for the second meal but of course that was free. I really do wonder how many plates one could eat before an additional cost was incurred! Don't think I'll be putting it to the test.

Anne's helpers are apparently looking for somewhere to buy in the area. Anne had seen a house for sale nearby on some website or other so after lunch we went on a magical mystery tour of Taboada council area looking for this mythical house... in which endeavour we failed dismally. Very scenic drive though, winding up hills and through tiny hamlets along the Miño.

It was getting dark by the time we got home. I went to shut the chickens in and heard a flapping from next to me. I thought a sparrow had got into the pen but it was much bigger - a sparrowhawk was stuck in

DECEMBER

the outside pen. S caught it (after putting his gauntlets on) and I got some photos of him holding it. Not at all aggressive, I reckon he could've been trained (the bird that is, not S obviously!!!) The chickens were all fine so don't know how long it had been there.

Wednesday. Still wet! Thank you for my cards and my presents. I was running short of knickers so thank you, and Aunty Jean, they are just right!! I made myself a lovely birthday lunch. We had Chinese pancakes with Peking rabbit (in the absence of any duck) and vegetable noodles, then chocolate soufflés and cream for afters. This afternoon I got to fill my half (and a bit, as S has generously offset the shelves in the middle so I get extra!) of the newly completed wardrobes. Didn't take long to fill up my shelves and hanging rails but at least that is a few more empty boxes out of the attic. S hung his clothes too, though he didn't empty as many boxes in the process! We even used the polystyrene from the wardrobe doors as insulation round the water pipes. That's recycling for you haha.

Love you tons and tons
XXXXXXXXXx

I had decided on a stay at home birthday this year after a disastrous day the year before.

I have always thought that I was born in the wrong hemisphere. I am a sun-worshipper, definitely not a winter baby. I have never skied, fall over on ice, and hate the cold. I like to try and go somewhere warm for my birthday whenever possible but having the house and so much work to do on it (and a distinct lack of ready money) meant a birthday here. I didn't mind, as Galicia was still new and exciting. The previous year we had planned a trip to Lugo, our closest large city, to do some essential shopping and visit a Mexican restaurant I had seen advertised. I hadn't had Mexican food since we had moved to Galicia.

One of the few things I miss here is the wide choice of cuisines which are available in England, or pretty much anywhere else. This was going to be a treat and Mum's birthday money would cover it.

The morning had started reasonably, with us unearthing some interesting wall tiles in a new tile shop we had found. The upstairs was all fancy glass and ceramics with eye-watering prices, but when I explained we were looking for something cheaper, the lady immediately showed us the 'bargain basement' – literally a huge open warehouse on the lower floor, stacked high with end of range or leftover boxes of tiles at seriously bargain prices.

Over morning tea and tortilla, I had tried to access my emails and birthday wishes but without success. I felt very down and isolated from my family and frustrated that I couldn't get online. I even tried to find a new mobile 'phone as mine was getting old and very slow but that too was a failure.

At lunchtime we made our way to the Mexican restaurant. I was full of enthusiasm for one of my favourite cuisines, S slightly apprehensive that it would all be overly spicy. I was sure we could ask them to reduce the spice a little.

As it happened, there was no need for S to worry about spice – there wasn't any... at all! The menu was short, consisting of meat sauce with rice, flour tortillas, or tacos and with or without hot peppers. The meat was either spicy beef or non-spicy pork.

DECEMBER

S had the pork with rice, I opted for the hot beef in a soft tortilla. They both looked identical. They both tasted identical. Both sauces were identical. Neither had any discernable flavour and looked remarkably like tinned 'savoury mince'. Desserts were all bought-in, cheap, plastic-tubbed *flan* or ice cream. We declined and paid the ridiculously expensive bill, vowing to stick to *Galego menú del dias* in the future.

On the way home a blizzard had whipped up, obscuring our vision and making the way back treacherous. By the time we had crawled our way to Taboada I was already vowing to stay at home the following year.

And that is exactly what I did. I cooked my own special dinner whilst S put the finishing touches to the built in wardrobes then spent a happy afternoon filling said wardrobes with bundles of clothes I had entirely forgotten I had, although I did wonder at my decision to bring ball gowns and high heels to Galicia when I spent my time in wellingtons and fleeces.

It was a magical birthday and proved once again that the best days are often those where nothing is planned nor expected.

Diary Thursday 3rd December Still raining
S has all his pipes for the hall chimney now but of course he can't fit them until the rain stops as he needs to cut through the roof. Maddening!
Ginger was chuntering this afternoon and Blondie was sitting on the nest. She eventually laid a tiny 'wind' egg... all egg white and air. Still, Ginger looked as proud as punch!

This year's youngsters were now fully grown. Blondie was the first to lay an egg, albeit one the size of a sparrow's, and the boys were both crowing madly and strutting about much to the amusement of their father, Buzz Lightyear.

There was no need for Buzz to assert his dominance as yet but he occasionally chased the youngsters off if they came too near to 'his' girls. The younger hens, for now, belonged to Ginger and Lucky.

Lucky had recovered completely from his earlier attack and subsequent rescue. He was a smaller, slimmer version of Buzz: white and brown with a flat top comb and caramel tail and wing feathers. Ginger was altogether sturdier. He was dark brown and chestnut with a magnificent full comb and the air of one who will be the boss. I think he was already looking forward to starting his own dynasty at Jayne and Richard's. It was almost time for him to head off to his new home.

Diary Tuesday 8th December Wet
Up very late to a horrid scene. Through the window I could see a pile of chestnut and brown feathers in the chicken pen. S was already on the scene by the time I had grabbed my trousers. He had chased the buzzard away but not before it had killed and part plucked poor Ginger. RIP pretty boy. I'd like to think our handsome boy had died trying to protect some of the girls but he was probably just busy preening and cockledoodling and didn't see the shadow descend.
S plucked and cleaned the remains. At least the buzzard had done most of the gutting and feather plucking for us. I locked the rest of the chickens in (horse, stable door etc) before going onto the allotment to continue putting the potash (wood ash) and mulch onto the rest of my trenches for next year's beans.
Once Ginger was cleaned and in the pot S found some wooden posts and set to extending the 'safe'

DECEMBER

roofed over area. Don't know what else to do. Chickens unaffected as still had 3 eggs. Angel chuntering so probably ready to lay too.

We have sadly lost many chickens to predators of various kinds since that day, and every single one hurts. But that one was probably the most painful.

The chick we had lost earlier had, I'm ashamed to say, not really had time to make an impact on me, and with Lucky's wondrous escape its demise was pushed out of my head. Ginger though was a fully formed personality; big, handsome, and full of bravado.

Although I'm not normally a violent person, if I could have caught that buzzard at that moment I would have strangled it. And yes, I know it too has to eat but it doesn't help when my poor cockerel is lying disembowelled on the ground.

Thursday 10th December. Sunshine in Lugo.
Dear Mum,

The only good thing to come out of poor Ginger's demise is that Lucky earns his name twice, as he is now off to Jayne and Richard along with Amy and the second blonde hen (now called Rita), instead of going into the pot. We had Ginger soup today. Very sad as he was so handsome, though of course I'm pleased for Lucky who is definitely a survivor.

We took the three of them over this afternoon and they seem to have settled in well. We left them to it and all adjourned to Lugo for a bit of a shopping trip. That is; visiting AKI (tools and interesting man things), Chino Antonios (no idea as usual but spent 20€ and got a free wall calendar), supermarket (boring but essential food stuff). We ate at the new (and, I feel, soon to be ex) Japanese place on the Ronda. Nice enough food but very expensive by Galego standards and absolutely empty, except for the four of us.

We stayed at Jayne's chatting 'til after 1am then got stopped by the Guardia on the way home. That was no problem until S reached under the driver's seat for his driving licence. As he came out, rear end first, I noticed the Guardia chappie had his hand on his gun hilt! S slowly showed he only had a driving licence in his hand but it could've been nasty if they had been trigger happy.

Our young hens have started laying. Blondie was first and the ones we took to Jayne and Richard should be laying soon. Only Baby to go.

We exchanged Lucky and the hens for a duck (already plucked) so next time I do Chinese pancakes we can have genuine Peking duck (although it would have to Galego/English duck of course!) My rabbit version was pretty good though.

We actually have sunshine today. Yesterday I put the washing on first thing, which is of course the kiss of death for any fine weather, though it didn't actually rain. It didn't dry the washing either.

S has finished extending the chicken pen. They now have three times the 'safe', wired over, space so we can happily leave them shut in if we are out, or at night time.

We didn't used to have such a problem with the buzzards. I think the crows in the huge pine tree chase them off most of the time. It's mesmerising to see them gang up on the much larger buzzard, mobbing it and turning cartwheels in the air around it. The crows are much more manoeuvrable and agile. I guess that now the buzzards know there is an easy meal, or ten, here they will keep coming back. We will have to remain vigilant. What we need is an old woman to stand there waving a stick about... any volunteers???

I have been digging over the allotment as it is so mild. There does seem to be a lot of it. I stupidly thought that once I had dug it all over that first year the weeds would not come back... how daft am I? Am trying to mulch the beds now to keep in moisture (it goes so dry in summer), and try and keep down the weeds. I sowed green manure on some beds but how do you stop the weeds growing quicker than the green manure stuff? So I've left the weeds as 'green manure' too. In fact, the allotment is totally green now! As it is so sunny I've also been planting my tubs with overwintering salad leaves. It's so mild, the red plum has flowers on.

Friday: As we have had a couple of nice sunny days, S has managed to get the stove

*chimney pipes through the roof and all connected up. Yippee!! We moved the stove into position and will try it once his cement has dried out. It will be nice and cosy sitting in our new central living space (and should warm up our bedroom a bit too).
Love you tons and tons
xxxx*

This year's projects were completed. We now had two bedrooms, a bathroom, and an internal sitting room upstairs and, most importantly, we were both bat and draught free up there. We had a new project or two for next year but for now we had almost three weeks holiday – other than the usual jobs and trying to sort out our forthcoming marriage... if we could only find our elusive mayor or *alcalde*.

Sunday 13th December Warm and breezy
Spent the morning making Christmas cards whilst S put the waterproof stuff around the chimney pipe on the roof. Walked over to CJ for Christmas lunch. Took a roulade and chocolate truffles for Gala (her favourite).
Delicious Christmassy meal – roast chicken with all the trimmings and even a Christmas pudding.
Got a lift home from friends so back in time to light the new stove, which didn't smoke. Count that one a success then!

Monday 14th December Sun and cloud. Sleet pm
Into town to post our Christmas cards and collect a copy of our empadronamientos from the town hall. No alcalde to be found so couldn't get the things signed! Went into the architect's office to get maps showing the route of the new motorway... do I really want to know?

DECEMBER

It had been almost two years to the day since I first found out about the plan for a brand new motorway to be built across our little valley, and two years since my world had fallen apart. At the time I had been devastated. We had only had the house four months, and I could not comprehend the idea of a motorway destroying our peaceful existence.

In the two years since, there had been a couple of meetings. We had attended one at the town hall. The hall had been packed, the meeting presided over by a number of officials, all looking stern and forbidding. The meeting started with a statement to say that this motorway was going to happen whether we liked it or not and, more importantly for many, that no one would get compensation unless they could prove ownership of the land which was to be compulsorily purchased. This of course was a clever ploy to save money. Many older *Galegos* have no deeds for land they farm, it has just been in the family for years.

I believe the same happened when the Belesar dam was built in the 1960s and land was compulsorily purchased for a miserly four pesetas a square metre. I read of someone saying they didn't have a choice under General Franco. It seemed not so much had changed.

The plans showed that the motorway would cut across our valley via a bridge, some 50 metres west of the house, then swing across and over the hill. I was still devastated but also more sanguine. Our neighbours told us this new road had been threatened for years. Money would appear, then magically disappear into someone's pocket.

A *Galego* friend once told us a joke:

"There is a building job out for tender. The first builder, a Portuguese guy, comes in and says he can do the work for a million euros. The second, a chap from Madrid, says it will cost two million. The third is a local guy, a *Galego*. He says the work will cost three million euros.

'But,' says the mayor, 'why so expensive?'

'A million for you, a million for me, and we let the Portuguese do the work,' is the reply."

Even funnier to me was a true story from that time which made the headlines in the local paper... '*Work halted for want of five letters.*'

It seemed that, for reasons known only to the official in charge, land for the motorway had been purchased not by area but alphabetically, by name. Thus, the Alvares through to the Rodríguezes had been paid for their plots but then, disaster. The money had run out (again). Hundreds of plots of land owned by all the Vasquezes and Veigas remained unpurchased and in the way of any further progress being made.

It was hilarious, and the incompetence of the local functionaries cheered me enormously. With a bit of luck I'd be long gone by the time they got the road started.

We finally collected our *empadronamientos* on the Tuesday morning, finished tidying up our new master bedroom, then packed for our trip to Vigo.

One thing we had been told was necessary for our wedding to go ahead was for us to sign an affidavit to swear we were single. As we had no *fe de vida* it was the only way to prove our status (providing one is honest, obviously).

We had made an appointment with the consulate in Vigo, which was now up and running though Aruni had left. The new honorary British consul was a lawyer called Maria, and we were to sign our oaths in front of her on Thursday. As we had some time off owing we thought we would take the opportunity to explore Vigo, another Galician city we had not yet experienced. We would leave early on Wednesday and enjoy a day at leisure.

Or maybe not.

DECEMBER

On Wednesday morning we awoke to a whiteout. Snow had already settled thickly on the ground and was still descending in a swirling blizzard. We sensibly decided to delay our departure and continued sanding down and varnishing the skirting boards for our bedroom.

By lunchtime the snow had slowed, and by afternoon it had turned to rain. We decided to try for Vigo. Half an hour later we managed to actually get the car out of the driveway and onto the village road. It was slipping and sliding on the slush giving no grip, no matter what we tried. Perhaps in hindsight we should have taken that as an omen.

It is 107 miles to Vigo from our home: 107 miles of freezing fog and heavy rain. There was no sightseeing to be done that day. When we arrived in the darkness of a winter's evening, we found a veritable chaos awaited us.

There were roadworks seemingly on every major road. There was far more traffic than we are used to even in the (admittedly tiny) metropolis of Lugo, and parking was non-existent. For every parking space, there were four cars waiting patiently, hazard lights flashing in the gloom. It was still monsoon weather and we could hardly see through the rain streaked windscreen. Eventually, after what felt like days, we found a *hostal*.

The owner was somewhat surly, but the room was clean and the shared bathroom acceptable, if not luxurious. I stood outside whilst S manoeuvred into a newly vacated space right in front. A young Asian chap asked me if the *hostal* had vacancies. I replied that I thought so as it looked quite empty when we checked in. Two minutes later he was back outside, still clutching his bag.

"It is full," he said with a resigned sigh.

I shook my head and apologised: for being white and for the human race. I knew that *hostal* wasn't full.

TOMATO, FIG & PUMPKIN JELLY

Once parked up, we decided to explore and try to find the consulate. Our appointment was for 9.30 the following morning, so a bit of preparatory work was in order. The weather, whilst still icy cold and miserable, had at least decided to spare us a further drenching, satisfying itself with a nice steady drizzle. We set off to walk to the consulate. I forgot to bring the email from the consular office with the address on it, but a bit of asking ensured we easily found the place.

No, it didn't.

The office building we were directed to was abandoned and empty. On the door was a faded piece of paper saying the consulate had moved to Rua Colón.

Off we set once more, street map in hand. Rua Colón is probably the longest road in Vigo, and of course we started at the wrong end. Halfway up the road there was a café advertising burgers. It sounded like an excellent reason for a break.

MacD's this was not. The house burger was magnificent. It was the largest bap I have ever seen stuffed with meat, bacon, cheese, lettuce, onion, mayo and ketchup. I was finally happy with something in Vigo. The rain had even ceased.

Our destination, when we finally found it, was a building at the very top of the hill. It had no sign pointing lost souls to it. There was only a teeny tiny brass name plate below the press bell, saying Honorary British Consulate. (I did ask why there was not a larger sign when we met the consular official and were told that they didn't want people wandering in off the street.... no, I guess that would be most inconvenient for them.)

On the way back we bought a couple of doughnuts for supper, confident we were sorted for the morning.

We had to vacate our parking spot by 9am and had already figured out that the underground

DECEMBER

parking nearby wouldn't cost much for a couple of hours. At 8.55am we left the *hostal* to move the car around the corner. Except that our normally reliable Escort wouldn't start. Probably it was as fed up with Vigo as we were. Luckily Linea Directa, our insurance company, was excellent and the English speaking operator promised a breakdown truck as soon as possible. We couldn't leave the car, now illegally parked, unattended to visit the consulate so I set off walking. S awaited rescue. And to explain to any loitering traffic warden why the car was parked in a no parking zone, if they looked like writing a ticket.

Because of our reconnoitring the previous day, I arrived at the offices early. A lady responded to my pressing of the buzzer and led me to a lift. We shot up to the fourth floor whereupon the lady produced a key which she used to take us further upwards.

I had been sitting in a small waiting room on the fifth floor of the building for around half an hour when Maria appeared. I explained about the car trouble and she said it was fine as we could make a start without S. My other half joined us a further half an hour later having had the battery jumped and sat idling the car for 20 minutes to charge it, before moving the car to the underground car park *and* then managing to find his way out.

As neither of us felt comfortable swearing on a bible, we had to hold our hands in the air and repeat that we were single and free to marry. This little speech would cost us 574€ to be put into print and then the banns would be published.

Maria showed me the wall where the banns would be pinned. It was in the corridor of the office. An office with no nameplate outside, on the fifth floor of a building where the public lift went only to the fourth floor. A very public place then. I did later suggest that all our friends should make a special trip to Vigo to view the banns just to annoy the consulate.

TOMATO, FIG & PUMPKIN JELLY

We decided we had had our fill of Vigo for the time being and headed back to the car park. Half an hour later we found the correct entrance and subsequently the car. Vigo's car parks, like its streets, were a chaotic confusing muddle. Built beneath the streets and stretching for many hundreds of metres, the pedestrian access points bore no relationship to the ones for vehicles. Thankful to have rediscovered our trusty Escort we drove straight home, stopping only for a restorative hot chocolate and *churros* on the way. At least we were, possibly, one more step closer to this wedding thingy.

Eleven years on we have still never properly visited Vigo, a lovely city... I am told.

Diary Friday 18th December Drizzly
Yuk, woke with a cold. I blame Vigo! Porridge for breakfast cooked overnight in the cocina which restored me a little. Dug some of the allotment whilst S was fixing the new window blinds in the sunroom.
Got to the swimming baths to find the front tyre was flat! Sadly only noticed after our swim, shower and sauna. Had to empty the boot to get to the spare tyre and find the rug for S to lie on as he changed it. Perfect!
Called to visit CJ but didn't stay late as totally bunged up and fed up. I am a very bad patient!

Diary Saturday 19th December Snow again and cold
Lit the stoves and pruned some bits off the vines (not really sure what I'm doing) then drove to Santiago to drop Linda and Martin off for their flight back to England for Christmas.
On the way home we decided to call on the other new couple we met at the market on the first, John and Fiona. Happened to notice that they had

DECEMBER

removed their cocina and it was sitting in the garden. We cheekily asked if they were reusing it and then cheekily offered to take it off their hands. They were more than happy to give it away and help us into the car with it too.
It looks pretty much brand new, or at least unused. Same as ours, a Lacunza number 9, but minus the water boiler. Only the cast iron top was missing as the chapara man (rag and bone) had already beat us to it. Propped it carefully in the long barn for when we renovate the rest of the kitchen.

Although we had renovated the ceiling in the kitchen, and ground out all the old plaster from our lovely granite sink, there was still plenty of work to do in there before it was the kitchen of my dreams. John and Fiona had kindly helped bring us one step closer to that dream with their generosity.

Sunday 20th December 7.30pm. -3°C on terrace last night. -7°C given for tonight.
Dear Mum,
   We have both stoves going. There was ice inside the living room window this morning - takes me back to my childhood! Mind you the overnight setting on the electric blanket is a luxury we never used to have at Coro' in the old days!
   The new stove is taking the edge off in the hallway but unfortunately the instructions specifically say you have to season it by running it only gently for 20 days. Think we may get fed up well before that haha.
   Until we can get it running at full heat we are staying put in the current living room, so it will be after Christmas before we uproot

again. We are spending time finishing little fiddly bits... surprising just how many of those there are!

We managed to unload the cocina front we procured from John and Fiona. They are a lovely couple. Boy was their house cold! They had a small wood burner but hadn't been able to get any seasoned wood at this time of year so it wasn't burning well at all. He was saying that they have a great wood burner with a back boiler but have found they can't run it without water in the system (in case it explodes I guess) and of course nothing is connected yet. Brought back happy memories of our first year!

Apologies for the lack of letter last week. I don't know what happened. One minute it was Sunday, the next Thursday!

Good job the lad managed to finish the chimney and seal it all before Wednesday when we went to Vigo as I think it would have been too icy to do anything since and having the stove going, even at gentle heat, is better than not having it at all.

The chickens don't like this weather. On Wednesday no one was outside but I could hear Buzz crowing away. They were all inside the house, Buzz crowing from his perch and the others covering their ears haha.

Brownie has been in the nest box every morning this week but hasn't given me an egg. I swear she is just keeping warm... 'I'm

DECEMBER

laying an egg Mum, honest I am.' Wish I could send you and Aunty Jean some eggs. I'm getting 5 a day. I used a dozen today baking and still have two dozen in the fridge, and Baby hasn't started laying yet. Egg recipes please! (Preferably ones using 6 or more at a time... surprisingly difficult to do). Jayne says at least one of hers has now started laying so she is pleased. Apparently poor Lucky is still being bullied by the hens. I guess he will grow, then he will show them!

Bunnies' new treat is chestnuts. Brown bunny gets very excited and grabbed S' finger instead of the nut the other day. Good job she didn't bite hard.

I was thinking this would get to you by Christmas if I posted it tomorrow, but if you are off to brother's on Wednesday it may not. Never mind, it's still sent with love. Hope you like the book. I remembered seeing it a year or two ago and liked the title. I do hope your parcels arrive you say you sent. I will ask at the correos (post office) tomorrow but if they were there he would have delivered them. No Christmas card from Jean nor letter from you either so it's probably the Christmas post your end.

Hope it's warmer tomorrow as we have been summoned for the matanza (pig killing). Not going to be pleasant if it is snowing! I shall wear a few extra layers just to be on the safe side. I have prepared some oats and belly fat ready for making this year's black puddings. I am determined to get it right eventually!

Tuesday evening. Damp!

Oh well, so much for a nice day for the matanza. At least it was warmer than yesterday and I was brave enough to decline going off to the river to clean the tripes this year. I do think twice is enough!

We brought the blood back. Luisa showed me how to keep stirring it as it cools to prevent it clotting. She then sieved it through some clean straw into my pot. We have made a sort of blood porridge then stuffed it into the (bought) intestines and simmered it gently. They have gone the right colour and haven't burst so I will fry one for tea and see about the taste.

We have frozen the liver, kidneys, heart, tongue, and the caul (for my faggots).

Wednesday. Actually saw the sun...I think!

Our pig was 78kg this year. They are getting bigger. Only 10 months old and fed entirely on vegetables (pumpkin, cabbage, and beetroot) and chestnuts. Delicious! Very little fat this year. Luisa thought it didn't have enough fat on it. She is quite right that you need fat for the taste but it looks good so we shall see. Think we are getting quicker at butchering as we had the loins, belly, spare ribs, fillets and two shoulders chopped and frozen by 7.30pm this year, though we have another full day tomorrow doing the hams and sausages.

DECEMBER

Thursday. Back to rain.

We were invited to tea with Gala this afternoon. As it was still pouring we drove rather than risk being soaked before we arrived. We also didn't want to be late! It was a very pleasant tea with some very fancy unusual Ukrainian cakes. We have just got home and the new hallway stove is still burning so that is a definite plus in its favour!

I think we are ready for Christmas. Tree decorated, overnight bag ready for Lugo, hams salted, sausagemeat made. Tried our black pudding but I think it needs more body. Either more oats or something and definitely more salt. I shall have to keep trying. The Spanish use rice in their morcilla so I shall try that next year. We have the sweet cure hams in their plastic tub and the sausagemeat ready for stuffing. I've done three lots this year; leek and apple, Cumberland (onions and spices) and herb (sage, thyme and onion).

I have made a nice Christmas wreath for the outside door. It is ivy, holly and vinca as they are the only greenery around. I think it looks pretty good anyway! We took our Christmas photo with us sticking our heads out of the hatch in the door!

We will be thinking of you all on Christmas day. I think there are nine of us for Chinese this year. CJ is in France visiting his sister. We wanted to invite Gala and her mama but as we are staying overnight we wouldn't be able to give them a lift back. Mama had dinner with us last Sunday. She was worried about us walking back and asked if we had lights on in the village. She seemed rather pleased when I replied 'Da, spasiba' (yes, thank you) - two of my four Russian words!

Get rid of that cold of yours. Think I am copying you. I have a chest cold despite avoiding all ill people, and now I have sciatica down my right leg. Hurry up and get well before I catch anything else from you! Need you fit for next year.

Love you tons and tons
Xxxxxx
Feliz año 2010.
'Appy noo 'ear you one eyed B...

Diary Friday 25th December Cold in Lugo
Painted the bedroom wall where I had missed behind the skirting with the nice dark red... looks very Christmassy. S knocked all the anti-cow posts back in along the track (someone's tractor seems to have demolished them all!)
Met Anne & Simon in Lugo after booking into the Hostal Grand Via and having a shower and a cuppa from our travel-everywhere-with-us kettle.
Excellent lunch as usual at China Town Restaurant. We shared, which is always better with Chinese, including something called 'hormigas subiendo un arbol'... ants climbing a tree! It was chopped fried chicken and vegetables with fried noodles which neither looked nor (thankfully) tasted like ants. At least not like the ants I tried in Indonesia in 2003. Had a wander round the Roman walls, before going back to the hotel.

DECEMBER

Checked my emails and sent out Christmas messages using the hostal wifi then watched ET in Spanish. Great fun.
Out in the evening for vinos at bar Museo. Think the owner was relieved Mum was not with us this year after that huge brandy! Back to the hostal to watch Happy Feet... also in Spanish. We shall be experts on children's films in Spanish soon.

Diary Saturday 26th December Cold in Lugo but dry
Lazy morning in bed then breakfasted at the Café Azul on chocolate and churros, as is traditional! Popped into AKI (also traditional when in Lugo) for some shelves for my storeroom/pantry. Found some green plasticy ones which look okay and were on special offer. Wandered around town looking at the Christmas market, and around the provincial museum. Had a bocadilla for lunch then delivered cake to Jayne and Richard before wending our way home to light the stoves and feed the animals.
Tried to put the new shelves together for my preserves but nowhere near enough bolts supplied. Hopeless!

On the last Sunday in December, we moved our sitting area to its third temporary home in three years (including the brief spell in the bathroom). The new stove was burning well and it seemed pointless firing up two stoves all evening, especially as the sunroom-living room lost its heat so quickly with the single glazing still in that section. The sofas, cupboards, stereo and coffee tables went into the new hallway, and we moved our bed into *our* bedroom.

That evening we lit the stove for our first night sitting in our nice new living room and sleeping in our nice new red bedroom, looking (or in my case peering short-sightedly) at the mirrored wardrobes five metres away.

We covered the remaining furniture in the sunroom, ready to start work in the new year. And we carried the remaining stack of plasterboard sheets out of our new bedroom into the utility-room-to-be.

Then, on the final day of the old year, we sealed the door from the Big Barn downstairs with plastic and sealing tape. This was to prevent dust, and the cold air, seeping upstairs from the dirty and still uninsulated barn area into our nice clean and warm living and sleeping area. Little did we know at the time that that door would remain sealed for the next 11 years!

We'd had a busy but productive year. We had decided to get married and almost managed to sort out the Spanish red tape for it. More importantly, we had put up a new, woodworm free ceiling in the kitchen and got our main upstairs rooms completed. We are not the fastest workers in the world (too meticulous, too many distractions) but it was not a race and we were becoming more comfortable each year we lived *casa nosotros*. Our next big project was the sunroom. That was for the new year, 2010.

JANUARY
Things folk leave behind

From the front as you enter the gates, our house looks like a single storey hacienda with a low roof and a square, covered terrace area in front of two doors.

Those doors cause all sorts of problems for delivery men.

Our main entrance to the house is an old low wooden door with an interesting sliding panel in it at chest height (or head height for an elderly *Galego*). To the left, up four stone steps, is a relatively modern wooden door painted burgundy - at least that's what it said on the tin, though I'd say pillar box red. This looks like the main door, and I often find delivery men standing at the top of the steps waiting patiently.

They would have a surprise if they opened that door. It leads to our utility room and outside toilet: a toilet which for two years and three months sat in our living room, quietly hiding behind the sofa.

Looking back up at our house from the valley below, it seems enormous: two stories of 15 metres in length with small, evenly spaced windows on the upper storey and three tiny slits on the lower. On the eastern upper corner is a huge window, facing south towards the water mill on our little river. Another two and a half metre long window faces eastwards along the valley to my *huerta* and beyond .

TOMATO, FIG & PUMPKIN JELLY

Those windows were the cause of so much heartache.

From our very first viewing of *A Casa do Campo* I had envisioned large picture windows for that room, which we had optimistically designated 'The Sunroom'. We had discussed options and finally, in the spring of 2008, had ordered the windows from the same company which had eventually fitted our other windows. Those first windows had taken us eight months to obtain. We were promised that these ones would be ready in just three months. Why I believed this after our previous window related disasters I have no idea. Call it unfounded optimism.

During that summer, S had built new concrete pillars to support the roof beams, which we had found didn't actually span the room. He wanted to get on with cutting out the new window apertures during the good weather.

But the windows did not arrive in July as promised.

They didn't arrive in August, which is holiday time in Galicia. Nor did they arrive in September, when everyone goes back to work. In fact our windows finally arrived at the beginning of October, just in time for autumn. Luckily we had an excellent autumn that year and, with barely a week's notice, S was able to get both two metre by two and a half metre apertures cut out before the rains (and the windows) arrived.

The window people turned up at 7pm on a damp autumn evening and set about fitting the two huge frames. The window fitter was a tall, well-built rugby player type of a chap. He was also totally alone except for Paulino, our friendly but not altogether accurate window measurer. Paulino managed to ably supervise the work whilst keeping well clear of actually participating.

JANUARY

The first window frame proved more unstable than the fitter thought as he ended up sprawled beneath it on our ex-bedroom floor. Luckily, neither fitter nor window frame were damaged, and I managed not to laugh at the sight of him laying perfectly framed on my nice newly varnished floor. The poor man fitted the two frames without further incident. He left at 9pm, returning the following day to fit the double glazed panels.

Finally on 3rd October 2008, a year and two months after we had arrived at *A Casa do Campo*, we had the view I'd longed for from our sunroom-to-be, and the room began to look like the sunny room its moniker suggested.

That Christmas Mum had stayed with us at the house for the first time and we had converted our ex-bedroom, now with the two, almost full length windows, into a cosy bedroom for her. The adjoining sitting room (complete with toilet) was Mum's personal en-suite for the duration.

But these rooms were not yet completed.

Our first project for the upcoming year was to remove the dividing wall between these two rooms, building a new wall, just behind the lurking toilet, to form a larger living area accessed through the old wooden door from our new internal living-hallway. This would finally become the 'sunroom'. The new smaller area, with the toilet now in its rightful place, would become a separate utility accessed from the terrace through the newer of those two pillar box red doors.

We were keen to get started.

Diary Monday 4th January Cloudy but mild
New year, new project! Made a start on the sunroom by cleaning the first row of chestnut ceiling boards. These are in better condition than the bedroom ones. They are also tongue and

groove and have not been whitewashed (thank goodness!)
S re-jigging one of the old wooden bed frames for use in bedroom one.

Now that we had moved our furniture into our nice new bedroom, we were a bed short in the guest bedroom. We had decided that one of the old bed frames I'd cleaned up would look perfect in there. The wood was, as ever, beautiful old sweet chestnut with a tall, carved headboard, and a lower footboard allowing an uninterrupted view through the window down the valley to the river and the water mill.

We had one problem. The original bed had been of a typically *Galego* shape: five feet ten inches long and three feet ten inches wide. The non-springy spring base had been discarded. (In fact, that statement is a lie as it had actually been used as a frame around one of our compost heaps.) S needed to extend the side runners then cut and shape new wooden slats for the bed base. With a new mattress it would look lovely, and I was pleased that we were reusing the beautiful old furniture from the house rather than buying new stuff.

Tuesday 5th January 8pm. Cold but definitely not minus 6… yet!
Dear Mum,
  Please tell Aunty Jean her faggots are ready for collection! Have some leek and apple sausages for you. Though I could've done with your help. S had to assist as it is definitely a four handed job. We managed 32 sausages and 12 faggots.
  I left the pig's head in a big pot on the stove while we were out over Christmas and it was cooked beautifully! Made three big

JANUARY

pots of pressed chawl. Have the bones to cook for soup/stock and the fat to render - very little fat this year, too little really, I needed to use some of last year's belly fat for the sausages.

We had an excellent Chinese on the 25th. Only us and Anne and Simon in the end. Jayne and Richard cried off as they were busy trying to get their new boiler going so they could get some heat. We called in on the way home with a cake. Richard was not happy as the boiler wouldn't fire up. He and S put their heads together and by the time we left it was roaring away.

We had the duck that Jayne & Richard gave us for lunch on Sunday with homemade Chinese plum sauce and mash. It was exceedingly tasty. There was lots left so I made a duck wellington, with butternut squash and some of the plum sauce inside the pastry, for the freezer. If you are lucky I might keep it for your next visit!

S is currently 'making' the bed for your room. He has found the correct pair of runners for the bed head and bed end and has fit a very neat piece into them to make them long enough for a normal mattress rather than a short Galician one. We need to buy some wood to make a slatted base and hey presto. I have moved your clothes into your wardrobe and chest of drawers. There is still plenty of space for more! Should be all ready for you by spring. Tell the hospital to pull their fingers out so you can catch the fine weather.

We had a smashing New Year's Eve with Cris & Steve up in Ortigueira. They asked how you were and I said 'impatient for her new hip'. We drove up on the Thursday afternoon and arrived in time for dinner. We wanted to take them for a meal but Cris said they had plenty of Christmas leftovers so we pigged out and were chatting so much we missed the midnight bongs entirely. But it was a most pleasant end to the old year (and beginning to the new one!)

We came home with a boot full of empty five litre plastic water bottles. I saw an article somewhere where someone had used plastic bottles to make a greenhouse. I also know that plastic bottles filled with water have good insulating properties, so I've a mind to see what I can cobble together. (Not, I fear a full sized greenhouse, I'm thinking more a cold frame!) In the meantime the bottom barn is a bit full.

I also have my kitchen wall tiles. CJ kindly picked them up in France for us. I couldn't find anything I liked here, as you know. These are small (4") tiles, some in white and some the same red as the outside doors. I want the kitchen to be red too. The picture tiles are of a French coq, and the large, six piece picture is of two cockerels facing each other which reminds me of Buzz and poor

JANUARY

Ginger. The pinny and oven mitt you sent for Christmas will match nicely if I can keep them clean until then! We will probably do the kitchen in the summer.

I have now cleaned all the sunroom ceiling. It looks beautiful. I will polish it once we have finished making a mess in there. We removed everything that was left in the sunroom this morning. We have a pile of cushions, the spare armchair, and the mattress off the day bed blocking the little lobby next to the bathroom. S has taken the door off between the two rooms prior to (gently) knocking that wall down. I am glad to see the back of that blue door! Although I'm sure we will find a use for it somewhere down the line haha.

We spent a while moving the furniture about in the hallway-living room until we were happy with it. We decided on the sofa as near to the new stove as we can, with its back to the sunroom door to keep the draughts off.

The matching armchair of Aunt Annie's is in the far corner under the chimney.

The chimney rises at a 45° angle from the top of the stove so we get lots of heat staying in the room rather than losing it all outside.

I put my slippers on the marble plinth under the new stove while I popped downstairs to make supper tonight. They are toasty warm now and the stone wall behind the stove is starting to warm up too so it is really quite pleasant and cosy in here.

It has even started to warm the bathroom, though it was a bit smoky earlier and we were worried the ceiling was on fire. S went up into the attic just to make sure. Thankfully all was well. After the debacle of getting a double, insulated stove pipe to fit, he made a Heath Robinson affair from an old, holey tin bathtub filled with fireproof rockwool. It seems to be fine so far, and luckily the smoke was just the new paint burning off the stove!

Wednesday 6th January. Dry and mild. Los Reyes Magos (the magi kings).

It is Russian New Year today so we had been invited by Gala for tea. Had one of Gala's incredibly sweet creations with condensed milk icing, and Christmas cake. She also did us a special Russian sweet soup they have for Christmas, of bulgur wheat, nuts, sugar, and poppy seeds.

Our stove stayed in while we were out and kept it warm in here though it's still cold outside. More snow forecast. Jayne says their temporary boiler is eating the gas and they don't seem to be able to get heating and hot water. For all its faults, I still haven't seen a better and cheaper system than our wood burning stoves. I was too hot in bed last night whereas before we had been leaving

JANUARY

the electric blanket on all night to keep warm. Luxury!

CJ has kindly volunteered to come over tomorrow morning to help S move our tree trunk into the sunroom. Do you remember 'helping' us to move it last Christmas? It is nicely dried out now, though still rather heavy.

S knocked down half of the wall in there this morning but has left the door frame as a support until we have the new 'prop' in place, though it probably doesn't need it. It should look good. A piece of real Galician sweet chestnut. I've promised him cake and tea in exchange (CJ that is, though no doubt S will have some too haha).

11pm. Just finished my book. Bit sloppy at the end and odd that the only time no one died was during the Great War. Enjoyed it though, thank you. Now nibbling cherry liqueurs. Very tasty, thank you Santa! We certainly have plenty of films now. Reckon we have around 15 or more film nights - you do get carried away. Please show this to Aunty Jean with a BIG thank you too.

This will be late again as today was a holiday (again). I hope you hear something soon from the hospital. Did you ring again? Maybe they will get fed up with you ringing and say 'come in now'.

Give my love to Aunty Jean and Aunty Jan. But most of all looking forward to having you here again to view the changes and

help with the chickens. August seems a long time ago!
Keep warm, Love you tons and tons
Xxxxxxxxxxxxx

Weather wise, January of the new year seemed to be carrying on from December of the old – with more snow.

That winter turned out to be the snowiest ever in the 13 years we have lived in Galicia. Although older neighbours recall snow some three metres deep being a regular occurrence in years gone by, we have seen very little since that year – the start of our third in Galicia. In fact only one other snowy period comes to mind, and that almost caused a disaster for both us and Mum. But that was years in the future. (And another story.)

Diary Thursday 7th January Frosty with snow off and on.
Put the washer on as it was sunny first thing. Mistake! Dried the washing in the kitchen on the rack above the stove. S started axing the huge tree branch 'prop' to reduce its diameter and weight, and to remove the soft outer layer. It has dried well with no splitting.
Popped to town to post Mum's letter and check emails. Arrived back at the same time as CJ. Tea and cake then the lads carried the tree into the sunroom.
Lunch: Ham and chicken pie (Ginger) with butternut squash chips and apple, raisin, and carrot slaw. Stewed plums and chocolate sauce.
S measured the prop, cut and jammed it into place. Unfortunately he didn't jam it too well as it fell out and put a nice big hole through the floorboards! S stood the prop up again while I helped hold it in place. He then nailed it (securely) to the ceiling

JANUARY

beam. He continued knocking down the other half of the wall while I sanded part of the attic platform in the hallway downstairs.

Other than the incident of the tree trunk, which we don't talk about, work on the sunroom went pretty well. The trunk, once sanded and polished, became a talking point. And the hole in the floor, once repaired and hidden under the daybed, was not mentioned at all. Most of our visitors pat or stroke or cuddle our tree as they enter the sunroom. It is rather tactile and the constant touching helps to keep it oiled.

Our tree trunk prop in the sunroom is not the only recycled item we have. The brass rail from the front of our old *cocina*, or range cooker, is now a bannister rail. Our other bannister rails in the house are tree branches or, in a wonderfully selfless act of serendipity, a small chestnut tree which had grown out of the stone wall of my allotment in a perfect bannister shaped curve.

Where we have needed new doors, we have used rescue ones (and no, Leo, you can't have them back now they are cleaned and polished.) Even S' workbench top is an old brown painted door our neighbour was throwing away.

In fact, we appear to have a bit of a reputation for being collectors of what other people may call junk. I think of us as Wombles, after the delightful animated 70s TV series. Things that other people throw away, we will use.

Our friend rang one day to see when our council rubbish dump was open as theirs had, for inexplicable Spanish reasons, closed. We invited him for lunch of course. Unfortunately the day he came, van loaded with his rubbish, our tip had also, again for inexplicable Spanish reasons, decided not to open. Rather than having to cart it all home again, we told Graham to leave the stuff with us, and we would dump it next time they opened. This was not altogether altruistic as we had spotted some useful items.

First, there was an old gas cooker. Most of the metal panels from this have since been used to repair other things, and the old metal hob rings are useful for weighing down covers on the allotment and preventing my garden fleece blowing away. There was also a large cast iron 'pig swill' boiler. The top of that now graces our new wood burner in the Big Barn together with two half cast iron tops from old *cocinas* which S angle ground (or grinded? I'm never sure) to form a lovely stove top.

Diary Saturday 9th January Very cold though sunny
Fiddled with the rustic bookcase I'd made out of the old wooden trunk (previously used to house rabbits prior to us moving in). It is now going to be a lovely rustic shoe rack at the top of the steps to the upstairs rooms, for guests' slippers and shoes. Just thinking what a tale that trunk could tell in its 4th or 5th reincarnation!

I suppose I've never been a spendthrift. Growing up we were by no means on the streets poor, but we didn't have money to burn either. The day I left home for university my dad thrust an envelope into my hands. In it was £70. That was a lot of money in those days. He explained that it was the 'leftover' child allowance they had saved. I don't know if that was the case or not, but I suspected he had been saving up for a while. I was incredibly touched by the gesture and that 70 quid lasted me the three months until my grant came through.

When I met S, I found a fellow recycler. We both enjoy the challenge of reusing stuff instead of buying new.

JANUARY

I have found that having a book out there means being at the mercy of folk wanting to know all about you. One subject which comes up frequently is that of money – or specifically of how I managed to 'retire' at 42 and buy a house in Galicia.

I don't smoke (thank you Mum and Dad for putting me off that for life, you have saved me a fortune). I don't spend on make-up (never got on with it, and it seems cruel to make S wake up to a totally different and even scarier me!). I don't spend on designer clothes (most of my wardrobe is pre our move here. But then again I'm generally gardening or building, so other than regular wellie replacements I don't need a lot). I don't go to the hairdressers (the photos will confirm that one) and of course we grow most of our own veggies and a fair bit of our own meat, fruit, and nuts.

Galicia is a cheap place to live, in comparison to the UK. Our house when we bought it (in a totally ruinous state remember) cost less than a small garage in London, or a tiny flat further north. Because we did every bit of the renovations ourselves, these added maybe another third to the price... so a slightly larger garage in London or a flat with a view in northern England. Our slow, 18 month roof renovation cost us 5000€, a saving of at least 30,000€ over the cost of a 'professional' job.

Day to day costs here are small too. A three course *menú del dia* still costs 10€ a head with wine and bread, and an evening *vino* (with tapas) is now a whole euro and ten cents. Spain has wonderful healthcare and good council services. We have everything we need.

And that is the nub... everything *we* need. Because of course our lifestyle here would not suit everyone. I know people who have moved back home because they missed English sausages, Costa Coffee shops, or English language cinema. People are all different, thankfully, but for us this is a move I've never regretted (except on those occasions when the inevitable Spanish bureaucracy has worked its magic).

Tuesday 12th January. Very heavy rain and very windy overnight
Dear Mum,
  Got your text - that's rubbish isn't it? Bet they're not full if you wanted your hip done private. We could have a go here with the hacksaw and a bit of old cow bone if you like?
  As it wasn't raining last night (until the middle of the night from when it poured and we were subject to Chinese water torture due to a small and persistent drip in the attic above the bedroom) and the snow had melted a bit, we decided to walk to town and pay Luisa for our pig. I had worked the price out and written it down. It was 78 kilos. The price is the same per kilo as last year, 600 pesetas which is 3.61€. Luisa only knows the price in pesetas though and has a special calculator to convert it to euros. The thing is, the peseta-euro exchange rate remains static, so why not just remember the price in euros? Her calculator wouldn't work and eventually she just took my word for it. Good job we are honest. I'm not sure maths is taught well here. The lady at the swimming baths last week said 'that's two sandwiches at 1.80€ each and two wines at .50c each, 3.60€.' 'No,' says I, 'it's 4.60€'. 'No,

JANUARY

3.60€.' she replied. I gave her the 4.60€ but she still looked bemused.

Anyway, we did okay last night as a new friend kept us in vinos. A tubby stranger in a red beret came in to the bar. I nearly said something about Santa but something stopped me. He got chatting about independence for the Basque country, and for Galicia. I pointed out that I didn't feel either was strong enough to manage outside of Spain and the discussion got quite heated. S then pointed out that the red beret is a 'badge' of the Basque separatists (ETA). So there's me in a bar, drinking vino and discussing politics with a possible terrorist sympathiser in a foreign language that I, at best, only half comprehend! When we went to leave he said he was buying and that he hadn't enjoyed such a good argument for years. He then put his red beret on and left.

The chickens don't much like this weather. No one would venture onto the white stuff yesterday. They all huddled under the bike shed. Sarah did go outside eventually, then I couldn't see her. Good camouflage being white!

The robin has learnt how to hop through the chicken flap and peck the crumbs they leave behind. We also had a little wren in the Big Barn. I thought it was trapped so opened all the doors, but once it realised we were probably harmless it continued eating

- one of our hibernating butterflies it had found. It seemed quite happy, though our peacock butterflies will suffer this year.

I had what one might call a religious experience in the allotment. I went to check my autumn onion sets after the rains and there, in the middle of my onion bed, half buried, arms outstretched - was Jesus! He is about 6" high and made of brass and was standing upright. I know he wasn't there last week. Very disturbing! I'm glad it's not Easter or I'd think he had resurrected in the onion bed! I've asked him if he can hurry your op along but obviously not too successful so far.

We had our banns back from Vigo yesterday. Poor postie turned up through all the snow. I had to laugh when you asked on Saturday. I thought you might have guessed when I wanted my full birth certificate last year. And as if we would get married without you... I wouldn't dare!

Anyway we still need to sort getting the birth certificates legalised before returning to the dragon, as we call the registrar, to set a date. We will let you (and everyone else) know but aim for late August/early September... possibly.

This morning we had fun turning the wood-burner around 90° so now it faces into the new sunroom. Not as easy as it sounds as it is very heavy, and of course we couldn't disconnect the chimney to make it easier. I *sort of stood on pieces of wood to anchor it down and S twisted it. But we did it.*

S is now putting up the new stud wall between the sunroom and the utility to be. At the eastern end the wall will divide the old living room window in two. We have a 'new' old wooden window for the utility side but need to think of something for the sunroom side which will only be about a 6" gap. I think a column of glass bricks would be nice and let some light into that corner of the room.

On Sunday I was supposed to be meeting Jayne to discuss our vegetable seeds for the year but we had to cancel as the snow had settled rather heavily and we couldn't get the car out of the drive again. We ended up retiring indoors early with the stove lit and the scrabble board. I won, but only by 7 points.

We did have a pleasant walk on Sunday afternoon, after our rabbit stew. It was frosty when we set off but quite pleasant. We went up and over the hill opposite, to a village called Castro, then on to a village where some people we had met last year have a house. The village seemed to be closed until spring! Then it started to snow… obviously! We came back over the tops to the village at the far end of our valley. Looked like little snowpeople! Took some good photos of the river and the chestnuts in the snow. Do hope that by summer we can take you on some walks. Tell the Doc that your daughter needs you to help on the farm so to hurry up!!

And to help eat our pig. I've run out of room in the freezer for the hams. Have one collar joint and two gammon hams frozen and two bacons on hooks. Had a pork boney stew for lunch yesterday, good winter warming fare.

Love you tons and tons
xxxxxxxxx

Those bacon joints are still hanging from the rafters in our kitchen. I *was* going to freeze them once I had made space, then I thought I would try for some *jamón serrano* and then... well they just stayed, and stayed. Now, 11 years later, they are a talking point. They have never gone off and look the same as when they were hung - just a little smaller and darker. One day maybe, just maybe, we will try them!

Diary Friday 15th January Mild and drizzly
Up early (9am) to go to Jayne's. Spent all day chatting, discussing seeds and drinking tea.
S meanwhile went over to Jen's house with CJ to look at some roof leaks (they had promised to keep an eye on the place). They dug up some bamboo and asparagus (which Jen's dad had promised me) then came back and cut and ferried the dead apple tree across from the allotment, between restorative cuppas and cake of course!
To Chantada for our swim and bathnight. Asked Angela about having my hen do there. She seemed concerned that we would want a full meal but I explained that a cold buffet style supper would be fine - just like the niños have! Left her puzzled but agreeable.

JANUARY

Diary Saturday 16th January Mild with less rain
Made cake then off to CJ's to print out the Foreign Office form for the official stamp needed on our birth certificates. S stayed home and 'thunk' about electrics for the utility and sunroom.
Lunch: Pasta, sun dried tomatoes, sesame, carrot, ham, raisins and red cabbage.
Limed two cabbage trenches on the allotment and mulched this year's root patch. S put the electric wires through for the sunroom. Noticed the asparagus S dug up from Jen's looks remarkably like fennel... smells like fennel too!

Diary Monday 18th January Drizzle again
Posted our birth certificates off to the UK Foreign & Commonwealth Office together with the form and fee for the apostles or whatever the stamp is called. S retiled the hórreo roof now it is calm enough to get up there. The tiles had slipped in the high winds. We both then put the old uralitas from Anne and Simon on to the chicken shed roof to provide a bit of extra shade and waterproofing.

Our 'officially-stamped' birth certificates were supposed to be back in a week or so. Then we would need to get them 'officially-translated' over here using an 'officially-registered' translator. It was slow work but I was starting to enjoy the game of trying to defeat Spanish bureaucracy.

Meanwhile we continued making our sunroom into our show room. S cemented concrete blocks around the wood-burning stove to act as a heat store, as the ones around the *cocina* in the kitchen did. He also wanted to make some rustic shelving using the old holey floorboards from Bedroom One.

Nothing, but nothing gets wasted!

The shelving would go around the corner of the room at waist height, and behind the newly turned-around stove. More shelves, on the new plasterboard wall adjoining the utility, would hold our collection of CDs, cassettes and Discworld novels. Completed, the old floorboard shelves look stunning and are remarked upon by everyone who sees the room.

I, meanwhile, ordered the floor tiles for the kitchen and storeroom. I had seen some I liked in the builder's merchant, but when I asked I was told I couldn't have them. We had been in Galicia long enough by now to know that a negative response doesn't necessarily mean 'no'. It's another sort of game. *Galegos* tend to reply with a negative before you have even finished the sentence sometimes. It can be frustrating but I persevered. 'Could you ring and find out maybe?' José waivered. 'We want 36 square metres.' Okay, he would ring, but he wasn't hopeful. Of course the tiles were there a few days later.

As I say, it's a game.

Diary Tuesday 19th January
Sunshine this morning so I decided to have a go at pruning the vines. Started raining off and on. Not really sure what I am doing anyway so went to collect more chestnut leaves for my leaf mould.
Surprise visit from Mark, the estate agent, this afternoon. Showed him around but he didn't make many comments, busy telling us what he had been up to and making the place look small as most of our doorways are at his neck height.
To Taboada in the evening. Played dominoes in Scala. No one has played threes and fives here so they were totally bemused. The old boy was in. He must be 102 by now!

Sunday 24th January. Actual sunshine.
Dear Mum,
Excellent news! Was so pleased to get your text. S says maybe the 'phone call to the

JANUARY

hospital did the trick after all. (Or my allotment Jesus came through for you!) February is good. I guess by the time you get this you will have already re-washed everything in sight and cleaned the house from top to bottom, just so you are ready.

Lunch today was our new sweetcure ham. Very tasty, not as salty as last year. One jar honey, one jar golden syrup in the big plastic tub with water, salt and spices. Afterwards we set off down the track for a walk. Took a small track by the little waterfall which is shown on our map as a road. Of course it descended into jungle, but we hacked our way through prickly gorse and clambered through some chestnut woods and a farmer's field then ended up at a derelict house on the road above. Took us two and a half hours of battering! The house is a village all of its own with its own name and must have been quite stunning when it was built. It has views over the valley and a big garden next to it. On the other side is a beautiful barn and walled garden. The outer wall has a big crack down it and the lintel over the main gateway (into a covered courtyard) has split so it won't last much longer. So sad really. If I ever won the lottery I would buy up old houses just so I could renovate them, I hate to see such lovely buildings fall down... especially when the new flats they throw up are so hideous.

Luckily it was still light at 6.30pm when we got home. Very pleasant anyway. Cheese on toast in front of the fire for tea.

Tell Aunty Jean that Jesus is definitely only brass. He cleaned up well using half a (used) lemon and wood ash. S says I should put him back on the allotment to bless the veg or some such. I may hang him in the car like the taxis drivers do. It's probably the most dangerous place around here!

Had 7 eggs today. Five from today and two I found in an old tub. They were very well hidden. Our two new girls I think, probably they are being bullied so decided to find their own quiet spot!

As we have so many eggs I made a couple of pots of orange curd. Very tasty in a tart and a good standby if visitors come for dinner. I froze the bit which didn't fit in the jars (why is there always a little bit too much?) as a rich ice cream.

Monday 6.30pm. The gas man turned up today which was odd as it isn't his week. But he wasn't delivering gas, he had brought his secateurs to cut my vines. He always comments on our vines and tells me what I should be doing and when. One day, ages ago, he was telling me I hadn't pruned them properly and I joked that he would have to come and show me. So that's what he had done! He grabbed our ladders and I spent an hour hanging onto them while he dangled at alarming angles snipping here

JANUARY

and there and, it seemed, generally enjoying himself, his truck abandoned in the lane, his customers waiting.

He told me to pull all the moss and old bark off (which I duly did this pm). He then pruned a bit of the pear tree and dispensed advice until it was lunchtime.

He refused payment or a drink and toddled off. I can't imagine any of our services men in England popping over to do some free pruning!

My broad beans seem to be growing again after their battering by the wind, rain and snow. No purple sprouting broccoli yet so the allotment supplies are down to carrots, parsnips, leeks, a few cabbage, leaf beet (excellent, has lasted almost 12 months) and landcress - not that bad really I guess and still plenty of tomato sauce. Oh, and some dried mushrooms too.

S has been busy concreting round the stove in the sunroom to make a big 'storage heater' so we don't lose all the heat through the walls. I just tried to draw it for you but it looks like a Dalek encased in, well, concrete I guess! Will have to send you a pic...

(Just reread that bit and thought I had put pie! My writing gets worse.)

Tuesday: Sunshine!

Thank you for your letter. Look forward to viewing the new suite - do I need to bring dust sheets to sit on or do you provide? Ha!

TOMATO, FIG & PUMPKIN JELLY

Do you remember the old bath CJ donated to us when they had the new shower fitted? It was one of the tiny Spanish hip baths which CJ reckoned fit his small toe! Well, we finally dug it into the ground today. The idea is to make a small wildlife pond at the bottom of the allotment to encourage toads and other insect eaters. We have a deep part which the bath sits in, then a shallower part around with a liner under. The sods of earth and grass will be put back around the edges and the whole lot left to fill with water over winter.

Linda and Martin from down the road popped in today at lunchtime (al fresco, first time this year, lovely) to ask if we can take them to the airport on 6th February. They are going back to the UK. It seems Stefan is saying he wants to strip the roof over the summer so wants them out. They are sad to be leaving and have really fit in well here. They offered us three boxes full of DVDs and a load of books which they don't want to lug back to England, plus a number of pairs of wellies and an old but functioning VCR player! We, of course accepted all gifts! See you soon.

XXXXXXXXXX

PS Was I supposed to say 'yes'? What should the question have been?!

Those three boxes of DVDs became the start of a huge lending library. S decided he would take the DVDs to the next market day meeting in Monterroso

JANUARY

and see if anyone wanted to borrow some. He stuck them in boxes with a sign saying 'if you have any DVDs you don't want please donate them.' We now have over 800 films, series' and documentaries. I did the same with the books. My 'library' is over 700 paperbacks of all genres, but we are running out of space in the house.

Diary Friday 29th January Back to rain!
Drizzled all day on and off. Decided to try the new bed in the guest room last night before offering it to future guests. It didn't collapse so that's ok!
Lunch: Blue cheese, mushroom, sweetcorn and sun dried tomato omelette. Salad. Frozen orange curd with a couple of those biscuits you get with coffees out. Scrummy!
Boiled and peeled a dozen eggs to pickle. Called to see CJ after our bathnight. He bought another dozen eggs from me.
Pinned Angela down to a price for the hen night. 6€ a head including vino. She can do sandwiches and tortilla and stuff. Sounds perfect. Anyone who wants to swim can come in on our ticket. Just need to sort transport. Wonder if we can get the bus? Also wonder what S is going to do. Told him he has to have a separate stag do.

Diary Sunday 31th January Some sunshine first thing
Excellent boiled eggs and soldiers for breakfast in the sunshine.
Pruned the roses as it is full moon... is that right? Finished cleaning the balustrades around the terrace. I think it's been a few years since they were last done, then started knocking the cement off 'Belle's wall' by the kitchen. It needs quite a lot of cleaning up before I repoint it and is annoying me sitting there with bits of brick stuffed in holes while we have our morning cuppa.

Lunch: Pork cooked in milk (very tender) with mash, roast apples, broccoli, and stuffing. Orange and apple tart using the apple cheese I made. Excellent also!
Poured with rain in the afternoon so S carried on cementing around the stove surround. It looks quite 60s. Like it! I finished decementing (is that even a word?) the terrace wall.

I guess the question is: are we Wombles or hoarders? I would say the former as we generally reuse anything we collect. S, for many years, had a collection of Smartie tops. Those plastic ones which came in different colours in the days before Rowntrees was taken over and the plastic tops disappeared. I found this collection shortly after we met and was intrigued to say the least. A Smartie top collection may seem to many, including me, to be a hoard. But this year he finally used his collection, as he had always intended, to create a work of art.

A large cream backboard sits overlooking the staircase in our newly completed Big Barn. Upon this board are columns of brightly coloured circles. Close up one can see the columns are arranged alphabetically. It looks splendid and is a constant reminder of the usefulness of things folk leave behind!

FEBRUARY
Family Tree

At long last things seemed to be coming together for our Galician wedding.

At the end of the February, I was off to England to help Mum after her hip operation. I planned to sort out more 'weddingy' things whilst I was there. Here in Galicia, we needed our documents back from the UK Foreign and Commonwealth Office and then officially translated before approaching the dragon once more. I couldn't wait!

I feel I ought to point out at this stage, that this book is not meant to constitute a 'how to' guide to getting married in Galicia. Neither should anyone considering getting married in Spain be put off by our experiences. The wonderful thing about Spain is that whatever adventures you may have trying to beat the bureaucracy, you can bet someone else has sailed through the process. And vice versa.

When we first arrived in Galicia, we had no idea how to go about accessing the health care services. We simply wandered down to our local GP surgery and asked. Within days we had our health cards and social security numbers. When I told our friend CJ this, he replied that it was impossible. Apparently he had to go to the social security office in Lugo with a load of papers in order to register. I showed him our Social Security number. He still maintains it was impossible, and I tend to agree. We were fortunate.

TOMATO, FIG & PUMPKIN JELLY

On this occasion, and for this particular piece of bureaucracy, fortune was not exactly smiling on us.

Diary Tuesday 2nd February Frosty am. Sunny and warm during the day
Washing on, once the hose pipe had defrosted that is.
Into town. Queued endlessly at the Co-operativa, eventually gave up and came home foodless. Emailed the official translator in Chantada as our apostilised (or whatever) birth certificates arrived back today. No reply.
S started measuring for the next lot of book shelves, in the alcove in the sunroom. It will be a lovely reading room.
Lunch: Bean burgers with rice salad. Orange tart and ice cream
S cut some leftover floorboards for the shelves whilst I cleaned the terrace wall ready for jetwashing tomorrow.

Wednesday 3rd February. Sunshine
Dear Mum,
At last, February seems to have brought us some welcome sunshine (and frosty nights, but it's far preferable to the rain). I have finished mulching my cabbage and bean trenches with old chestnut leaves raked up off the track. Concha spotted me collecting and came over to tell me I was too late for chestnuts as they would be rotten by now. I tried to explain that I was collecting the leaves for the huerta but not sure I succeeded.

I have put a leaky hose in the vegetable beds, which will eventually be connected up

FEBRUARY

to our big tanks at the top of the allotment for irrigation. We will see how well it works before deciding if we get any more.

We bought a persimmon tree at Monterroso market on Monday. (Diosprynos, I think if you look it up.) It is supposed to like hot summers and it has big orange fruits in winter. We have planted it on the allotment and mulched it well. Wonder how long it takes to start fruiting?

I borrowed CJ's jetwash again today. Tell Belle that as the stone chipper never finished her job (you can't get the slave labour can you?) I have finally given in and finished her wall on the terrace. I had fun blasting it this pm. With the newly jetwashed balustrades it is looking quite cared for on our little terrace. I need to paint the balustrades white now.

8.30pm. Just back from Lugo. Fire roaring up the chimney. Had to get S a new phone as his died two weeks ago. He is busy reading his instructions (in Spanish) and muttering!

We called to see Jayne and Richard on the way back. The chickens seem happy, though Jayne says Lucky has gone for her a couple of times. Once flying at her and trying to use his (thankfully non-existent) spurs. Guess he is growing up!

We will try to order some kitchen worktops when we go to Santiago on Saturday. The floor tiles are on order with José in town and we have the wall tiles, so once it gets warm enough to not use the cocina we will make a start in there.

I will post this in town. Don't know if I will get in another before your op but will post one for when you get out. Behave yourself and do as you are told. (Don't forget to tell them you need a bathboard and a raised toilet seat for upstairs.)

I do hope you are going to be good while I am in charge. I don't get to be in charge often so I shall make the most of it! Are you all packed and ready? At least you don't have to stay in hospital very long. The situation with the MRSA bug sounds quite scary, and you should take a goody bag of food with you too if the hospital fare is as bad as you have heard!
Love you tons and tons
See you soon
 XXXXXXXx
PS Just missed a job in Walsall today. I hadn't picked the email up in time. Still, it's nice to be remembered!

One would think that when it comes to official things like weddings, there would be a definitive guide listing the process and the documents needed. As we had already found, the lists were very different depending on where they came from. Our dragon at the registry office didn't help. Nevertheless, we were exceptionally surprised (no, I don't know why either - you would think we were beyond surprise by now) when our friends John and Mike got married six months after us with no hassle

FEBRUARY

whatsoever. They popped into their town hall, the banns were published there, and the mayor rang them with a date, all within a few days.

Diary Friday 5th February Drizzle
Tried to ring the translator again this morning. No reply.
Cleaned up the last of the wall on the terrace and put everything back, then decided to make a start on the wall under the utility window. Think the map of Spain chiselled into the old plaster will have to go too. Decorative though it is!
Lunch: Dorada with ginger and stirfry veg (last courgette thingy)
To Chantada for our bathnight and swim. Tried to find this interpreter as no reply to my email or calls. Found her mother, eventually. It seems her daughter is in England until Easter. Plan B!

Monday 8th February. Dull, where's our February sunshine gone?
Dear Mum,
 I guess you should get this when you are all done, bionic hip in place! I'll see you soon xxx
 We are cracking on with the sunroom. S is making some rustic shelving around the room for our CDs, cassettes and books. He is using the old floorboards from bedroom one. They look really good, especially the 'leg' which has a hole in the middle of it. We don't waste much do we haha! Now we are counting the CDs and tapes so we know how many shelves we need!
 On Saturday we had to go to Santiago to drop Mart & Linda off. They are off back to

TOMATO, FIG & PUMPKIN JELLY

England. It was sad to say goodbye to them as I think they would have loved to have stayed and they have become good friends. On the way home, we called into Leroy Merlin, the DIY shop, to look at worktops for the kitchen. We eventually chose some oak ones as a contrast to the grey and white granite round the cocina.

They are quite expensive but very solid looking and 4cm (2") thick. Pretty heavy too. I plan to oil them like the ones I had in Doveridge. As they are 8 foot long, S will collect them when he drops me off for the flight over at the end of the month, so that has all worked out well.

I decided to let the chickens out into the garden for an hour last night for a treat as I was outside. Of course they soon blotted their copybook by digging up my chives and parsley seedlings! Then they scattered the lettuce seeds I'd sown. Then Buzz tried to lead everyone 'over the wall' onto the track. S had to chase them back along the ledge for me. I think they enjoyed their hour of destruction, though I was exhausted. Only Veronique refused to come out at all and stayed in eating all the grain. She says 'when chickens go out that door they don't come back.' I may wait until I have a chicken sitter before trying that experiment again (Mind you, Sarah found herself two snails straight off so at least she was some use.)

FEBRUARY

I have managed to point up the walls on the terrace and that 'map' of Spain has gone. It was specially cemented in with a different mix. I almost got it off in one piece. Anyway, I think it looks better without.

Our walk on Sunday took us two and a half hours as there was some scrambling (isn't there always!) to get alongside the river, so we had a rather late lunch. Luckily the rabbit stew (with bacon, mushrooms and cream) had cooked nicely in the cocina while we were out. Pudding was a custard fool with blackberries which I had made earlier. Always feel I deserve dinner after a bit of exercise. Do you remember when we went on holiday and Dad and I would always go off for a jog down the prom while you made breakfast. Bacon and eggs always taste better on holiday!

Weds 11pm. Cold but at least we don't have snow! Hope yours is gone in the morning for you. I spent a happy morning in my kitchen baking. I made a root vegetable and chestnut pie for lunch, egg custards, leek and potato soup for tea, cheese and meat pasties to freeze, and meatballs for tomorrow. Then this afternoon I made a tongue and ham galette (like a pate but more solid).

S spotted this advert for a DVD on the back of the crossword you sent. We were amused by the title... 'Attract birds to your garden' with an illustration of a sparrowhawk! Poor blue tits!

Friday pm. Sunny but still biting cold wind and -3° overnight.

Brother says you had an epidural for the op. Brave surgeon! Bet you never stopped talking to him. Will ring you when you get home.

S has been chopping up that dead tree that came down on the allotment. Said he found a few grubs in it for the chickens. There were a dozen HUGE things. 4" long and very fat. The chickens enjoyed racing round the pen with them anyway. By the way, did I tell you that I am a bit concerned that one of the young ones (known as Blondie) appears to have a BRAIN? Very worrying! If I go in with their food and a corn cob behind my back, the others all go for the food but she stands and looks at me until I pull the corn off the cob. She can outstare me too.

Went over to Jorge and Kath's to collect some donkey muck on Thursday. They don't use it and are happy for us to collect. They are coming to the fiesta on Sunday (bone stew fair) so we went into town tonight to book our table. It was icy in the bar. I asked for room temperature wine (tiempo) but it still felt like it had come out of the freezer!

Cris and Steve are coming Sunday morning with the dogs. I hope they behave this time (the dogs that is!) as both bunnies seem to be nest building. S has cleaned out

FEBRUARY

the barn for the dogs and the people are in the guest room! This is all weather permitting. Steve said they went into As Pontes last week and were turned back on the way home because of snow by the windmills on the tops. Don't know how they got home as it's a long trek round either costal way!

Had a surprise this morning. S was outside and I could hear shouting. The postman was standing by the gate yelling but S couldn't hear him! When I went out, wiping my hands on my pinny, to rescue the poor man he had a parcel. A large jiffy bag inside an even larger plastic bag. The plastic bag had a map of New Zealand (pretty distinctive) on it and the letters NZMAFF. When I opened the jiffy bag, there inside were the onion sets you sent me before Christmas! Of course by now they had started to sprout. So the question is how on earth did they get to New Zealand? The address by the way was perfectly correct. I will plant them tomorrow. They are certainly well travelled onion sets!

I'll pop this in the box tomorrow. You will probably be home before it arrives, and I'll see you in about a week from when you receive it.

Loads of love
xxxxxx

S had been struggling with his increasing deafness for a while. It affected me more than him, as I am very poor at talking clearly and loudly. He says he can hear Concha perfectly. One day we saw an advertisement on the notice board in town for a free hearing test. It seemed worth a look.

We opened the door of our small town hall building to a cacophony of noise. The sort of noise only a couple of score of hard of hearing *Galegos* squashed into a tiny hallway could make.

We pushed our way into the mass, shaking hands, kissing, or nodding to the people we recognised. The door to the architect's room opened and a smart young man poked his head out looking rather flustered.

"¡*Silencio por favor!*" he said. "It is impossible to conduct the hearing test if it is not quiet."

He closed the door, upon which I noticed a large sign hung. '*Rogamos silencio*' it read. We beg silence. They have the same signs in the doctor's surgery. They don't work either.

The peace prompted by the young man's complaint lasted maybe two to three minutes before the volume began to creep up once more. Beside me, an elderly gentleman in the regulation beret started to quiz me about my health, home, and background in an extremely loud voice. His wife hissed at him to be quiet but to no avail.

By the third time (since we had been standing there) that the young man poked his head out to 'beg silence', his expression was one of resignation. The huddle of folk had not diminished a jot, and of course there was no type of queuing system. (The Spanish don't do queues, though woe betide anyone who jumps in front as everyone knows their exact place in the non-queue.) So far we had only seen one chap emerge from the test room so things were obviously not going to plan. At that moment a friend of ours came in the door.

"You don't want to buy these hearing aids you know," he said. "¡*Son muy caro!*"

FEBRUARY

Very expensive?! We looked around the milling crowds, enjoying a chat with their friends and decided our day, and our pockets, had more to offer. We left.

Years later, S bought a pair of hearing aids from the Specsavers chain in England. He never really got on with them and eventually killed first one and then the other, by washing them under the shower. To this day S continues to manage without hearing aids, and I occasionally remember to speak up.

Diary Sunday 14th February Sunshine but cold
Feira do caldo de ósos in Taboada. Cris & Steve arrived at 11am. Quick chat and tea then into Taboada for more tea and a preliminary bowl of pig bone stew. Bought a soft cheese with walnuts in at the feira. Onto Bar Mencia to meet everyone else for our famous three course pig bone stew menu. Absolutely stuffed full!
Showed our guests their nice completed room with newly renovated Galician bed. CJ rolled up so more tea and cake (for those who could manage it). More chat, more tea, and supper.

When we met up with Cris & Steve there was always plenty of chatting went on. And still is, although sadly we see them less frequently now they have moved back to England. We stayed up chatting until the early hours then retired to bed.

I was just nodding off when I heard a loud thud. I woke up S. "What was that?"

"What?" he murmured sleepily.

I was just about to explain when I heard a stage-whispered voice outside our door. "Are you two awake?"

"Yes," I whispered back. "What's up?"

"The bed collapsed," replied Steve.

I stared at S and he back at me, then we simultaneously jumped out of bed. We both struggled to get dressed and ran into the hallway. In the guest bedroom was Cris, trying her very best not to laugh, and beyond her was our lovely new bed - now in an interesting V shape. It had broken right across the middle.

Luckily our friends both saw the funny side as we all dragged the wrecked frame out of the way and positioned the mattress on the floor. Cris even allowed me to take a photo of her looking horrified, for posterity.

"But don't you dare tell anyone," she threatened.

"I'll just tell them that there was too much acrobatics in bed," I replied, grinning.

By morning they had both decided that was an acceptably amusing story. Just as well because I've dined out on it for years!

Diary Monday 15th February Nice in sun. Not hot
Found another official translator online. He is called Nacho and lives in Lugo. Agreed to meet him on Wednesday. He says the minimum charge for translating is 50€ but he will do both birth certificates for that price.

Diary Wednesday 17th February Cool in Lugo
To Lugo for the usual shopping in Chino Antonios and AKI, then drove round to Parque Rosalia Castro to meet Nacho, our translator. Took ages to find parking so we were late. Luckily Nacho was typically laid back about time keeping. Nice looking lad too... just saying!
We chatted about the English language and some of the dire translations we have seen in documents. He says that sadly many organisations use a relative who did a couple of years of English in school for their translations or worse still, Google. Said he could have the birth certificates translated by 5pm.

FEBRUARY

Walked up to Café Recatelo for lunch then finished our shopping at Lidl and checked my emails in El Galeón.
Back to the café in the park to meet Nacho. He had a question about the fathers' occupations. My certificate says collieryman. Nacho had found the translation for a miner (minero) which we agreed was the same thing. S' certificate gave his father's occupation as linesman which confused poor Nacho completely. We agreed on telephone engineer after a long explanation. 50€ still seems a lot for 2 words, even if they were complicated ones, but it is done so we are another step closer. Back to the registry tomorrow. Let's see the dragon complain this time.

Me and my big mouth.

We did return to the dragon's lair the following day. As usual, there was an air of desolation about the place. Our dragon stood at the desk, silently watching us traverse the empty floor. I plonked all our papers on the table, smirking, and muttered under my breath, "read 'em and weep."

"*¡No!*"

My smirk faded.

Apparently, according to our dragon's twisted logic, the consulate affidavits which had cost us almost 600€ were not legal.

Not even bothering to argue this time, we left. On the way home we called in on CJ and Gala for tea and sympathy. Gala immediately agreed to accompany us straight back to the registry office.

We returned to the dragon's lair with Gala in tow. The dragon was as surly as ever, but she had met her match in our wonderful friend. In a clever bit of psychology, Gala asked the dragon about her begonia, which had grown even larger since we first saw it almost a year ago. This innocent question caused a stunning transformation. The dragon lady smiled as she and Gala chatted about the beloved plant and its care. Our dragon still assured us that the documents were no good, but Gala persisted. We could, she allowed, come back the following Wednesday '*if* we wished'. Gala assured her that we did indeed wish to return.

It felt like yet another completely wasted morning to me, but Gala was confident that success was around the corner so we got on with our house renovations and awaited our appointment.

Friday 19th February. Sunshine and showers.
Dear Mum,

I hope you are behaving yourself at brothers? Remember I'm on my way soon and I get to be in charge… please?

S has been busy making some longer runners for the guest bed after our disastrous evening with poor Cris & Steve. Good job we have understanding friends. The runners had broken where he had joined two pieces together to make the bed longer, even though it was over-engineered to start with. These athletic types haha.

I trust you are not being too athletic as yet but are doing your exercises. We shall have to do the circuit of the Avenue when we get home. Everyone can cheer you on!

We had our 'last' Christmas card arrive today. It was from our Wendy. She had put the address as 'Lisa Wright, Taboada, Galicia, Spain'. I was so impressed that the correos had managed to deliver it that I went in to thank them. The chap in the post office seemed surprised. 'It says Taboada' he pointed out. 'Yes but I know there is more than one town of that name.' He shrugged this off, so I said 'it doesn't have a village name.' 'Ah,' he replied 'but once it got to this Taboada we knew who you were.' I'm not entirely sure now whether that's a good or bad thing!

He was telling me with some pride that one letter they received just had a name and postcode on it. I think the puzzles give him something to do. Still hope for your postcard from last year arriving then haha.

Veronique, one of our original chickens, is unwell. She has a prolapse I think, so will sadly have to go. The others are all doing well. We sprayed them all yesterday against red mite. It's that organic stuff we bought in Ashby, seems to work. Some are easier than others and Baby actually pecked me! We are getting 5 or 6 eggs a day now. Luckily CJ likes them so I have a customer, although Gala said she prefers shop ones as they are all a uniform size, which of course ours aren't.

CJ took us to see a house that a friend of his is selling. I thought it might suit a certain someone. It is a lovely house (well, it could be), not too big and in its own garden, but a bit further away from us than I would like. When are you going to say yes so we can look properly? Then I can be in charge permanently... as if!

TOMATO, FIG & PUMPKIN JELLY

I've been hoeing and putting up bean poles for when I get back. The weather has been very mixed this week. Sunshine and showers, with intervals of persistent downpours and howling winds. If it stays like this I'll be glad to be in England, though it doesn't sound like your weather is any better at the moment.

At least we all enjoyed the pig bone stew fair last weekend and the sun came out for that.

There were 8 of us at lunch. We were going to invite a new couple too, but they are vegan so we decided pig bones were not likely to be an ideal meal for them... nor was a fair dedicated to pig products sadly!

I have had a bit of a cough so I told S that he had to do the talking at the feira but that didn't work did it? So now I'm more hoarse than ever!

I'll ring you Wednesday at brother's though I hope my voice comes back or it will be a bit of a one-sided conversation!

Love you tons
And see you very very soon
XXXXXXXXXXX

The weather deteriorated further that week with high winds, thunder and lightning displays, and rain coming horizontally. I was off to England on Thursday but first we had another appointment in the dragon's lair.

FEBRUARY

Diary Wednesday 24th February Rain coming sideways, thunder, lightning, the lot...
I do hope this weather isn't an omen for our encounter with the dragon!
Collected Gala and drove (carefully) to the registry office through floods. Gala engaged our dragon in a discussion about her beloved pot plant again whilst I sat nibbling my fingernails. At last there was a pause in the conversation and I heard Gala say 'Gracias, hasta entonces.' Until then? Until when? Why? What? We then filled in yet another form but... We have an appointment to see the judge on the fifteenth of March!!!
Our wonderful, diplomatic, clever friend has done it. I could have kissed her!
Drove home then helped S move the slightly damp red pine for the sunroom seating, which José must have delivered whilst we were out. Field below is completely flooded and the river is roaring.

The following day I was due to fly to England to stay with Mum for two weeks whilst she got used to her new hip. We awoke early to continuing heavy wind and rain. A walk around the area showed extensive flooding of fields and tracks and, not for the first time, I was pleased we lived on a hill.

At noon, after removing the back seats of the car, we set off for the airport. S was to collect the wooden worktops we had ordered from Leroy Merlin on the way home.

At the airport I was stopped by customs. My comb apparently has a metal piece all the way through it and had set off alarms. Who knew? Luckily the customs men in Santiago are pretty laid back so they didn't arrest me, and even let me keep the comb.

I landed in England safely despite the weather, but S had had more problems at Leroy Merlin. He had arrived at the large DIY store in a driving rain.

TOMATO, FIG & PUMPKIN JELLY

Knowing the worktops would not fit in the lift from the underground car park he had had to park outside. The outside car park is on a slope…

(S)Diary Thursday 25th February
Drop L off then drive to Leroy Merlin for worktops. Struggle to get them in the car (2.5m x 650mm x 38mm). Very heavy. Very wet. Trolley blowing away down the car park in the strong wind. Use feet, arms, and body block to hold it still.
Back in for light, glass bricks for sunroom corner, pencils and sander. No suitable cheap worktops for utility.
Worktop jammed up against windscreen, in the middle of car, as the only place it will fit. Have to look off to one side through windscreen. Probably not quite legal.
Home 1730. Struggle to get worktops out of car. Big, heavy and awkward.
Put some uralitas back which have blown off the chicken shed roof and rescue the plant trough Lisa had put on the balustrade.
Tea, Lisa's pork pie, beans and a yoghurt
Put car back together. Bed.

Back in England I planned to cook and clean for Mum, and generally make sure she was okay.

Mother, in her inimitable style, had other ideas.

When I arrived at the house with my hire car she had already made us a stew for dinner, despite the fact she had only had her hip replacement two weeks previously. Each time I got her to sit down, she would jump up to remind me to do something or tell me how to cook something. She was, is, and always will be, impossibly wonderfully anarchistic.

I finally managed to get her to sit down by opening up the photograph box and letting Mum tell me some of our family history whilst going through the old faded sepia prints. This never failed to enthuse me.

FEBRUARY

I once traced our family tree back to 1752. In that year, King George II was on the throne and in England, the New Year started on 1st January for the first time. England was late to change to the Gregorian calendar from the Roman Julius one, but in 1752 the calendar act was adopted. This meant that not only did the New Year start on 1st January but September was an unusually short month. Eleven days were simply erased from the month, which went from Wednesday 2nd September straight to Thursday 14th September in order to come into line with the new calendar.

In 1752, the Wright family were still coal miners, still living in a small East Midlands village, and still using the same half dozen male names for the children. I finally got stuck in that year as two Wrights had a male heir of the same name within a few years. The marriage certificate of one William Wright didn't give me an age so there was no way I could decide which line to follow back.

There have been some interesting events in our close knit family tree. In 1896 my Great-grandfather, John Wright, jumped out of his bedroom window in order to elope and marry the woman he loved, despite his mother's objections. There were six children in that generation. Two sons, Thomas and Joseph, were killed when their pony and trap overturned in 1909. My then eight year old grandfather, John's son, was also on the trap, but thankfully survived.

John's two remaining brothers did not marry and neither did his only sister. So I am doubly lucky: that great grandfather John was a man of his convictions, and that his son, John Thomas, survived a tragic accident – otherwise, I would not be here.

Mum was the repository of the family photos, some going back to the first commercial photographers. In these early pictures, the poses were as rigid as the cardboard backing, the figures unsmiling. In many, I noticed the women appeared to be pressing down rather harder than necessary on their husband's shoulders.

By contrast, the early photographs of me show a smiling, gap-toothed child in polka dot dresses, holding impossibly large cuddly toys.

By the time I came along in 1964, my eldest brother was already 13 years old. I'm told he brought all his mates to peer in the local cottage hospital window at his new sister. For much of my childhood I had all the advantages of being a single child but with the unconditional love of two siblings. My brothers were the ones who took me on my first train ride and my first rock concert, to see Meatloaf in 1982. They bought me my first pet, a golden canary called Lemon, or Lemans after my younger brother's Moto Guzzi Lemans motorbike. He was also the one who took me on my first ride on a motorbike, to nearby Donnington racetrack when I was 14.

My brothers both got married and had wonderful children of their own. Those children now also have children, ensuring the Wright family line will continue for years to come.

I had never really had a desire to get married, or to populate the world. I was pleased my brothers had done the deed for me, though I knew Mum would have liked a grandchild from her only daughter. Still, she would have the next best thing, she was going to have that daughter married, to a man that mother thought the world of....

(S) Diary Sunday 28th February Another wild and windy night
Clear all the bits of uralita up from by the chicken shed which had blown off and broken. Put ALL the plastic covers back in place on the allotment. Brew time already!

FEBRUARY

Finish the last pieces of insulation and plasterboard on the utility side of the sunroom wall and continue with the electrics.
Radio dead. Recharge batteries.
Lunch: Leg 'o rabbit with boiled baby potatoes and spinach.
Ring Lisa. Phone dead. Recharge it.

One thing I had promised myself I would do whilst in England was look for a dress for the big day. I rarely wear dresses, preferring the comfort and ease of trousers or shorts, but I felt a wedding called for a bit of effort. My aunty suggested I try the local cancer charity shop in Swadlincote. She told me the lady there had a special wedding section and had contacts with many well-known designers.

St Giles charity shop has a narrow frontage down a small road. Inside is crammed hundreds of books, clothes, and china – the usual charity stuff in fact. I spoke to a friendly lady about a dress. She in turn called on her companion who ran the wedding department. Together we climbed the narrow staircase behind the shop to a vision of weddingness!

The entire first floor of the shop was given over to special occasion dresses. There were comfortable chairs for mothers of the bride or friends to wait in. Racks and racks of dresses of all types, from miles of froth to sedate suits, lined the walls. There were hats and gloves, shoes and veils. Even to a shopping and dress hater like me, it was a wonderland.

I wasn't looking for a traditional wedding dress. I was hardly a virgin at 45 years old. I tried on a couple of coloured dresses but neither looked quite right. Then the lady pulled out a cream wedding dress.

"No, I don't want a wedding frock."

"Just try it, I think it would really suit your figure."

TOMATO, FIG & PUMPKIN JELLY

Reluctantly I agreed. The dress slipped over my head and fit as if it was made for me. Sleeveless, with a low cowl neck in the front, the bodice was decorated with tiny beads. The back of the dress was open to almost the waist, the skirt falling into a short train. It was nothing like I had planned.

As I was still dithering, my new friend showed me the mirror, and I had to agree it really did suit me. More importantly, this dress was actually comfortable to wear.

The lady told me that the dress was brand new. It was a donation from one of the wedding stores. She explained that St. Giles often had donations from bridal shops of ex-window display items, as well as 'only worn once' donations from happy brides. My 'posh frock' cost me an astronomical £35. I was overjoyed.

My only concern now was how I was going to explain to Mum that I no longer had the wedding ring she had given me years earlier in a fit of hopefulness.

Whilst we lived in Rochdale we often worked away from home for weeks at a time. On one such occasion we had a break in. The neighbour called S' brother, Bob, who attended with the police.

When they arrived, the police asked if Bob thought anything had been stolen. They were concerned that we had a TV cabinet but apparently no TV. Bob thought we didn't have a TV, but was not entirely sure. The police asked where we were working. Bob didn't really know as we moved around. The police asked for our phone number. Bob thought he had the right one, but wasn't certain. The police, by this point, were probably wondering who this man pretending to be a relative really was.

We were told that they all then spent a happy hour looking for our house 'phone in order to ring us. S, ever the artist, had painted his plastic wall

FEBRUARY

'phone to match the door frame on which it sat. It doesn't inspire much confidence in the police's powers of observation that not one of them could find this disguised telephone, until our elderly neighbour had the bright idea to go back to his house and ring it.

The burglars had managed to break our double glazed window unit, leaving a small entry hole in the corner. The child burglar (we knew exactly who they were, though of course we couldn't prove it) had ransacked the house, turning out my entire chest of drawers. I was more mortified that Bob had had to see all my knickers scattered on the bed than about the burglary. The thieves were obviously not after money, as our change pot in the hallway was overflowing with pound coins. Nor did they want electronics. My elderly Walkman cassette player was untouched.

They were looking for something specific.

Whether they found it or whether it was just sheer bad luck, but the only things stolen that day were an old digital camera and mum's wedding ring, which I kept in a small felt bag in a drawer.

We went around town to each and every pawn shop asking about that ring but were met with sullenness and enmity from every single one. No one was willing to entertain the idea that they may have received stolen goods, even inadvertently. The police never found or prosecuted anyone. The upshot was that we never did recover the ring but, as I was not planning on ever getting married, I never broke the distressing news to Mum. Now I had to.

"At least you already have a ring," said Mum one night.

This was the moment I'd been dreading.

"Ah, well, I don't."

I explained what had happened but Mum was not as upset as I had dreaded.

"Never mind, I have grandma's wedding ring, she had a diamond put into it, I'm sure it would fit you if you would like it."

I was incredibly grateful to Mum for her understanding that day. Though if I could ever get hold of the little toe-rags who stole the original I would gladly kick them to the end of the town and back.

MARCH
The last posh frock

(S) Diary Monday 1ˢᵗ March Still wild and windy
To Monterroso market. Buy screws, bolts etc for sunroom seating. Lots of people at the meeting. Sell two dozen eggs. Lunch at new pulpo place. Pulpo must be extra as menu more expensive than expected.
Guardia stop and breathalyse me on the way home. Reading zero-zero so okay.
Start to assemble sunroom seating.

(S) Diary Wednesday 3ʳᵈ March Rain (gentle) all day.
Continue with seating in the sunroom. Think I know what I'm doing now. Have radio on all afternoon. Good stuff, 60s and 70s rock.
Visit from CJ for tea and cake and to buy a dozen eggs. He says Jen's house is sold.
Tea: Callos a la me. (L told me I had to use up the tripe.)

The sunroom window seating was an idea we had to use up some of the melamine coated chipboard we bought for kitchen cabinets we didn't end up needing, and to create some much needed storage. I am still amazed how, with a house the size of ours, we manage to run out of space to put things.

The picture windows in the sunroom start 60 centimetres above the floor. The space below, all the way around the corner, was the perfect spot to box in for some window seating. S made a frame with red pine then fixed the white melamine chipboard into the spaces. Add a melamine removable top and we had oodles of ready-made storage space (which is now full, obviously). The bonus was some insulation for the holey brick wall. It was a beautiful sunny room (when it wasn't pouring with rain of course).

(S) Diary Thursday 4th March More rain
Fed up sanding bits of wood. As rain stops briefly, decide to put water pipe across track to connect rainwater tank in barn and those on allotment.
Check no tractors due imminently. Hack out trench in sunken track. Set up concrete mixer. Measure and lay pipe across track. Have brew then throw three barrow loads of concrete over the pipe in the trench. Clean up and have lunch. Pork pie and pickled egg.
Back fill rest of pipe. Connect one end to tank in barn. Go to connect other end to tank on allotment. It's 15cm too short. Pipe must have moved. Thought everything was going too well.
Dig out tank and move it 15cm up to the pipe. Connect it all up. Brew.
Sun pops out so do a bit of gardening, pulling brambles escaping into Long Barn. Watch lizard scrambling up wall.

(S) Diary Saturday 6th March Cool no rain
Fiddle with the hose on the car to see why it wouldn't start yesterday. Must do something right as it starts. Leave it running while I walk into town for yet more screws from 'Arkwright's'. Tea and cake then drive over to let CJ peer into the car.
To swimming baths as didn't make it yesterday 'cos of car. Arrive 1920. Closes at 2000 so she lets me in for free. Café and sauna both closed.

MARCH

Meanwhile in the UK I was trying to be bossy with mother and failing dismally.

She was supposed to exercise her hip regularly. That was not an issue. She exercised willingly and enthusiastically. The problem was getting her *not* to exercise: not to bend down to pick imaginary bits of fluff off the carpet and not to stand peering over my shoulder while I was cooking. She meant well, but was not used to having someone else in charge of her house. If she had told me once how to light the fire, she had told me dozens of times. I had lit a fire a few times myself.

Mother-daughter clashes apart, we had a good time and Mum's hip was healing well. I had my frock, which Mum loved, and my godmother, Aunty Jean, had offered me a beautiful bejewelled necklace to wear. I even went into a secondhand shoe shop to buy some high heels (well, a half inch which I felt was the highest I could manage and not make an idiot of myself).

It may be obvious by now that I am not a particularly girlie girl. I don't wear make-up, nor perfume (I'm allergic to the stuff). I don't drip with jewellery. Mum insisted I had my ears pierced one holiday as she wanted hers done. I wasn't keen, and even less so afterwards as I thought it was ridiculously painful. I wore earrings for a while but they seemed to get tangled in my hair or caught on things, so I gave up. I think the holes have long since healed over. I am happiest in wellies and ripped camouflage pants or my much-loved, much-patched, jeans.

I remember one episode of my favourite comedy, '*The Good Life*', where Barbara Good is lamenting the demise of the last posh frock she owns. She complains that Tom, her unsympathetic husband, sees three sexes, male, female, and Barbara. I'm perfectly happy to be a Barbara!

TOMATO, FIG & PUMPKIN JELLY

That wedding frock was the first dress I had worn for probably 25 years. Since the day I was volunteered to meet the queen when I worked at the Public Health Laboratory in Colindale, northwest London.

I had been the newest and youngest member of staff at the facility when Queen Elizabeth II came to inaugurate the new building. I remember being summoned to the director's office and wondering what on earth I had done wrong this time. He told me that I had been chosen to hand over the traditional bouquet of flowers to her majesty.

"But I don't really want to," I said.

The director looked rather put out by this outrage but ignored me and rang the palace something or other to find out what colour outfit I was allowed to wear. Apparently protocol demands that one does not clash with her 'Maj'. As if!

Realising I had no choice in the matter, I asked if trousers were okay. My normal work clothing at that time was a pair of ripped Levis, a T shirt, and a Levi red label denim jacket with my teddy bear poking out of the top pocket. Over the whole ensemble was a white lab coat. The director looked at me in horror before telling me that I had to wear a skirt. I was not happy.

On the day in question I turned up in ripped denims just for the fun of it, but I had a smart skirt (my only one) and a lilac jumper my grandmother had knitted me in a plastic bag – just in case I couldn't get away with it.

Obviously I couldn't. I had to approach her Majesty, curtsey, and hand her the bunch of flowers I had been given. I told my grandmother that 'Liz' had admired my beautifully knitted jumper. To be honest she just mumbled something and turned away. A work colleague gleefully told me HRH had handed the flowers to an aide who immediately

MARCH

threw them onto the floor in the back of the car. Charming! What a waste of time and expense.

That was my last recall of skirt wearing. But I had to admit that this frock was stunning. The shoes I bought were brocaded in pinks and golds with a sling back and pretty beading on the front. More importantly they were not too difficult to walk in. I did however draw the line at a veil.

§

By the time I returned home on the 11th March, with my pretty frock and fancy shoes, S had completed the sunroom seating and sorted out his mysteriously shortening pipework. The tank in the long barn would now fill from the four metres of guttering along the roof, which S had also lengthened whilst I was away, and in turn fill the tanks on the allotment without us having to lay a hosepipe across the track. As a tractor would inevitably come along each time we unrolled the hosepipe, this should be a time saver. From the allotment tank we had a leaky hosepipe connected to the raised beds we were creating. This was all designed to reduce our watering load and save precious water over the summer.

The weather had also changed whilst I was away: from wet and windy to sunny and frosty. We couldn't test our new system quite yet. I was almost looking forward to rain! Meanwhile, the leaves I had collected back in January to mulch the vegetable beds were keeping the moisture in, and the soil warmer.

I met our friend Simon on the 'plane from England carrying a bag of eggs.

"But you have loads of hens. Why are you buying eggs, Si?"

"These are for Anne, she wants some special hens. They're from a breeder in England."

TOMATO, FIG & PUMPKIN JELLY

If it seemed odd to be carrying two dozen eggs back to Spain, I knew Anne well enough not to query her needs. We offered Simon a lift to Lugo to catch his bus home and told him about our wedding plans, to which he smiled ruefully.

I soon got back into our day to day routine. I hoed the allotment and sowed some shallots I'd bought in the UK. I sowed peas and mangetout. I checked my broad beans, which had suffered in the snow and frost over winter. Most of the plants now had blackfly, and ants farming the aphids. The soapy water spray came out. The broccoli had not come through at all but the first lot of tomatoes were doing well and were almost ready to transplant.

We had the most scrummy eggs for breakfast. After two weeks of shop bought eggs ours seemed especially delicious, and were perfectly cooked by my husband to be. I continued sanding, varnishing, and cementing. The idea of me in a frock receded from my mind.

In fact I gave no more thought to the wedding at all until the following Monday, and our appointment with the judge.

Monday 15th March. Sunny and hot now I'm home

Dear Mum,

Well, I think we passed our interview! We arrived at ten to ten with Gala, and waited, and waited, and waited! Eventually the lady judge appeared and called S over. I followed but she said 'wait outside'.

It appears that as we are not Spanish we have to be interviewed to make sure it's not a marriage of convenience. As we are both foreigners I can't see there would be much benefit to such a thing but I wasn't going to

MARCH

argue. S and Gala seemed to be ages. As he came out, S whispered, 'my hobbies are swimming and reading, yours are gardening and cooking.'

I went in on my own as I thought I'd manage okay but I hadn't thought to ask Gala what the Spanish word for hobbies was, so it took a bit of creative mime when I was asked what my pasatiempos were (bit obvious really as it's the English word pastimes.) The judge asked how long we had been in Spain, did we come over together, do we live together, what family does S have and have I met them, what hobbies do we have, what work do we do, and what are our plans for the future? I even made the dragon smile when I said we wanted to continue living here!

She then said 'go away', so I asked what next and the dragon said she would ring in a month when the papers were all ready. Talk about slow! Maybe they are going to give us time to change our minds haha.

Oddly the judge didn't have any problem with our translated documents nor our lack of a 'fe de vida'.

We were just sitting down by the fire tonight to eat our tea and beep, beep, beep. José's helper with a lorry load of floor tiles, cement and grout. Just finished loading them inside as it went dark (7.45pm). The Big Barn is full again! Will now have to empty the storeroom again so we can plan *how the tiles will go. We thought we would do the storeroom and hall first so we will get a good line through into the kitchen.*

I have so many jobs piling up now the weather is better. I have planted shallots and peas (mangetout) and carrots, and sown cabbages in trays in the barn. The tomatoes are getting proper leaves on in our bedroom, and I've just hoed the spud patch.

S has done a lovely job of the window seats so I'm varnishing the wooden frame now. I've stuffed our two draught excluders with some of the (cleaned) sheep's wool from the old mattress. They work well thank you! I will stuff the rest of the seat cushions you made once the frames are varnished.

S is now working in the utility. He is fitting the bidet and we have painted the plasterboard wall white. The toilet is of course already in place now the wall has been erected behind it. Clever eh?!

We have taken both the bunnies back to Carmen's boy rabbit with instructions to do it properly this time, as neither had kits. The chickens are still doing well. The lad had 4 dozen eggs stacked up when I got back. He says he ate two a day and sold some to CJ and some to John and Fiona, but couldn't stop the girls laying!

Tuesday 9pm. Pleasant, some cloud but warm.

The buds are breaking on the red plum, the hoopoes are back, and the ground has

MARCH

completely dried out! Sowed my onion sets and the soil was drying out as I turned it.

S has just been showing me some photos he took while I was in UK. The river was even higher than on those I showed you. He said they had two 'hurricanes' and loads of rain. CJ had water in the house again.

We went into town today. The clock maker has done a good job of making my ring smaller… only charged me 3€. We also went into the Town Hall and found our names were on the wall! They have posted the banns there. After all that! The young justice of the peace said the mayor could marry us. We can either use his office (which seats four at a push) or have the room below the library which is for the use of Taboada residents. He didn't mention a charge. He said we need to agree a date with the mayor once the banns are complete and the paperwork sent to us. So we are still aiming for the last weekend in August, providing the mayor isn't on holiday of course!

Weds 10pm. Very warm and sunny today. Wish you were here!

Well, it was supposed to rain today but despite me putting the washing out it has stayed fine and hot. Of course now S has connected the rainwater tanks it won't rain at all.

I've painted one of the walls on the terrace today (the utility wall, above the exposed stonework). It looks much brighter. S has put all his seating back together in the sunroom now I've varnished the wooden frame.

CJ came over this pm for his tea and cake. He has promised to give me a lesson rendering the storeroom wall so we shall have to order more sand and cement. We thought we might concrete the horno floor (outside oven seating area) at the same time. So it's all go still! Hope you are behaving for Drena. Bet the house is sparkling by now. I suggest if she is that good you let her at the garden too! Looking forward to seeing you May/June all being well with your hip. S promises to have re made your bed by then!! (He is having some design issues).

Love you tons and tons

XXXXXXXX

PS We have planted my blueberry and cranberry plants from Wilkos on the west side near the corner seating gravelled bit which we cleared last Christmas.

I forgot to tell you on the phone but I was stopped at customs at Stansted. They said I had liquid in my bag. I said I definitely hadn't, but they wanted a look. Well, you know how tightly packed that bag was with the material and clothes and DVDs and plants. They wouldn't let me unpack but just pulled everything out and threw it on the table. When he found the blueberry bush he held it up as if I was carrying a bomb then took it away to be 'tested'. When he came back, he said that was what had set off the scanners as it contained liquid. I couldn't resist saying that, as it was a plant, if it didn't contain any liquid it would be dead! That's probably why he left me to attempt to repack my bag on my own. Of course nothing would go back in properly. I was not in a good mood by the time I got to the plane. And we were half an hour late landing. Luckily S was there and had even brought some peanut butter and marmite butties with him. He knows me so well!

Love you tons and tons

Xxxxxxxxxx

With the dragon defeated we could at last start to plan our wedding activities. Or rather I could start planning and S could agree where necessary. One of the things we did agree on was that we wanted to share the 'English' business around as much as possible. Taboada and its residents had been so welcoming to us that we felt this was our chance to repay some of the many kindnesses.

Obviously our guests would stay in the (only) hotel in town. There were 10 rooms, so we hired the lot for the bank holiday weekend. Of course in Spain the last Monday in August isn't a bank holiday as they have all been on holiday since July anyway, but we wanted to be sure.

We were having the wedding feast at Bar Mencia – once we had agreed a *menú* that is. Negotiations were still ongoing as to a price. I would suggest one, Luisa would lower it, I would counter-offer a higher price, and so on. It was like a reverse bartering. We would certainly use Bar Scala for our evening gatherings, and I planned activities every day for a week including *menus* out in various local establishments to ensure no favouritism.

I made up and printed invites in dual languages for neighbours and friends living locally, and sent email invites to England.

Mum had already said she would bring her sister, Aunty Jan, (which would boost the shoe shop sales) and her friend and neighbour, my godmother, Aunty Jean. These three were to be known as the Golden Girls and turned out to be *very* popular in town... but more on that later.

A number of S' friends also wanted to be here for this miraculous event. S asked Les, his best friend, and our wonderful roofing helper, to be his best man. I think he neglected to mention the duties which traditionally go with the role.

I checked schedules for Ryanair into Santiago or even Oporto, over the border in Portugal. There were no direct flights from the North of England and no other international airlines flying into Santiago, making it a problem for most of our friends from Rochdale. But everyone made super-human efforts and went to extraordinary lengths to make it for our 'big' day. One friend even ended up paying twice for his ticket due to an administration error by Ryanair, but he did so uncomplainingly (well, almost uncomplainingly) and turned up on time for the event.

Diary Thursday 18th March Sunny and warm but windy
Picked nettles for soup. Boiled a dozen eggs for pickling.
Call from Les, in a bit of a pickle himself, as he wants to know if he has to do a best man's speech. I said 'of course', which was probably the wrong answer!
Bullfinch back eating all the plum buds. He is so pretty with his pink breast but the bits of buds are

flying all over the place. Now he seems to have brought the family along too as I counted at least six of them. Hope they leave a few plums for us!

Diary Friday 19th March Sunny
S laid land drains in the horno area ready for concreting and eventual tiling. I cleaned the beams in the storeroom. They are quite holey and rough but in good condition once you get the outer layer off. Got thoroughly filthy, with woodworm dust in my hair and my eyes. Good job it's bath night.
Later: Swimming baths shut for father's day (San José). Perfect timing as ever! Called into CJ to say we weren't staying as we were not fit to be indoors. Back home for a shower!
15°C in Chantada at 8pm. Salamanders out all the way home. Had to keep stopping to move them to the side of the road out of harm's way. First cuckoo today.

Diary Monday 22nd March Sunny
Decided to go on holiday. Animals fed, plants sorted, car filled with petrol and out of the door by 11am.

Now the house was more comfortable and we weren't in such a hurry, one of the things we wanted to do was explore more of the wonderful area of the country we call home. Galicia has so many unique places that to see everywhere in one lifetime is virtually an impossibility. That year began our annual attempt to visit Galicia, one area at a time.

As we have the animals and crops to care for these 'holidays' usually take the form of two days with one night between, staying in a spot we particularly like. As most areas of Galicia are within an hour and a half drive from us we have plenty of time to explore. We often take off in late October, when the autumn sun can still be surprisingly warm, or early in the year during the first spring-like period we have. March or even February can be sunny and pleasant, the garden is not yet planted up and the coastlines are quiet. We have the beaches and towns to ourselves.

On this occasion we headed due west towards the coast, travelling along the National VI and the new A6 motorway for an hour towards our first stop of the day.

Betanzos is a reasonable sized, pretty town, near to the beginnings of the west coast Rias. It was founded in the 13th century by King Alfonso IX. By the 16th century, Betanzos was the capital of one of seven Galician provinces. The main town is built on a hill overlooking two rivers, the rios Mendo and Mandeo, which wind in a horseshoe around the base of the hill. The old town, climbing the hillside, is compact with a lively café scene and a large market square on top of the hill. Below, at river level, are a shopping centre, parks and the *two* football grounds.

From Betanzos we headed towards the coast and an interesting looking spit of land. The municipalities of Sada and Oleiros form this small promontory which separates the estuary of Betanzos and the bay of A Coruña.

Sada is a small, seaside town with a stunning art deco building right on the sea front. La Terraza was built in 1912 by the architect López Hernández and became a National Historic-Artistic Monument in 1975. It looked like a huge glass liner washed up on the roadside but was sadly uncared for when we visited.

We successfully found the tourist information office, which was both informative and friendly. The helpful chap there directed us to a nearby hotel. It was slightly more expensive than the inland areas of Galicia at a whole 50€ for a double room, with breakfast.

MARCH

Bags dumped we set off to explore. Outside of Sada we found a small and totally deserted beach where we sunbathed and read the afternoon away. Later we adjourned to our hotel to shower and change before heading into the surprisingly windy town centre for a *vino* or two.

I have noticed that wine on the coast is generally more expensive than in the interior, and we are often given Rioja when we ask for red wine. Rioja may be Spain's most exported wine but it is not Galician wine and, to be frank, it is not for me. I find Rioja generally too oaky and too strong for my palate, whereas our local red Mencia-Garnacha mix is a fruity and very quaffable liquid delight.

On one occasion in Bar Scala, I sent my wine back, telling Silvia I didn't like it at all. I admitted it wasn't 'off' but tasted funny. She looked baffled but took the wine away to reappear laughing only a minute later. It seemed their new barmaid had poured me a rather expensive Rioja instead of their own, very tasty red. I know nothing about wine, but I do know what I like.

In Sada it seemed that every bar wanted us to have Rioja. Each time, I asked for the house wine but was told the Rioja was it. At one bar I had a pleasant conversation with the barman who promised I would like *this* Rioja. Needless to say I didn't. We did enjoy our evening out though, and the *tapas* were pretty good too.

The following morning after a modest breakfast, or what passes as a breakfast in Spain – sweet buns and coffee, we set off northwest around the peninsula. We followed a sign for a small beach called San Pedro where we spent a happy morning rock pooling, investigating the sea anemones and crabs and limpets. Again, the beach was deserted. Having fully explored the small area we continued towards Mera, a small town in Oleiros municipality with , it appeared, large pretensions. The front at

Mera was lined with brand new flats and houses overlooking the wide, sandy beach. We couldn't resist peering into an estate agent's window and were surprised at the low prices of the new flats.

There were a few shops but only two restaurants that I could see, and a total absence of residents. But the new buildings gleamed and the brand new promenade boardwalk wound its way along the sea front and over the headland to a quieter beach overlooking artificial mussel beds out in the bay. We spent another pleasant afternoon on the beach reading and watching the fishermen, before packing up and walking back across the headland. We arrived home in time to collect the six eggs laid in our absence and feed the animals, and to eject the rather large adder from the chicken pen.

Wednesday 23rd March. A bit cloudy now but lovely at the coast.
Dear Mum,

Bit late to be starting your letter but the week has flown by... again. We had a lovely couple of days at the coast. Another part of Galicia to take you to when you visit next. You will have to move over in order to get to see all these places with us!

It was nice to have a break. It's funny but although it was only two days it feels like we have had a proper holiday. Although I suppose every day is a holiday really.

I've been busy baking since we got home. My cake stocks in the freezer had dwindled whilst I was in England with you. (S says it was because he kept getting visitors but I know his sweet tooth, I bet it was cake for pudding every day.)

MARCH

I now have five new cakes in the freezer so am feeling rather content. Also made a blackberry and apple pie and a couple of loaves of walnut bread (last year's walnuts, keeping well).

Saturday was spud day. S digs a trench, I fill it with potash, and dried weeds and plonk a row of spuds on top then S covers it and digs the next one. We are a bit slower than most of the old Galegos who just dig dig dig like little automatons.

I remember the old chap behind us when we had the flat in Monterroso, I used to watch him for ages going up and down the rows hoeing. Very relaxing (the watching that is!).

We also spent ages on Saturday fruitlessly searching for the spare phone chip (the one with money on it) so I could ring CJ about his rendering lesson. The mice must've had it away (actually more likely the giant ants - I reckon they could carry me off if I sat still long enough).

Luckily CJ turned up at tea time anyway. He says he smelt my chocolate cake - which had already taken a battering as S said he ought to try it, despite having had dinner and pud. And, of course, yours truly couldn't be left out!

It's Cris' birthday this week. I had a card for her but couldn't find it (mice again) so thought I would print one of our pics off and make a card. The printer was playing *up so it came out blue! In the end I gave up and sent her an email!!*

Thurs. Mild and a bit cloudy.

They had forecast rain all week but we are doing rather well so far. I planted my last row of spuds today. It's light 'til after 8pm now so we are working until 7pm or later.

I have also been varnishing the lad's shelves in the sunroom. We decided on varnish rather than polish so it won't matter if things get spilled or put on them. They look nice, and very rustic. Would probably have cost a fortune to buy 'distressed' stuff like this!

Can't wait for you to see everything. Seems ages since you were here last.

The plum trees are looking magnificent this year and the peaches are just blossoming, so we may get both together this time.

S has been clearing the horno area out ready for concreting with CJ on Friday, now he has done the fixtures in the utility. He is making a brick and concrete platform at the back of the horno area to put plants (or cups) on. He is also digging out a driveway... more on that next week.

Pumpkin time. Music has ended so off to bed

Love you tons and tons

xxxxxxxxxxx

Remember to ask the doc when you can fly so we can book you into this B&B haha.

MARCH

And I must get the handyman to finish remaking your bed!
See you soon, we hope
  xxx

With the tiles having arrived for the kitchen and downstairs we wanted to cement render the old brick wall in the storeroom. Then I could paint the walls and tile the entire ground floor – ideally before our visitors arrived in August.

We had steadily filled the storeroom with rubble, ever since we dug out all the old rabbit muck two years previously and ended up with a three foot step instead. We had welcomed rubble from anyone who had it to spare, often returning home to find black tubs of broken bricks and concrete sitting by the gate. Sometimes there would be a note, oftentimes not. We were grateful for all the generous donations.

In October we had concreted the floor. Now we were ready to render the thin brick walls. CJ had once more promised to come and help, and to show me how to do the cement rendering. The weather conditions promised to be better on this occasion at least.

Our fickle *Galego* weather had other ideas. On the Thursday evening it started to rain, heavily. And rain and rain and rain...

Diary Friday 26th March Pouring all night and all day. Wild and windy too
Message from CJ that he was not going to come and cement today due to the weather. Very sensible if you ask me!
At least we can check the water tanks now. Should be full pretty quickly in this rain.
Varnished the tops of the shelving in the sunroom instead and tried to jam the polystyrene insulation above bedroom one to stop it flapping madly and

loudly in the wind. I don't think we would go the polystyrene insulation route again somehow.
S continued chiselling the beams in the storeroom (my efforts weren't good enough... of course!)
This afternoon, S had to put an overflow pipe on to the rainwater tank in the barn as both the allotment ones and the barn one are full already. That works then!
To Chantada for our swim. Confirmed my hen do on 27th August with Angela and promised to confirm numbers at least a week before. S still has to decide what he's going to do. Told him we couldn't have a joint do. I hope whatever he does it won't involve him being tied naked to a lamppost in town!
Bought some sunshine yellow paint for the sunroom walls.
To CJ and Gala for tea and chat. Agreed to do the cementing on Monday.

Diary Sunday 28th March Back to sunshine again!
Scrummy boiled eggs and soldiers. Spent the morning painting in the sunroom. Now it really does look sunny. I love the colour with the dark chestnut shelving and the green and gold cover for the day bed. Need a green rug now methinks.
S continued digging out some of the driveway to make a gravelled turning circle. Big holes everywhere!
Lunch: Pig's cheeks slow roasted, with mash and mushy peas (ours, dried). Very good. Bread and butter pudding made with orange marmalade.
Very full so off for a long walk. Set off at 3.45pm to parallel the main road towards Monterroso. Very pleasant except for one bit which had flooded (due to all the rain do you think?). Had to cut across to the road for that bit. Ended up at the parillada San Martiño on the main road. Whilst having a cola there I mentioned booking a table for one of our

MARCH

wedding lunches. They seemed happy. Had a vino to celebrate, which was paid for by Carlos from the ferreteria. Home finally at 7.45pm

Luckily, we awoke to sunshine on the Monday morning and CJ arrived as promised to help render the wall. At that precise moment the sun disappeared and the rain returned.

We bravely did the cementing anyway.

I thought it was going well until the whole bottom half of one wall fell off. CJ blamed our poor sand - too coarse apparently. However, CJ is never one to let a job get the better of him so he insisted on staying to finish the wall. He refused to stop for any lunch or even tea (must be serious) and finally declared himself, if not happy then vaguely satisfied at 3pm. We had a rather late lunch which CJ declined to join us for and, as it was by that time really doing the Galicia rain thing, we retired upstairs to light the fire and for me to continue my wedding planning.

Tuesday 30th March. Wild and windy again
Dear Mum,

Trying to write this and play S at scrabble. He has just made up a dubious word and has gone to look it up. 'Agaze'... he says our dictionary is rubbish which I gather means it wasn't in!

We have been to Jayne and Richard's today as S had promised to help them with some concreting. They decided to go ahead despite the awful weather and managed to get quite a bit done whilst us girls huddled in the polytunnel sorting out seedlings. We hope to sell some plants at the hotel on the first. I think we have enough for the whole of Galicia.

We had a very nice lunch of shepherd's pie and apple crumble and got to call into Lugo on the way back for some lights (for the sunroom, instead of the funny temporary ones we put up) and yet more paint. And S only got slightly wet!

I think he is getting used to being wet, what with the identical weather yesterday for our storeroom rendering day. S was on the mixer for that too, whilst CJ and I were indoors in the dry. He had pulled the cement mixer under the overhang of the horno roof but that meant he was stood right under the drip line. Poor lad! At least Richard put a bit of an awning up over his head.

The weather really has been dreadful. One friend said all the polytunnels near her had gone this morning, blown away in the wind. At least our driveway project is going well, S is busy digging it out and we will then lay a membrane and gravel it. All this of course has to be done by August too!

Wednesday: Still wet! Thank you for your letter and cutting from the Telegraph. Another chicken shed project? We will have a complex soon. I liked the Suffolk seaside house painted baby blue with a shingle roof. Especially the little shutters on the windows, I'm sure Mr Fox would enjoy opening them.

MARCH

It would be like an advent calendar!! One hen a day! And only £7,000!

There is a wine tasting in town later on. It's supposed to start at 9pm.

Later: Arrived at 9.30pm and had a drink in the Gema first. There was a lovely smell as we walked in. Maria was cooking up a batch of torrijas (sort of eggy bread). Delicious!

By the time we left the Gema, the main event had started. There were about eight boxes of wine set up on little trestle tables in the market tent in the main square. A chap was selling pottery cups which when we got home we found had 'bone stew' written on them so obviously recycled haha. These were 1.50€ each. You bought a cup then just went round helping yourself to wine! I think S managed 5 (small) cups. He enjoyed the white one.

There was also a BBQ set up with 3 men in charge, one of whom S kindly pointed out was extremely handsome in a Bryan Ferry lookalike kind of way. I also noticed he was a very good dancer later on (not that I was looking you understand! I swear I hadn't even noticed him 'til S pointed him out!)

Anyway Bryan Ferry and his helpers were cooking huge amounts of bacon and pig's liver on the grill. There were thick chunks of bread and later on cheese made an appearance.

All the food was free, so for our 3€ we both got sloshed and well fed. Oh and to watch Bryan Ferry dance. I wonder if he can sing? I could hire him for the wedding!

Strangely, there was still plenty of wine left at the end and no one was lying underneath the barrels with the tap open (just a passing thought). Cannot imagine this happening in the UK.

Glad you are progressing well. Bet you are eager to get on and do things in the garden eh? Everyone here has been asking how you are getting on.

All the fruit trees are flowering here and the tits are all back. Long tailed tits and coal tits today plus a blackcap, and the grey wagtails are nesting. My daffodils are looking good this year, even if we did seem to lose all the more interesting pheasant's eye and doubles, and the Christmas roses are stunning under the vines.

Love you loads
Xxxxxxxxxx

APRIL
No such animal

I don't know if we have more wildlife here in Galicia or if we simply notice it more. I remember when S and I were newt catching back in England, people would come up to us and reminisce about how there used to be more newts in 'the old days' when they were children – when we weren't being abused by irate wildlife lovers who thought we were stealing their newts that is. I used to ask 'when was the last time you fished in a pond with a net looking for newts?' 'Not since I was a child,' was the usual answer.

Here in Galicia we are outside for ten or more hours a day, digging, eating al fresco, weeding, or just walking around this most beautiful of regions. We have plenty of opportunity to wildlife watch.

I do think it helps that there is more small-scale farming here, with correspondingly small fields, usually bounded by dry stone walls. We have few large corporations, harvesting fields the size of a small country with nary a tree to be seen. We have plenty of hedgerows and bramble patches. Old stone barns abound, and here in the centre of Galicia we are blessed with oak and sweet chestnut forests full of squirrels and birds.

Diary Thursday 1ˢᵗ April Sunny but cold
Awoken at 8am this morning to a tap, tap on the

window. When I wandered into bedroom one there was a young greater spotted woodpecker sitting on the windowsill vigorously pecking at the glass! He didn't fly away until I was almost on him. I'm now wondering just how strong double glazing is.
To the market at Monterroso. Bought pelargoniums for the terrace plus a thyme bush, and a load of ironmongery for S.
Sold 2 dozen eggs at the meeting and a load of veggie seedlings with Jayne.
Bar Mencia for lunch. Had a long and possibly productive chat about the wedding meal. Many side lines as usual and all in rapid fire Galego/Castellano but we may have agreed a menu… or then again maybe not!
Took the cover off one of the vegetable beds on the allotment. 3 slowworms (female), 2 lizards (one a Schreiber's lizard), and a skink under it.

Reptiles seemed to have an affinity for my plastic covered vegetable beds. The black plastic and old linoleum quickly warmed up in the spring sunshine making it a perfect basking spot. I would be fascinated to see what I would find each time I removed the covers. If the various species didn't run or slither away as soon as I uncovered the bed, I would carefully pick them up and translocate them to a safe area where they wouldn't get disturbed again. I loved all our varied wildlife and revelled in discovering new species. The Schreiber's lizards (*Lacerta schreiberi*) are stunningly beautiful in a vivid, speckled green with, in the breeding males, a blue head. Including a full tail they can measure around 30 centimetres in length.

One day I was carefully relocating a slowworm when Carmen saw me. She looked horrified.

"*Un serpiente,*" she said.

"*No, liscante,*" I replied holding it gently in my hands. "They are good for the garden, eat snails."

APRIL

As I lowered the bemused slowworm to the ground, Carmen backed away. This snake phobia is by no means restricted to Galicians. It seems to be a natural fear for humans the world over. Rather sad for our poor harmless (and legless) lizards.

Diary Friday 2nd April Cold wind
Up rather late as it was overcast. Picked veg in the rain while S tidied the rest of the area around the stove in the sunroom ready for me plastering it.
He has made a new step for the sunroom entrance, using a huge chestnut plinth. The original step down was a bit much for my little legs. I got to sit on the step to hold it down while S screwed it to the floor!
Lunch: Trout with bacon, mash and purple sprouting broccoli.

Diary Saturday 3rd April Easter Weekend More rain
Popped into Taboada. Bread shop shut, no internet working anywhere. Rang Canon service centre about my printer not working but they are closed until Tuesday. Why do things always go wrong on a bank holiday!
Lunch: Pasta putanesca. Apple charlotte with caramel sauce.
S wired in the new lights in the sunroom and I plastered round the stove ready for painting.

Some wildlife is not as well liked as others, even by me. One of our main battles every year is with the field mice which wander into the house when the weather gets cooler and decide to set up home. Part of the problem is that our 70 centimetre thick stone walls are built as two layers, with an infill of rubble and whatever else is around (old corn husks and shoes appear to be favourites). For a small mouse this is a superhighway, from the ground floor to the

TOMATO, FIG & PUMPKIN JELLY

roof and through the whole house, they just emerge wherever they like.

One of my fun things to do at night if I can't sleep is to listen to the mice running along the beams overhead. Sometimes they manage to get into my walnut store in the barn on the lower ground floor. Then we hear a scratching noise as they push the walnut up into the roof space. This is often followed by a rattling slide as the nut rolls all the way down the roof again. Think the poor squirrel in the film *Ice Age* and you are there!

Most of the time the mice cause no serious problems (other than when they were nesting in the chimney of the *cocina* our first year here). They will, however, nibble our food in the storeroom. For this reason I keep everything in sturdy tins or old plastic paint tubs (washed out of course).

In the allotment they are a much bigger nuisance, eating the walnuts before we can get to them and even climbing the stems of the soft fruit bushes to nibble at the berries.

That year I discovered an ally in my battle against the mice. One day I was uncovering a part of a vegetable bed for planting and there, beneath the plastic, was a smallish adder (or viper) enjoying its dinner. Its jaws were open to their fullest extent as a tail was disappearing down its gullet. The outline of the mouse was clearly visible through the snake's body.

Monday 5th April.
Dear Mum,
Actual sunshine! Quite hot once the mist cleared, at around 11am. I managed to get the washing on and dried - first time for ages. Had to wait for the hosepipe to defrost though! Will be good once we get the washer

APRIL

all properly plumbed in the utility rather than on the terrace.

Thank you for your letter, it came this morning so Easter Monday is not a bank holiday here. Sounds like you are doing really well with your new hip - hopefully won't be long before you are allowed to travel. I have a job waiting for you... buzzard warden. It's a bit like air raid warden but you have to give the alert to the chickens if there is a buzzard nearby!

They had fun today, we let them outside to play. Poor Buzz was clucking himself hoarse with treats for the girls and he had only taken two steps outside. So exciting, especially when we started digging up crickets and grubs. They did miss the one S landed accidently in the old wash tub though. They were looking all around the base but no one thought to jump inside the tub!

We had a double walk on Sunday. Did our cleaning in the morning and, as it was sunny, set off after lunch. Got only marginally lost. We arrived back home at 7pm with a lovely, but unidentified plant (which I've scribbled in the margin). It's about 4" high with sword shaped spotted leaves like an orchid but 6 equal, pink petals and a drooping head. It was growing in the leaf litter along the track. We also collected a discarded beer can full of frog spawn for our new pond.

TOMATO, FIG & PUMPKIN JELLY

Over tea we looked at various frog pictures but couldn't decide which tadpoles they were, so in the evening we set off with torches and spent ages going up and down the track and the field. Found two frog species, some palmate newts and some larger larvae which could be crested newts or more likely salamanders. Difficult as none of our UK books have salamander tadpoles in. Most enjoyable trip down memory lane - though only S managed to get muddy.

Our horno project is coming along nicely. S has built a low brick wall inside at the back, with drainage through it. He cemented inside that this afternoon to make a shelf. Once it's dried I will tile the top with some of the old red and white quarry tiles we found in the barn. In the corner he has made a larger raised platform for the lemon tree to sit on in winter. The floor, which he concreted last month, I will tile with the same tiles as the kitchen and storeroom. It will be a nice area for outdoor eating and entertaining. Because it faces south, it gets the sun all day in winter but the overhang ensures it is cool in summer when the sun is higher. And it has a lovely view across the valley too.

I have also been plastering the new stove surround in the sunroom. If you remember, it is designed to act as a sort of heat store. Plastering inside the surround is fun

APRIL

though. There is only just space for my little hand, so if I tilt the spatula too much all my plaster drops onto the hearth! It may not end up looking perfect!

Tuesday: Cloudy today. Just back from town. When I got to the car this morning I couldn't see a thing through the wing mirrors. They were all smeared up. Very odd. Then, after I put the car away and was checking the plants, I heard a funny tapping and rustling noise. A blue tit was sitting on the wing mirror going absolutely mad, pecking at its own reflection and spitting on the glass! We have cut up some old socks and fitted them over the mirrors. The blue tit is probably happy he has chased his rival away.

Buzz is in competition with Carmen's cockerel. Each time hers starts crowing, Buzz joins in but louder and more frequently. When his 'rival' finally gives up, Buzz carries on for a bit just to have the last word.

Our new driveway is getting deeper and deeper by the day. We will brick around the edge then gravel it. Concha asked if we were digging a swimming pool! The hoopoe loves it, he comes pecking in the newly turned soil with his long beak.

Can't wait for you to arrive. There will be so much new for you to see.

Love you tons and hope to see you soon
XXXXXX

TOMATO, FIG & PUMPKIN JELLY

One of our other projects for this year was to make a gravelled driveway. After the fun we had in December trying to get the car out on a slippery grass drive we thought gravel would be a better option.

Our neighbours were fascinated as we measured and then dug out a circle. The excess soil was piled to one side on what became known as the 'first tee', the only flat bit of our garden and an interesting three shot across the track to the allotment.

Concha had obviously heard that all English have a swimming pool in their garden. When I explained it was a driveway for the car, she seemed somewhat disappointed. We said that once it was completed we should sit on the gravel in our bathing suits, inflatable dinghy by our side, as they walked the cows to the field. I think our neighbours would have found it hilarious.

One welcome visitor we had frequently during our drive making was the hoopoe. This European bird is a rare visitor to England and we had never seen one until we moved here. That first time, Jen's dad had spotted one and was trying to describe it…

"It's pink."
"A parrot?"
"No, it has barred black and white wings."
"A magpie?"
"No, it has a comb on its head."
"A chicken?"

We were enjoying this game. Jen's dad, not so much.

"It has a long curved beak."

This was too much. "Naw, ain't no such animal."

When we got home, I looked in my bird book and found Harold's bird. A medium sized, stately bird, the hoopoe loves nothing more than disturbed ground where it can push its long, curved beak into the soil to hunt for leatherjackets and grubs. It is fearless, often refusing to move when approached.

APRIL

On more than one occasion I have had to stop the car for one which steadfastly refused to hop out of the way. The hoopoe makes a delightful 'oop oop' sound giving it the wonderfully onomatopoeic Latin name of *Upupa epops*.

We apologised to Jen's dad the next time we saw him and from then on his nickname became Hoopoe Harry.

The gravel for the driveway arrived on the Friday in three, one tonne sacks. Our new drive was completed in time for our wedding, but sadly we never did sit in our bathing suits on the newly created 'swimming pool'.

Thursday 8th April Warm and pleasant
Sitting in the sunroom. We moved the sleigh bed/chaise longue back in this morning, and the stereo system. The sun has kept it nice and warm in there so we are listening to music (S allowed me to christen the new room with my favourite artist, so long as I promised not to sing!) and I am playing about with aligning the rug and filling shelves with books and CDs (alphabetically of course).

Sunday 11th April. Hot this afternoon
Dear Mum,
What an exciting day we have had! I started off jetwashing all the old quarry tiles for the horno 'shelf' - they are actually quite bright cleaned up. I also had a go at the storeroom walls, though I don't think the smoke stained walls will ever come clean in there. I quite like it really as it shows the original use for the room (chorizo smoking room). Lots of tarry soot came off so at least they are clean black walls now!

TOMATO, FIG & PUMPKIN JELLY

S was still gravelling the drive and grassing over the levelled bit of lawn, 'for camping' he says! The hoopoe was enjoying a dust bath in his newly excavated soil. The driveway is very bright, lots of sparkly bits... which you are NOT allowed to steal!

After lunch S decided to go into the cool of the barn and I was mortaring a bit of the outside wall when I heard a right kerfuffle going on next door. I peered over the wall (nosey that I am) and could see Carmen was in the barn. Her cockerel was going mad which of course set Buzz off too.

A bit later, I thought her cockerel sounded like it was lower down the track. I looked over the wall again and there was the cockerel on my allotment with Carmen trying to call it from her huerta. He is a nasty piece of work. She has told me she has to take a broom into the chicken pen with her. Handsome brute he is. He had somehow got out and wasn't for going back. I shouted 'hold on' and grabbed a stick and reinforcements (S). Unfortunately I only had sandals on and the giant ants were soon biting my toes, but S ran across next door's walnut plantation to head him off. We chased him up the road and back again, across the allotments, down the track... We had a good three pronged attack going at one point, with him penned in in front of the horreo on the road, but he flew over the stick and was off again. S got our newting nets, and off we went onto the allotment once more.

After about an hour, we were tiring even if he wasn't. He was finally recaptured when S made a heroic dive, straight into a nettle patch, to grab him.

I'm sure the cockerel had quite enjoyed his afternoon and we had a beer from a grateful Carmen... and a further 15L box of wine. That is a slight problem as we still have a full one from last year, so someone had better come over soon and help drink some. We now have around six gallons of wine to get through!

We had just had a cuppa and I was trying to re-wet my mortar to finish the wall when Carmen and Pilar, the two elderly ladies (mother and daughter) from the next village, arrived for a chat. They had been on their usual walk. I really hope I can still walk so far when I'm in my 90s. The mother didn't stop chatting. She wanted to know where my lettuces were and was very concerned she couldn't see any so I had to show her the allotment. I got a gold star for my chicken cabbage at any rate! Did you know they walk from their flat in town to the village almost every day? Probably two miles, and uphill going back to town! Tuesday evening, in the sunroom enjoying the last of the sunshine and warmth.

We are sitting on our nice chaise longue with the fire going, watching the bats fly *out from under the tiles to start their evening's hunting. The poor moths don't stand a chance - they flutter at the windows trying to get at the light inside then... gulp and they are gone. It's a bit sad, but it is wonderful to watch the aerobatics.*

We have had a peaceful couple of days after Sunday's fun and games. I have hoed the little seating area on the west side while watching all the butterflies. We have a large one called a Queen of Spain fritillary. It looks very majestic as it sort of floats around the place, inspecting everything. I can imagine it saying... 'you've missed a bit there.' I also saw a treecreeper on the old walnut tree. So tiny, and so cute with his little curved beak.

S has finished putting the turfs back on the 'first tee' but every time he places them carefully, the blackbird comes and tips them upside down looking for worms. It does the same with my carefully piled leaf mulch on the allotment. Rotter!

Wednesday: I think cockerels escaping must be a new pastime. Buzz got out again today. He must be jumping up onto the well and over the fence. Luckily the girls aren't interested in following him. At least he is easy to get back in.

Buzz is such a gentleman. He has never pecked us, even when we have been clipping his spurs. Not even the first time when we cut too close and he started bleeding - he let S bandage his leg without a murmur.

We also have bunny babies. Brown bunny has had four kits. White bunny is due at the weekend I think.

My garden is coming on. I have sown some sweet peas in pots in the barn (plus some special ones Gala gave me) and some nasturtiums, and have potted up the pelargoniums I bought. My onions are up and I have just sown some lettuce amongst them. Have planted the Jerusalem artichoke corms from last year and hoed the trenches ready for my tomatoes. The broad bean flowers don't seem to be setting though. There are plenty of bees around but also lots of ants. I wonder if they are taking the nectar somehow without pollinating the flowers.

The redcurrant we brought back last year is flowering and my new cranberry and blueberry bushes look okay. I have spotted my first asparagus spear (and a lone swallow last week) and there are lots of little tadpoles from the frog spawn and lots of lizards out sunbathing. The cherry is in blossom, the plums almost over and the kiwis leafing up so fingers crossed for no late frost this year.

Love you loads
Xxxxxxx

I can spend hours watching our wildlife, and I think I frequently do. Certainly the time seems to rush past as I'm admiring an industrious bee or the tiny treecreeper sneaking quietly up the walnut trunk hunting for insects. Even when we had masses of work to do on the house, we could always find time to wildlife watch.

Diary Friday 16th April Showers overnight, hot during the day
Hoed bean patch. Quite a few asparagus spears (from UK plants) are through. It's going to be difficult not to give in and pick some this year!
To Chantada pool. Met a new friend. Dasha is Czech, tall and absolutely stunning. She also speaks impeccable English. She invited us for dinner as they live nearby. As one can't refuse an offer like that we stuffed our cheese sandwiches back into our bag and agreed. Following Dasha's instructions we arrived at the house 15 minutes later.
The table was laid with Serrano ham, cheese and olives. We dug in happily and chatted to Dasha. A little while later her husband appeared carrying a large pot filled with churrasco from the local restaurant, fries, and wine. By now it was 11.30 in the evening and getting near our bedtime. But one can't turn down a free meal in such pleasant company, and the time flew by.

Diary Saturday 17th April Thunderstorms
Regretted the late churrasco! Couldn't sleep at all. Painting the newly plastered stove surround in the sunroom that lovely sunshine yellow. Very slow. S mortaring between the new quarry tiles in the horno... also very slow!
Had last night's butties for lunch.
Something is definitely eating my leeks again. The thing never seems to come to the surface but burrows underground nibbling at the bulb part of anything interesting. First sign of damage is when the things start to wilt because they have no roots!

APRIL

Put more traps in. These ones are a length of plastic tubing with one way doors at each end.
S took the old wooden side off the staircase in the storeroom ready for cleaning and removed a huge mouse nest. That's where they are hiding then!
Tea: Peanut butter, sesame, leek and broccoli pasta

Diary Sunday 18th April Sunshine
Spent the morning in the kitchen using up eggs! Made burnt creams, onion and bacon quiches for the freezer, egg custards and three cakes.
S cleaned all the window blinds from the sunroom (a bit dusty to say the least) and hung them on the line to dry. He then played with his new walnut dye, staining the new wood around the ceiling to match the old chestnut (green walnut husks with water and a bit of wire wool for the iron content... fixes the dye apparently).
Lunch: Stuffed pork belly. Roast potatoes and broccoli. Apple and blackberry pie.
Wandered up the valley looking for the flowering cherry we can see from our garden. More difficult than it looks as you can't see it once you are in amongst the trees. The track was full of tiny wild jonquil narcissus. So pretty. Collected wild strawberries, a honeysuckle cutting, some tiny unknown fruit tree, fungi to identify, and a saxifrage. Oh and two roofing slates. Very productive afternoon!
S put the blinds back up. I filled the new shelves with more books. Very happy day!

We have never managed to solve the problem of the 'beast'. The trap did catch one mole. Unfortunately we hadn't been checking it regularly. By the time we found the mole it had been dead some time and was rather bloated. There was no way we could get it out of the trap so we buried the whole thing in the compost heap until it had 'composted' sufficiently to clean the trap. I still battle each year with the *topos* despite the number of cats in the village, and each year I try a different trick to fool them.

§

On the Wednesday the rain came back in spectacular fashion, albeit briefly. The day began with thunder and sheet lightning as a prelude to the main act – heavy Galician rain. As outside work was off the agenda we decided to go and tackle our dragon at the registry office for our paperwork, which should have been ready by now. That they hadn't rung didn't really surprise me. The receptionist was as welcoming and cheerful as ever, but oddly she had lost the ability to worry me.

She made us sign something (I have absolutely no idea what) then snatched our documents back and told us they would be in Taboada by the beginning of the month (*quince dias*, obviously). Happy that she was still miserable, we celebrated with a tea and sticky bun in town before returning home for egg and chips.

The sun was out by the time we arrived home so I spent the afternoon in my allotment where there are no dragons or miserable *funcionarios*, only lizards and skinks, adders and slowworms. My sort of people!

That evening the rain returned in force. It seemed to have brought all its friends too as it gushed down our pathway, washing all the stones in front of it. Twice I had to clear the drainage hole in front of our terrace to stop us flooding. As it began to get dark, the sky turned an eerie orange-brown colour and the birds fell silent. There seemed to be dust swirling across the sky. Only later did I learn that the dust clouds were part of the ash plume caused by a series of volcanic eruptions from Eyjafjallajökull in Iceland which disrupted air travel for over a month that spring.

APRIL

Diary Thursday 22nd April Sun and showers. Thunder late pm
To the town hall. Told there is no need to make an appointment to see the mayor about officiating at our wedding as he is there every day at 12.30pm. Went back at 12.30pm. Mayor not there today!
Resowed swede as it seems to have disappeared, and the mulch has gone too! S planted the 'repollo' from Carmen and I did the 'col'... still not entirely sure what the difference is in cabbage terms. The chickens enjoy it anyhow.
Lunch: Pork and tomato stew with dried apricots (or peaches) and last year's green peppers (dried). Unearthed grandma's old rocking chair. Cleaned, polished and reassembled it. It will be perfect in the sunroom.

Diary Friday 23rd April Sunshine
To the allotment to pick broccoli. Picked two dozen slugs and snails off one tiny plant! Chickens will be happy! Sowed 24 sweetcorn in pots in the Long Barn whilst S was continuing to put new electrics in the storeroom.
Lunch: Dorada (is that bass or bream? I'm never sure) with mash, hollandaise sauce, broccoli and asparagus (just a couple of spears!). Meringue with chocolate cream and orange ice cream.
Spent the afternoon nursing a bumble bee back to health, hand feeding it until it could fly again. S did something more productive (though my bumble bee wouldn't agree). He fitted the new wooden boards along the staircase in the storeroom. Very neat job.
Bathnight so off to swimming pool then back to CJ's for tea, chat and pancakes. Delicious end to the day!

I've always had a soft spot for animals of all kinds. It really was a good job I never became an RSPCA inspector as I wanted. I even went vegan for a while but that didn't last more than five years. Now I prefer to eat locally, which means pretty much all of our meat is grown by us or our neighbour and we grow the vast majority of our fruit and veg too.

As a child, I had a school friend who had a pellet gun. He would shoot indiscriminately at anything and everything. My dad gave him some paper targets in the hope he would aim at those but he preferred aiming at wildlife. One day I was in the garden with my dad when something small hopped onto my shoe. It was a house sparrow. I bent to pick it up, surprised it didn't fly away. We noticed it had a pellet gun burn across its head and only one eye.

I put Horatio (obviously) into the canary's old cage and fed it bird seed. Mum insisted it stay in the brick built shed outside. It would, she said, likely be dead by morning. However, next morning Horatio was swinging on the canary's swing, whistling. We kept him for a week until he was strong enough to manage outside. I cried the day I opened the cage for him to fly away, but Horatio would return regularly for seeds and bread. We could always tell him by the odd way he held his head.

Some people find it strange that I can be such an animal lover and yet participate in killing animals to eat. I find this to be two sides of the same coin. I care about the welfare of animals and I hate an animal to be in pain. I worry constantly about the conditions in which factory farmed animals are kept, and it was one of the reasons I became vegan in my thirties. But, I personally felt that being vegan was not sustainable. I couldn't source all the elements of a vegan diet either locally or seasonally.

Our animals, and those of our friend from whom we buy our pig, are grown on local produce, looked after well, and killed humanely. If we have to do that ourselves to ensure they are not treated unkindly, then so be it.

APRIL

Diary Sunday 25th April Hot
After lunch we drove to Castelo then walked part of the Ruta Ider towards Vilar. Found an interesting water snake. It was very pretty, and fast, and seemed to enjoy being in the water. Must look it up. Lots of froglets too. Very peaceful route once we had got past the fishermen. Back to Castelo around 7pm. Stopped for a cola and chat at the café there. They had heard of us they said. Hasn't everyone?
Rang Mum.
S says something is eating the rabbit food.

Although we have many field mice (and some yellow-throated mice) we rarely have rats. However the invitation of rabbit food sitting in the feeders was too much for one particular family of black rats (*Rattus rattus*). S decided to set up a humane trap for them.

The first day we caught a small, very attractive young black rat. S took it down the track a ways. The second day we had another, then a larger female, and finally a bruiser of a male. A few days passed before we caught granddad: an old rat with greying whiskers and more than a few battle scars. He was released with the rest.

Unfortunately one of our neighbours spotted S carrying the trap down the track and couldn't resist asking what he was doing. 'Taking it for a walk' was his reply. Her face was a picture, as S remembered the Spanish don't do irony.

Wednesday 28th April. Scorcher. Forecast 28°C for today and it feels like it!
Dear Mum,
Don't know where this week has gone. We have failed totally to see the mayor about

our wedding. I was told that we didn't need an appointment as he is always in at 12.30pm. It was our third attempt today. We went at 12.30pm to be told he would be in at 1pm. so wasted half an hour wandering around Taboada. Returned at 1pm to be told he wasn't coming in because he had exams. Mayoral exams, S said. If I didn't know better I'd think he was avoiding us.

I've found out what the snake was from our weekend walk. It is a viperine snake. Not a viper at all but a small water snake in the same family as the grass snakes. It was only tiny but very pretty.

I wish your car cleaning gang would come here and do ours. It is covered in yellow pollen and full of tiny wasps' nests. They are small paper wasps but have taken a liking to all the little gaps between the door pillars and under the bonnet. Most annoying. We also have lots of solitary bees making little nests in the stone wall of the horno. Fascinating to watch them filling each hole in. We have cut some lengths of bamboo and popped those into some of the bigger gaps for them.

Aunty Jan rang today, she said she was worried about us having to collect her and take her to the airport. I said we can't exactly make people walk and we don't mind as it's a trip out. Will have to organise something for the wedding party mind as there will be too many of you for the car.

APRIL

Maybe we'll just strap one of you ladies on the roof rack haha.

Your 'poo' sounds like a hedgehog. You will have to go with the torch at night and have a look. They like cat food.

We had fun yesterday moving that big bread box out of the attic room. S wants to make a floor in that half of the room (the current floor of bent old barrel staves is not very safe). The box is 6 foot by 2 foot by 2 foot and weighs a ton. It's also a bit narrow and windy up those stairs. As I say it was fun, but we managed it eventually without damaging anything - though S did threaten to shut the lid on me at one point! He is now busy making a handrail around the platform at the top of the steps, which I cleaned in January.

Our chickens love snails! I will ask one of them to pop over for a holiday to clear them up for you. Perhaps you could take a hen home in your case in June then bring her back in August. I'm sure she would have a great time!

At least the chickens are paying for themselves now. I bought their food today using the egg money I've built up from the market. They are being naughty though. Yesterday everyone wanted to lay in one nestbox, the noise was deafening and in the kerfuffle one egg was jumped on and squashed. Then today I put two new boxes in the hut and one of the youngsters was scratching and jumping in and out of it. Later S found another squashed egg. I've told them they are all for the pot!

S has been mortaring the stone wall in the storeroom to keep the mice out. He found two, very flat, very dead mummified skeletons in the wall. There must've been a rock fall and squash! Yuk!

Later: Still light at 9pm and T shirts at 10.30pm walking back from town.

I spent most of the rest of today in the allotment. Have mulched my broad beans and put up sticks for Harold's 'rainbow' beans. I have planted out some of my courgettes as they are getting so big. Covered them with two cut off, large water bottles that Cris and Steve gave us, just in case of frost. If the frosts do hold off this next week or so, we are hoping for a bumper crop of figs this year - there are loads of little figlets on.

I sprayed the ants as you suggested with soapy water, but they don't seem very bothered to be honest. Tell Bill, I don't think I could possibly destroy ALL the ant nests on the allotment. I don't mind them generally as the bigger ones drag caterpillars and bugs back to the nest. They are decorating the mounds with pine seeds, catkins and twigs at the moment - quite fascinating!

Am looking forward to you coming over. We will find some nice gentle walks for you... when you are not on buzzard watch that is!

APRIL

Any date in June is fine by us, just get brother to find the cheapest price for you.
I shall post this tomorrow and ask if the mayor is in at the same time. I can but try!
Love you tons and tons.
xxxxxxxx

Ants are another pest on the allotment. Mum used to be a demon ant killer when I was a child. Boiling water down the nest in the garden was her favourite method of attack. I vividly remember sitting with Dad one day after the kettle had been employed, watching the ants scurrying around rescuing the eggs which they lined up on the rocks to dry out. Then, something happened which has stayed with me – the ants started to bring out the bodies of the dead and line those up on the rocks too. I vowed there and then never to use boiling water on ants.

I have no objections to ants per se. But on the allotment they do cause problems. The huge wood ants build undergrown nests many metres across then set off in a single determined line towards my broad beans where they farm aphids for the honey dew they produce. Not only do the aphids destroy my broad bean crop but the ants defend their livestock against all attacks. When one of those wood ants grabs hold of a body part, it doesn't let go!

Diary Thursday 29th April
Wow! Stormy night. Thunder, lightning the lot until about 3am. By this afternoon it was hot hot again. To the town hall. Mayor not in again! Took our preferred date and time up to his office and left a message for him to ring me... urgently! The lass there didn't think the 28th August would be a problem but said she'd pass on the message.

TOMATO, FIG & PUMPKIN JELLY

Lunch: Stirfry rice with broccoli, leek, cashew and fried rabbit. Eton mess with yoghurt, cream, cake crumbs and sugar. Very good!!
S fitted the new handrail around the platform near the attic room. That platform will make a good display area.
Both attempted to fit the new kitchen wall cupboards. The wall is exceptionally bent! If the first cupboard is level, the third one is almost 8 inches out from the wall. S decided to chisel off some of the plaster.

Even if we couldn't find the mayor, at least our house renovations were progressing well.

We had completed the sunroom, *más ó menos*. We had gravelled the driveway and concreted the new outside eating area. We had cemented the storeroom walls, with help from CJ, and were ready to start on the kitchen.

The kitchen wall units were the top part of the large second-hand display unit we had bought in 2008. The base units, complete with velvet lined drawers, were looking smart in the bathroom. The top part of the unit was surplus to requirements, and it was perfect for the kitchen – even if the wall wasn't.

One unit has full length glass doors. The other end has a large cupboard below more glass doors. My crockery went in the top. The large cupboard houses dry goods and bread, safe from the inquisitive mice. The central unit has two long shelves and more cupboards above.

S battled chiselling the wall and gouging out lumps of plaster to level it, but the three cupboards were in place by the Friday. The next stage of our kitchen renovation project was underway.

MAY
The heart of the Home

On the first of May we screwed the final wall cupboard up in the kitchen. At last I had somewhere for my spice jars and my all-important cook books, (the latter have a whole shelf of their own). The glass fronted cupboards were perfect for displaying glasses and our collection of cat mugs. And, most importantly, I got to empty a few more boxes from the attic room. It seemed that although we had emptied many boxes over the last few months, that particular room was as full as when Les stayed all that time ago.

Diary Sunday 2nd May Cooler
Cleaned the kitchen cupboards and the glass. S screwed everything back together and fixed the cupboard bases to the wall support he has put up. Off for our Sunday walk whilst lunch was cooking itself.
Up over the hill then along the river. Met a friendly farmer who showed us two more mills on our river. I think he thought we were like trainspotters, writing numbers down in a little book, as he told us there are 14 water mills altogether on our little rio. That will keep us going for a while!
Lunch: Rabbit, kidney and heart casserole. Rice pudding.
Emptied more boxes and filled more cupboards.

TOMATO, FIG & PUMPKIN JELLY

Diary Monday 3rd May Some sun but feels cold in comparison to last week.
Decided to move the washer into the utility room. Managed to somehow manoeuvre it up the steps where it will eventually be plumbed in. I shall NOT be moving that ever again!
Continued to empty boxes and organise my kitchen how I want it.
Cheese lady day. Bought one spicy, one soft.

Growing up in a rural area in the 60s and 70s, I remember well the visiting shops. Few people we knew had cars, and even fewer had two cars, so housewives had to walk to the shops if they needed groceries. Far better for those shops to come to us.

There was the baker, Mr Smith, with his van smelling of fresh bread and custard tarts; the fish man, weighing out cod and plaice fillets for Friday dinner; and the butcher, who set up his heavy chopping block on the pavement to cut up the sides of beef, lamb, or pork. Mr Robey, the vegetable man, came with his open topped cart carrying fresh fruit and vegetables piled up like a kaleidoscope.

My favourite was the tall van which one could walk into, like an tiny regular shop. This shop carried tinned goods and, most importantly, chocolate! If I was extremely lucky I got a creamy Galaxy bar as a treat.

Of course the milk man delivered daily. If we were early enough, the blue tits hadn't pecked through the foil top by the time we collected the milk from the doorstep. And in summer there was Edgar, the '*oakey*' or ice cream man, with his cheerful jingle.

The Corona drinks man was a bit of a speed merchant. Once, he took the bend near to our house far too quickly, the lorry tipping and spilling its load of glass drinks' bottles a matter of feet from where me and my friend were playing. Our parents were furious but, I believe, were persuaded not to complain. I tried fizzy drinks for the very first time when the Corona man 'donated' a number of bottles to the understanding locals.

These visiting vans died out in our home village as more people began to drive cars and shop in supermarkets. More women also began to go out to work, meaning no one was at home during the day.

In rural Galicia we still have those visiting shops.

The *panaderia* will bring your daily bread and, if you are out, hang it on a convenient doorpost or specially positioned nail. Our bread shop sells what would be termed artisan bread in England. It proudly displays its ingredients on the paper bag the bread arrives in: *fariña, sal, levadura.* (Flour, salt, yeast). Nothing more, nothing less.

The fish man visits weekly, his small van loaded with fresh fish collected that morning from the fishing boats in Coruña. It is always exciting to see what delights have been brought for our perusal. We have tried some delicious, and some unusual, treats. The conger eel was a delicacy that was definitely not for me... or the cat!

Isabel, our cheese lady, visits fortnightly, her van full of different cheeses from the local Diqueixa dairy. The fresh cheese is crumbly and tangy and makes a delicious cheesecake. The local D.O Arzua-Ulla cheese is creamy and soft with a sour bite whilst the '*piquante'* has a slightly hot paprika flavouring.

Milk lorries visit too, but to collect the milk from the local farms rather than to deliver one's daily 'pinta'. Here in Spain, virtually all milk is Ultra Heat Treated (UHT) milk rather than pasteurised. I love drinking fresh milk so this is my biggest disappointment here. Our local co-operative store did start to sell 'fresh' milk for a while, but it petered out due to a lack of interest. And I suppose drinking less milk might keep me slimmer.

Vegetable sellers, with or without carts, are unnecessary as most village folk grow their own. The same goes for butchers vans, in a rural community where meat is grown 'on site' in the majority of cases.

Our neighbours all grow rabbits, chickens, and often pigs to eat. Our nearest neighbour, Carmen, admits she hates killing them. "But," she says, "if I want to eat meat I have to be prepared to kill the animals." An admirable statement, though sadly I think fewer and fewer people would agree with it nowadays.

Wednesday 5th May 3pm, in Monterroso waiting for car pre-MOT
Dear Mum,
Boy what a difference in the weather. Last week T-shirts at 10.30pm. This week gloves, hat, two jumpers walking back from town - and I was icy! There is snow on the high ground at Pedrafita (past Lugo). I hope it doesn't freeze here as the fig is absolutely loaded, as are the other fruits, and I have courgettes and tomatoes already planted out on the allotment. CJ's friend Pete is coming this week so it is bound to be dreadful. Good job you decided to wait until June!

On Saturday night we were watching a film with the lights off when there was a bang from the fire and the lower half of the chimney began to glow red! Talk about panic. I thought the whole lot was going to melt, and imagined molten metal all over our wooden floor! Luckily it stopped once I turned the air intake off. S reckons there must have been a load of gas in one of the

MAY

logs and it ignited with a whoosh. Would have made a great pic if I had thought about it.

List of clothes etc you have here...

Toothbrush and toothpaste (but no charger), swimsuit if you feel able, two pairs jeans, PJs, 'teddy bear' cardigan, dark brown long sleeved top. Plenty of working clothes and jumpers but NO knickers!!

We have finally sorted out a price with Luisa for the wedding breakfast. She kept thinking of different things we could have. I have emailed wedding invites to everyone except you two luddites in Coro'. You will get posher, printed invites.

8pm. Just home with the car. They are still waiting for a new exhaust so we have to go back again tomorrow. Quite an exciting day really as we had two journeys by bus from Monterroso, where the garage is, and back. Just 1.25€ each but only 4 buses a day so timing is critical. We spent a fortune drinking tea at the hotel waiting for the bus!

Forgot to say, Luisa asked when you were coming next and I said 2nd June. She said you should stay permanently. I agreed. She said she would find you a house.

I hope they don't strip search you looking for that metal object you are hiding at the top of your leg. Mention you have a new hip at security when you come through. It may save hassle.

TOMATO, FIG & PUMPKIN JELLY

11.30pm. Oops, pen died on me. We have just had the second half of Doctor Who, thank you, followed by two hours of blank tape! We love you very much but please please tape something on the spare tape. Cartoons, Grand Designs, anything will do… even Carols from King's College, Cambridge (that one was most enlightening!). We put on the third Doctor Who tape (it says episodes 6,7,8) but that appears to be a film. At least it seems to be a complete film so we will watch that another night. We really do appreciate all your efforts with technology, and film nights are always exciting!!

Both bunnies definitely have babies so if you promise not to poke, you can play with them in June. They should be big enough to go into the ark by then.

Thank you for your letter, I don't think your scribble is any worse than mine. I'm not used to writing any more. Don't think I could do my 3 hour college exams now. My hand is aching already haha.
Oops 12 midnight, pumpkin time.
Xxxxxxxxxx
Only a month to go. Kisses are baking and should be ready on arrival xxxx

And one from the chicks x who say they are looking forward to seeing that funny woman who lets them jump on her head. (One of the babies was 5 foot up the peach tree today nibbling the tastiest leaves!)

MAY

Diary Friday 7th May Drizzly
Jayne arrived this morning with the chickens and Lucky for their 'holiday'. Had made up the lower chicken hut as guest quarters, separate from our lot. Wonder if they remember each other?
S finally sorted out his design issues with the guest bed. Moved it into position and made it up ready for our VIP in June! Cleaned and swept storeroom ready to start tiling the floor.
Found a vole 'feeding' station on the allotment very near to my leeks!
Lunch: Rice, sardines, asparagus (just a bit). Choc pudding and ice cream.
Both spent the afternoon measuring and drawing up lines on the new concrete storeroom floor for my starting point. Would be easier if any room here were square of course, plus I want the lines to be central when I turn the corner through into the kitchen. Chalk lines all over the floor by the time we had finished!
Bathnight. Spent almost an hour on the allotment afterwards collecting slugs and snails for the chickens.

Our house, when I was growing up, was a well-designed council property. We had a small pantry on the north side of the kitchen where produce always kept cool, even in the hottest summer. Outside was a coal shed for our all-important fuel and a large brick built 'outhouse' for storage. We had an outside toilet in the passageway next to the outhouse... very useful when working outside.

In the centre of the house was an open fireplace which heated the living room. Behind it was a back boiler which kept us in hot water year round. Backing onto this, in the dining room, there was originally a large range cooker. This also used the free heat from the coal fire to warm it. Mum says she cried the year the council took those cookers out.

TOMATO, FIG & PUMPKIN JELLY

The chimney ran up through the centre of the house, helping to warm the bedrooms.

Space was cleverly used. Between the main and second bedroom were built-in cupboards opening into one room or the other and providing some noise insulation between the rooms. Even the small, third bedroom had a huge built in wardrobe above the staircase.

Sub-consciously, I had tried to emulate many of the best features of my childhood home when redesigning *A Casa do Campo*.

Our wood-burning stoves heat the upstairs rooms and our *cocina* is the heart of the home, warming my kitchen, airing my clothes, and heating our water. We now (13 years on) have a back boiler to one of the wood-burners which heats the bathroom water in winter, and S has created clever storage solutions in many of the rooms.

Sunday 9th May.
Dear Mum,

You will be pleased to know that you have a bed, so you won't have to sleep on the floor after all! S has built a strong frame inside the original one so it should be secure now, though management take no responsibility for accidents caused by over-zealous use of the equipment such as trampolining!

We are sitting in the sunroom watching the swifts doing some wonderful aerobatics catching insects, and listening to Lucky crying… There is no other way to describe the noise he is making. Very un-cockerel like. S says he is calling 'Jayne! Jayne! please come back and I won't ever attack you again. I'm imprisoned.' He has been fine with me, but S says he pecked him this morning. Richard told us he had to poke a broom handle in his chest to stop him attacking Jayne one day. And he was such a cute baby!

You should see Buzz. He keeps flying at the fence separating them, feet first, trying to get at that cheeky usurper. I must get a photo of the two of them, they look so alike.

You are welcome to bring your spare books here for the club but don't overload yourself. And why do you need 12 pairs of pants? We have a fancy modern piece of equipment here called a washing machine you know. And it might even be plumbed in by then!

I'm positive neither you nor Aunty Jean will 'let us down' at the wedding. Have you visited the charity shop in Swad where I got my dress? It really is worth a look and the lady was smashing. It's very discreet upstairs with proper changing rooms and everything. You'd be surprised.

A friend asked if you needed to borrow a hat but I said that the bride's mother had refused to wear one (you can borrow my old Estrella Galicia sunhat if it's too warm haha). Tell Aunty Jean I would be honoured to borrow her 'jewels' again and thank her very much. I hope you will all come for a while. It seems daft to come just for the weekend when you don't need to.

Monday. Still wet. Will be glad when CJ's Rainman friend goes home! Just as long as the Snow Queen doesn't go and jinx it in June that is!!

I think we have a world record for size of egg from a small chicken today. Number One (our first ever chicken) laid one of 3¾oz! I think that is officially a goose, poor thing.

We have been busy tiling today. Well, I have been tiling and S cutting all the fiddly bits around the edges for me using his angle grinder. Have done about half of the storeroom floor so we are having a couple of days off! The car has its MOT tomorrow so we have to go into Lugo. Fingers crossed for the old girl! Then on Wednesday we have been invited over to Dawn and Stephen's for lunch (you went over last time... big house with the stone balcony).

Oh dear, that's the chickens arguing again. I'll be glad when Lucky takes his girls home. They are such noisy guests haha.

Tuesday. STILL wet!

Can't believe the old Escort passed again. 15 years and still going strong. Uncle George would have been so proud. S was hanging onto the handbrake for dear life. The chap gave us four tries then said the handbrake wasn't very good (we had noticed!). But at the end the printer threw out a white 'pass' sheet not a blue 'fail' one so that's okay for another year. If only cars could talk.

MAY

We met some new Brits in Bricoking today (as you do). Heard them talking. They have a sweet shop in Lugo. Very nice couple with a 9 year old daughter. They apparently saw our house a month before we did but thought it would cost too much to renovate. Funny how many of us have seen each others' houses.

Can you get a (large) bottle of HP sauce into your suitcase? A tiny bottle was 3€ in Carrefour supermarket. I'm sure it's not that much in the UK (though if it is, don't bother).

Back to tiling tomorrow as Dawn isn't well. Flights still seem to be off and on. Hope Jayne and Richard get back okay and we don't get stuck with this delightful cockerel who now keeps going for me too! They are due back Friday.

Wednesday evening: Just back from town and completed my slug hunt. Have covered my poor courgettes again and the runner beans seem to have rotted off in the damp. Shows you can't assume spring has arrived eh?

Luisa was telling S that she likes his 'happy face'. I said he sounds like the village idiot! He mainly smiles as he has no idea what she is saying. She also said (again) how beautiful you must have been in your youth as you have such good bone structure. I shall have to take her an old photo in to *prove she is correct. Funny, but she never says anything about me being beautiful, happy or even pretty... I'm feeling left out haha.*

My wedding cake is made. 3½ hours in the oven on low (16 eggs, 4lb fruit). It smells good anyway. Am just wondering where to hide it so a certain someone doesn't nibble his way through it before August. I used my big meat tin in the end as I didn't have a cake tin big enough. I made it square by putting some stiff cardboard across one end. I had some large round tins but square is so much easier to cut. Anne is making the marzipan and I think I may ask Dawn to do the icing as it's not my forte. CJ provided the glacé cherries from his stock and Jayne the dried fruit. My girls obviously provided the eggs and S even stirred it up for me, so it was quite a joint effort! We had to mix it in my big jam saucepan.

Had your letter today. England looks very blue! I saw on TV that Cameron has done a deal with the Lib-Dems. The only consolation is that the governor of the Bank of England said 'whichever party gets in will be so reviled because of the cuts they will have to make to clear our debts that they won't get back in for a decade.' Every cloud eh?

Love you tons and tons...only two weeks to go! XXXXXXXX

MAY

The storeroom, that I was busy tiling, was to be my domain. I always wanted a cool pantry like Mum's but on a bigger scale: a space for my preserves, jams, chutneys, dried fruits and pulses. A place to keep things cool but not fridge cold. I was going to have a large table in the centre of the floor for working at (the old one which was left in the middle bedroom when we moved in) and shelving units around the walls. I had already envisaged and planned the stocking of those shelves.

Even now I love to gaze at my labelled jars of produce lined up on the shelves in my storeroom. They are the result of all my hard work over the year and the promise of good food throughout the winter. It is very satisfying.

Diary Friday 14th May Cold wet stuff!
S put knobs on the kitchen cupboards while I thought about what other exciting things I can fill them with. Collected veg for lunch while S cut tiles for the edge of the storeroom. The slugs have eaten at least half of my red cabbages despite my nightly torchlight hunts! Think I'll just let the chickens loose out there, though they would probably also eat the cabbages, and ignore the slugs.
Lunch: Pasta with leek and broccoli and just a couple more asparagus shoots.
Continued tiling the storeroom floor.
Clara called later so drove up to Taboada to collect her. Met Pepe in Santa Lucia who insisted on paying for the coffees.
Bathnight. Dropped Clara off. Vino and bocadillos in the café at the swimming baths. Booked my hen night for 27th August.

Diary Saturday 15th May Cloudy and cool
Decided to paint the storeroom walls. S cut in (being the neatest) and I rollered. Loaded Jayne's chickens into the car and dropped them off on the

TOMATO, FIG & PUMPKIN JELLY

way to Anne and Simon's for lunch. Back home around midnight with strawberries from their garden. Pumpkin time!

Diary Monday 17th May Hot!
Potted up sweetpeas while S played with his electrics and cleaned out the animals. Heard a funny scrabbling noise whilst in the long barn. It seemed to be coming from the newly installed downspout. Got S to unscrew everything and a blue tit flew out! It must've nested in the gutter and been washed down the pipe.
Sowed two rows of white beans, planted out the 24 sweetcorn in a block plus 5 melons under cloches. After tea planted out tronchuda spring cabbages, kohl rabi, and white cabbage.
Lunch: Pork, ham and bean meatloaf with roast potatoes. I do like a bit of Meatloaf! Anne's strawberries and cream for afters.

Wednesday 19th May. Very very hot. Summer is here at last!
Dear Mum,
 I hope this lasts for you. I have finally put all the tomatoes, peppers and aubergines, squash/pumpkins and melons out. My corn and sweetcorn is in and the broad beans are finally growing proper beans on. Anne says bumble bees can be a problem as they can't get the nectar the proper way so steal it by biting into the back of the flower. I did have lots of bumble bees early on, I think they fly before the honey bees in spring.
 I also have flowers on my peapods (mangetout) so should have some veg for you by June.

MAY

We are looking forward to seeing you. I hope this silly dust cloud hurries up and goes. Still causing problems for planes I think. Be careful with my loaned jewels won't you? I think you should chain your bag to your wrist like they do in films!! I wish someone would sort out your tickets for August. I'm wondering if I can do it from here. Would hate for you to end up in the two man tent on the lawn!!

We didn't know anything was amiss in Thailand. Saw some pictures on the TV in Mencia last night but it is so small, and no sound so we had no idea what was going on. How cut off we are!

We had a visitor today, Pepe, whose Mum owned our house. He wanted to show us some firewood we could cut. Off we went. It's not far and I think his family own most of the valley...

'this is my aunt's plot, this is my cousin's' etc all the way.

Of course he hadn't been up there for 20 years and got hopelessly lost. 'I'm sure there was a boundary tree here.' Part of the boundary wall had collapsed too but I think he worked it out. He says we can take whatever we like which is kind, but it is virtually inaccessible except on foot so we would have to cut and drag it all back by hand. Not an auspicious idea.

He also asked when you were moving over. He has a house to sell apparently...

TOMATO, FIG & PUMPKIN JELLY

We went to Anne and Simon's for lunch on Saturday. Lovely meal but I had to overdose on anti-histamines because of all the cats (12 I think as they just bought a Persian from the pet store in Lugo... for 240€!)

Don't seem to have much other news since I spoke to you on Sunday. We have been busy tiling and grouting the storeroom. It should look nice by the time you arrive. I think we will do a points system again... a kiss for each new thing you spot. I shall have to add up how many there will be... Ooo lots I think!!

Before I forget, I've enclosed the contact lens solution leaflet and written 60ml on it so they know it is for the 'plane. If you have space can you also bring the following?...

Same contact lens solution but large 250ml size;

Yorkshire tea, 3 packets (loose leaf of course)

Vitamin B1 tablets from Holland & Barrett. They are for preventing insect bites.

A large packet of sesame seeds if they do them. If they only have the tiny packets don't bother as they are really expensive and I can ask Belle to bring one from the Chinese hypermarket in August. It can be our wedding present!

Phew! That's your bag full... good job you have some clothes here already.

Love you tons and tons and tons
xxxxxxxxxx

MAY

See you in 1½ weeks. I need my watering assistant. S isn't nearly as diligent with the 'ON!' call as you are. Just can't get the staff!
PS Is it definitely Sunday you go back?
PPS Anne gave me this slug recipe you might appreciate as it is so gruesome: To deter slugs either steep dead slugs in a bucket of water and water the resulting stinky liquid over the susceptible plants <u>or</u> roast slugs and sprinkle the ashes around the plants! Have fun xxx

We soon learned that one of the problems with having a well as our only source of water was that the mountain spring which fills the sump doesn't flow quickly enough in summer. It meant that while I was watering on the allotment, with the hosepipe stretched across the track, I had to listen carefully for the pump running or 'hunting for water'. This was often made difficult by the sounds of tractors revving or even chickens squawking nearby. When Mum stayed she stood by the pump and told me when it was running. She would then turn the power off at the switch until the pump reset. The 'on!' cry let me know it was safe to start watering again.

Our well water has far more advantages than disadvantages though. It is pure and clear with no chlorine or chemicals in it. The area, being granite bedrock, has very soft (acidic) water so no furring up of kettles with calcium carbonate. And I have lovely silky soft hair. It is also free unless we need repairs to the *bomba* (pump).

One of the other projects we had for the year was to improve on our solar shower.

For almost three years we had used the free power of the sun to heat our outdoor 'shower'. This was an old hosepipe attached to the outside tap and left in the sun for between thirty minutes and an hour. We then had a hosepipe length of lovely hot water. One learnt to shower quickly and efficiently. S thought that he could adapt this system to provide us hot water in the bathroom, without having to resort to using the expensive immersion heater.

Richard had brought the hot water tank from the UK for us. It had two heat exchange coils as well as the immersion heater. Eventually, one of the coils would be attached to the back boiler behind the (as yet to be started) wood-burning stove in the (as yet un-renovated) Big Barn. The second coil was for our solar water system.

We could, of course, have bought a sophisticated solar water system ready-made, but where is the fun in that? Cris and Steve had given us a boot full of plastic bottles, we had a new, long hosepipe, and S had constructed a frame on the back, south-facing, house wall.

Using the hosepipe shower as a starting point, S designed a zigzag system of hose pipe fixed to the south facing wall and plumbed through to the hot water tank. A top up tank ensured the system remained full, and some of Cris and Steve's small water bottles were threaded onto the hosepipe to provide some insulation and help retain the heat. Our do-it-yourself system worked surprisingly well. Over the years it has evolved – it is now made entirely with black poly-piping for instance. But it still follows this basic design and we can have hot showers every night from late May to October, when the sun shines. The total cost of our solar system was less than a hundred euros plus the free power of the sun.

Diary Thursday 20th May Hotter
Weeded on the allotment. S cut the first lot of tiles for the hallway. He also made some wooden

MAY

shelving to hide the electrics along the storeroom wall. More storage is always welcome!
Lunch: Tortilla, 'sandwiched' with bacon and cheese. Orange curd tart with cream.
Finished grouting tiles in the storeroom. Moved on to the hallway which is a real mess of levels, especially by the back door.

Diary Saturday 22nd May Very hot
To the allotment after scrummy eggs (chef forgot the day!) Hoed etc.
To Stephen and Dawn's for lunch. Chatted with Dawn while S and Stephen moved some roof slates. Left 9.30pm. Stopped on the way home to ring Mum as I hadn't warned her we would be out. She had already imagined all sorts of disasters befalling us, so good job I did!

Diary Sunday 23rd May 29°c on terrace. Thunder pm, no rain
Made choux buns as CJ said he was coming over. S took the kitchen door off for my next bit of tiling. Not easy as all the screws were welded on with rust. Continued tiling the hallway but not happy as the levels aren't right near the back door. It seems to be going in three different directions... very frustrating.
Fried rabbit legs with spinach and fried potatoes for lunch. Choux buns for dessert as CJ didn't show, and choux pastry doesn't keep does it?
Strimmed south lawn and had solar shower. S cut a wooden thresher for the back door.
CJ arrived 5.30pm. Oops. Good job there is always cake casa nosotros!

I never did get those levels right in the hallway. And it still irritates me whenever I walk in the back door. I once told Mum I wasn't happy with the tiling in the hallway. Her reply?

TOMATO, FIG & PUMPKIN JELLY

"Next time do it yourself."
Thanks Mum!

Tuesday 25th May. Some rain today but not really wet the ground. Given nice for next week so far!
Dear Mum,

We are very pleased that the mother of the bride has found a frock to wear - I had visions of bra and knickers being the order of the day! I told you that charity shop was good. Of course I won't tell anyone where you got it. Finding the handbag to match was great luck wasn't it? Jayne, who knows more about these things than me, says it is a very well-known brand. Oh! I haven't told anyone else... honest!

I had a very nice acceptance card from Aunty Jan today so the three of you are definitely coming! Are you bringing your outfit with you this time to save space? It can hang here without creasing that way. You have your own wardrobe now you know.

There was a poster up last week for a mobile blood donor van coming to town. As I always gave blood in England... do you remember me telling you about Colindale? Best blood donor place ever. Always sandwiches and cake afterwards and free Guinness (for the iron!). I persuaded S to join me and off we went. We sat down inside the adapted coach, all very clean and swish, and waited our turn. A lady came to take details but as soon as I said we were

MAY

English she looked oddly at us and excused herself. I thought (optimistically) she may be collecting an English speaking colleague, but no. A doctor came back with her and asked in Spanish if we were in England in 1999 and 2000. Well, of course. Then he said we could not give blood as we might have variant CJD (mad cow disease). Well, you know me! I was fuming. I felt like we weren't good enough. I believe CJD shows up within five years. Mind you I probably did look like a mad cow by the time I'd finished ranting... complete with steam coming out of my ears. The irony is that S was vegetarian at that time and I was vegan so we would be exceptionally unlikely (and exceptionally unlucky) to have the disease anyway. So much for trying to do our bit.

I opened one of your jars of bottled tomatoes last week as I am out of tomato sauce and they are excellent. S said what a good flavour they have and they are ideal as a replacement for tomato puree so I may have you making some more in August!

On Friday night, after our swim, we went to the boating club (Club Náutico) near to the iron bridge over the Miño, as they had advertised a 'crisis' evening (free tapas and cheap wine). Well, you know us - free tapas! We arrived about 9.30pm but no tapas to be seen. It was a hot night and lovely views along the river from the balcony though, so we didn't mind. We thought we must have been too late but no! at 10pm (I mean who but the English would come out before 10pm?) the tapas started arriving and the place filled up. We had mussels, bacon sandwiches, meatballs, and tortilla. Very nice vino too. As we left the chap asked if we wanted any more food. S says we should have had a bacon butty to take away. Nice looking restaurant too.

I'm pleased you have your August flights sorted. The lady at the hotel says there are only two rooms left as one is permanently occupied. She seems very disorganised with the names all just scribbled into a notebook rather than a proper diary, and all the bookings are in my name. (Well, actually all are listed as 'los ingleses'… we told S' friend Steve he was paying for everyone as his surname is Ingle!).

Wednesday. Wet! Hopefully it is getting it out of the way for you. This time next week you will be sitting in here too - good eh?

Have just been identifying a beetle S found bumbling around in the barn. It is a horned scarab or dung beetle. Rare in Britain apparently. He has a helmet with a horn on it. He keeps lifting his helmet up to peep out from underneath!

We decided to plant the rest of our sweetcorn today as the ground is damp and it is a full moon. The locals plant by the moon so we put the last lot in by the new moon to be perverse! Will see if there is any difference! First broad beans and first strawberries off today so that's good.

Well, I guess I won't be sending a letter next week as I can tell you our news directly!

Can't think of anything else. Don't forget those knickers! You have PJs here... did I say?

Really looking forward to seeing you and have ordered the sunshine for Wednesday.

Love you tons and tons
xxxxxxx

Diary Thursday 27th May Cloudy and cooler
S put the kitchen door back on (after sticking down the interesting 'U' shaped bits of tile round the door jambs) and took back door off so I can finish tiling the hallway.
Lunch: Sausages; potato, cheese, and onion bake and broad beans.
Finished tiling in the hall. Left the back door off overnight so the tiles can dry properly before we walk on them (though we couldn't make them any wobblier!).

Diary Friday 28th May Cloudy
Both cleared out the attic room. Incredibly dusty! S put down temporary floorboards to replace the barrel staves in the annex bit. (Next year's project!)
Both put the back door back on... and off, and on, taking a bit off at a time until it closes over my wobbly tiles.
To the swimming baths via the kitchen place for our quote for base units. No quote yet! How long can it take to draw up a quote for four kitchen cupboards!

TOMATO, FIG & PUMPKIN JELLY

Diary Saturday 29ᵗʰ May Some sun pm
Spent the whole day filling the new shelves in my new storeroom. Wonderful!
S meanwhile vac'd out the car ready for our visitor, cleaned the utility room, and hosed the terrace.

From the beginning of our adventure here in Galicia, we have tried to be energy conscious. I'm the first to admit we are by no means perfect – we still use electricity for example. But, thanks to my clever fella, our hot water now costs us and the environment virtually nothing. In summer we shower using the free energy of the sun. In winter the excess heat from our wood-burning stove gives us enough hot water to have a shower and to heat the bathroom radiator. And that I am pretty proud of!

JUNE
What's in a name?

When I was first writing of our adventures in Galicia, it seemed somehow fitting that S had merely an initial to go by. He is a private person, but more importantly none of our neighbours know his name. Don't get me wrong they have been introduced, of course they have, but his is one of those English names that not only has no Spanish equivalent but begins with two consonants.

The Spanish do not begin words with 'sp' or 'st'. Hence España, *especial*, Esteban (Stephen), *estupendo*. One of our neighbours, who lived in England for many years, calls my blue-eyed hubby James, and always has. I have no idea why as it bears no resemblance at all to his real name. The rest of our neighbours sound like they have a bad case of the stutters and generally resort to '*su marido*', your husband. So, 'S' he became.

S in fact does not use his first given name, which would be much easier for the Spanish to pronounce. He never has done apparently. This is the same with most of my family who either use a middle name, a shortened version of their full name or a nickname bearing no relationship to their real name. All except me.

As a child I always wanted a longer name such as Samantha, Charlotte or Georgina which I could then shorten to Sam, Charlie or George. Did I mention I was a tomboy? Maybe growing up with two much older brothers, from whom I inherited my Corgi car collection and plastic soldiers, and a father who loved to share with me his hobbies, such as woodworking or gardening, helped shape who I am. Or maybe it was just nature.

Diary Wednesday 2nd June Very hot and sunny
Up early to collect Mum from Santiago. Called in Leroy Merlin to look at kitchen base cupboards. Good price and in stock. As the other kitchen places still haven't got back to me, we bought them, and some oil for the new wooden worktops. Ate our butties at the little riverside picnic area in Melide. Spent the afternoon checking for and picking off Colorado beetles from my potatoes.

Although Mum was, of course, coming for our wedding in August, she couldn't wait that long and felt her new hip was now good enough to have a trial flight out. As usual we had a lovely time, exploring new places and showing Mum our work to date on the house.

One night we were sitting in the living room enjoying a chat when Mum suddenly said "It looks so nice in here now. I never imagined you would manage it you know?"

We had heard this before a few dozen times but I played along.

"What do you mean? You never said anything!"

"Well, I didn't like to but I cried after I'd seen this place the first time."

Nice to know my mother had such confidence in us!

§

On the following Monday we decided a trip to the coast was in order.

JUNE

According to the Conselleria de medio ambiente (conservancy council), Galicia has 1498 kilometres, or around 930 miles, of coastline and the greater part of it is undiscovered by tourists. Our mission is to visit as much of it as we can and we have found some wonderful places so far.

On this occasion we headed north toward the *Lucense* coast. Our first stop was the Castro of Viladonga, just beyond Lugo. As with many of the local Iron Age Celtic settlements, Viladonga was discovered by accident when a farmer came upon the ruins as he was cultivating his field. It is well worth a visit.

By the time we had looked around the partly excavated but extensive ruins and the informative museum, it was almost lunchtime. Luckily the town of Meira was nearby. The Mesón Pozo, like most Galician restaurants, had a three course *menú del dia* board outside. My eye was drawn to one of my favourite dishes: *rabo del toro* or oxtail. Oxtail stew used to be one of our winter treats when I was a child. Long slow cooking brings the meat to a velvet tenderness with a rich flavour, but it has to be done right. The chef at Mesón Pozo knew his stuff. The *rabo de toro* was the best I've tasted outside of my childhood memories of Mum's cooking. The meat was so well cooked it dropped off the bones, leaving the latter clean and white. The potatoes accompanying it were cooked in olive oil in the oven, tender and soft with a lingering fruitiness. The house wine was delicious and the desserts were sweet and satisfying.

From Meira we tootled toward the coast, stopping in Pontenova to admire the huge lime kilns which dominate the little town, before arriving in Ribadeo for the evening.

We had fallen in love with Ribadeo on our *Camino* trip some six years earlier and had long promised to take Mum there. We stayed in the same *hostal* and visited the same bar. The square in front of the *hostal* had been pedestrianized since our last visit, making it surprisingly noisier as the Spanish mingled and shouted to each other and children ran around screaming.

The following day we headed west along the coast to As Catedrais. These natural rock sculptures on the north Galician coast are part of the NATURA 2000 European network of protected natural spaces, and form huge cathedral like shapes on the sands.

Mum was also keen to see the cathedral in the pilgrim town of Mondoñedo, as we had heard it was quite beautiful. Unfortunately, despite my doing a full circuit of the place and asking everyone who looked like they might vaguely know, we failed utterly to get in. For a cathedral in a pilgrim town to be closed is unusual enough in Galicia to be worthy of a mention!

We paused on the way home at Abadín, a place I love mainly because it is pronounced the same as the Granite City in Scotland. And the fact that it has at least two excellent restaurants – always a good sign in any Galician town. (Our own Taboada has four restaurants which I would unhesitatingly recommend to anyone.)

On the way home I rang my older brother to check his arrival date and ask him to give me away. Old fashioned maybe, as this was not a church wedding and I was hardly a maiden to be handed over to her husband, but I wanted him there in place of my beloved father. He was chuffed to bits to be asked so we were all set.

After a few days at home, with heavy rain hitting the roof and drowning the Colorado beetles on my potatoes, we set off for another trip, this time along the Sil valley.

On the way home we stopped in Luintra, the site of the first house we had fallen in love with in Galicia. Above the tree line at 650 metres, the

JUNE

hillsides here looked barren compared to our little valley, but we stopped at the café there and chatted to Brian.

We had first met Brian, an amiable Irishman, some five years earlier. We had called into the bar for a coffee whilst looking around the area. Brian had come over and asked, hesitantly, if we were British. I complemented him on his English, a rarity in these areas.

"Yes," he said. "I am from Dublin."

It turned out he had been living in Galicia for so many years that his English was more than a little rusty. His Galician born wife had to translate some English words for him.

Brian worked incredibly hard in the bar, opening at 7am and closing when the last customer left, sometimes after two the following morning. He told us that the previous year they had decided to go back to Ireland for a trip, their first in over 20 years. The flight was an early morning one so he had had to politely ask his customers if they would mind leaving by midnight so they had chance for some sleep. Although being a bar owner in the UK is hard work, it cannot compare to Galician hours.

§

The fortnight had rushed past as usual. On Mum's last Friday, we visited the Club Náutico near to the iron bridge again. The tapas were really *raciones* and came free with each drink. There was no choice, but it was fun waiting to see what we would get next and the setting, overlooking the river, was just perfect. S thought this might be a good place for his stag do.

Mum was off home on the Sunday. She apparently had a million things still to organise before she returned in August.

Before she left, one of our *Galego* friends invited us to supper at their house – a wonderfully warm and kind offer. I explained Mum didn't eat seafood or *pulpo* or ears, or all the other goodies *Galegos* love so much, but was assured it would be fine.

When we arrived, the table had been set around the old wood-burning range or *cocina*, thankfully now unlit. We made ourselves comfortable on the long benches behind the stove and I managed to translate most of what was going on, though I don't have the flair for simultaneous translation which our friend Gala has. (Nor, to be honest, any talent in that direction whatsoever.)

There was almost a diplomatic incident though.

Men in Galicia tend to be rather macho and have very set roles. Pepe, the husband, would drive the car, do the shopping, and collect the wine from the bodega below. Otherwise, he was generally waited on by the three womenfolk. Mum used to wait on Dad in a similar way.

On this occasion, Mum passed Pepe a platter of meats. She held the heavy platter for a while as he stared at it, making no move to help himself. Luckily, his wife intervened, taking a choice slice of meat and placing it on her husband's plate.

Mum said later, "I may have waited on your dad but I wouldn't go that far. He nearly got the plateful in his face."

This was not an idle threat. Mum can appear quiet but if she is annoyed, beware. As I say, luckily the incident was avoided.

In rural areas, traditional gender defined roles are more likely to be strictly adhered to. Women were responsible for looking after the home and children, the cooking and cleaning. They also helped in the fields, hoeing and gathering corn. Men would cut trees and collect firewood, and drive the heavy plough using the oxen – and in later years the tractor.

This is much as it was in middle England, where I grew up, in the 1970s.

JUNE

Mum briefly got a job as a dinner lady at the local infant school. She had to wait until I had moved up to junior school, but enjoyed her role. This left Dad, when he was on 'days' at the colliery, having to cook his own dinner. When I say cook, I mean reheat. Mum would leave his meal ready, with instructions on warming it up. One day Dad had the task of reheating the previous day's gravy in a pan to go with his meal. He admitted that the gravy had not worked out. He had not thought to add a touch of water to thin the sauce and had not enjoyed the solid lump of gravy on his dinner. Mum did not continue her job much longer after that.

This is not a complaint against Dad, or against Pepe. They were both a product of their times. Times which are changing.

When we first arrived in Galicia 13 years ago, our favourite bar was the haunt of elderly men, smoking, playing cards or dominoes, and chatting in groups. The only females, other than me, would be the ones serving behind the bar. The only time we saw the men's wives, were at fiestas.

I remember one day in the supermarket seeing an elderly gentleman who was often in the bar, and who always made a point of chatting to us... in French. As I was queuing behind him and his lovely diminutive wife at the till, I said *bonjour*. Immediately he shook his head, looking sideways at his wife who was busy packing away the shopping (men pay, women pack – another rule.) and pointing in a rather pantomime manner. I shrugged, thinking no more of his odd behaviour until his wife had gone to carry the heavy bags to the car (men drive, women carry the shopping).

He turned to me as she left and stage whispered, "*mi mujer.*"

That much I had guessed, though I still didn't understand why being with his wife (or literally his 'woman') meant he was unable to acknowledge me.

TOMATO, FIG & PUMPKIN JELLY

I'm still not really sure, although I have the oddest feeling it had something to do with the fact that I knew him from the bar.

After the smoking ban came into force here on 1st January 2011, women did begin to enter the bars. Nowadays, although numbers are still not evenly spread, I no longer feel like a lone female in a sea of males.

Not that I have ever felt unsafe in any bar here. At one time, S had begun Spanish lessons in another town. I would often walk into Taboada to wait for him in the bar. Inevitably, as soon as I sat down one of the elderly men would join me, buy me a wine, and act as chaperone until S appeared, whereupon he would gracefully retire knowing I was safe. It was sweet and old fashioned.

Once in town, on a particularly windy day, I got a speck of dirt in my eye. I wore contact lenses at the time and my eyes started to water instantly, trying to dislodge the foreign body. Unable to get it out, I ran for the car leaving S standing on the street. The sight of a female, in floods of tears, running from a male told an obvious story to one *Galego* chap. He came up to me asking if I was alright and glaring at poor S, who was slowly walking to the car. I managed to say '*polvo*', dust, and point to my eyes which were of course red and puffy by then. The man wandered off, his concern not entirely assuaged. Again sweet, but his disquiet has darker roots – that of *violencia machista.*

The *Observatorio Contra la Violencia Doméstica y Género* (Observatory against Domestic and Gender Violence) records that there were 3 577 known cases of gender violence in 2019 (to October), and one murder per week in Spain can be attributed to gender violence. In Galicia, there have been 64 deaths since 2003 (when records began), including two at the beginning of 2020. Some 5 000 cases are reported each year.

JUNE

A recent local campaign included adverts on TV, posters, and even a helpline number on the paper bags used to wrap our daily loaf. It couldn't have been comfortable for S to have to collect our bread.

In 2004, Spain set an example in Europe by establishing domestic violence courts. Figures for 2017 show that Spain has one of the lowest rates of death in the European Community from domestic and gender violence: 0.12 deaths per 100,000 females. There were 54 deaths that year compared to 70 in England and Wales, and 123 in France. (Eurostat and the UN office on Drugs and Crime statistics.)

I hope that Spain will continue to lead the way in its action against this 'hidden' crime.

Tuesday 15th June. Cloudy.
Dear Mum,
You can rest assured it is NOT you. We had rain yesterday and it is still cloudy, though warmer at least, so you cannot be the rain goddess!
I have managed to get one load of washing on... have about 3 to go. Lots of it seems to be from our visitor, I don't know how you get through so many clothes haha!
I had to have a baking session today as someone pinched our elevenses. We thought we would stop on the way back from the airport and eat our cake, but it wasn't there. S remembered a plastic tub in your hand luggage so the thief has been identified!! I hope you at least shared it with Aunty Jean. (And can I have my tub back in August please?)

TOMATO, FIG & PUMPKIN JELLY

Now, what did you say to Sarah (our white chicken) before you left? I hadn't collected any eggs on Sunday morning as Olive was on the nest. When we got back, Sarah was sitting on all the eggs and refusing to move. And she is still there! We have managed to swap some eggs around and have shut her in the top part, moving the others into the lower pen so they don't disturb her. I have put three of her own eggs under her but as she rarely lets Buzz have his wicked way with her they may not be fertile. We will see in three weeks.

We have made a start on fitting the new cocina from John and Fiona. We now have a big sooty hole where the old range was. S has got the whole front off. It is really just that: a cast iron front with a tin box welded on for the oven. And, on ours, the brass water boiler. I guess that would have been kept permanently topped up with water in the old days, though it has long since rusted through and the brass tap had sadly vanished before we moved in. I do think a kettle or three are a simpler option. Granddad's big stainless steel kettle is wonderful.

You should have seen the state of the lad by the time he had the whole thing outside, the ash emptied, and the fire grate out. He looked just like a sweep!

Unfortunately, despite being the same model, the new front doesn't quite line up

JUNE

with the existing holes for the ash and fire boxes. S is having to knock bits out and cement other bits up! He did manage to get all the marble surrounds off, except the final one which was stuck solid and cracked in half. I may have a marble pastry board instead! We will have to visit the marble place in Chantada to try and get a matching piece.

We did successfully get the old brass rail off the front of the range. We shall use that as a bannister up the steps, for elderly parents to use. Haha.

Had a film night yesterday to see what else was on the latest video (it's always fun seeing what you have taped!) We had half of an interesting documentary about the Ganges and two silly DIY programmes - one of which showed nothing of the eco-house they are building only who was being voted off-site (like I care). Oh, and half of an odd film with Debra Winger dashing about with Berbers on camels after her husband had died. Enjoyed our eclectic evening! Thank you xx

I shall go and post this. I can hear S knocking bits of the kitchen out so a good time to escape.

Love you tons and tons

Xxxxxxxx

PS did the tomato plants survive their trip?

Addendum: In Taboada. I just popped into the hotel. I told you how slapdash their *booking diary was. She just turns to a new page and writes names and dates. Anyway, being Miss organised I couldn't leave it like that. I had visions of double-booked rooms, so I carefully produced a lovely colour coded calendar page for her with all the guest names, the type of room, the number of nights they are staying, and the dates they are arriving and leaving blocked out across the page. The lady stared at it for ages before shoving it under the counter and asking the most important question for her… do they all speak Spanish?!! Can't say I didn't try.*

PPS No I'm not changing my name. I rather like the one I have!

Loads of love. Hurry back

xxxxxx

I had already decided I was going to keep my surname. I had been a Wright for 45 years, or as I liked to say, I was born Wright. And I couldn't imagine being anything else.

In fact, the problem never arose. In Spain one keeps one's birth name throughout life. The double barrelled Spanish surname consists of the father's and mother's first surnames. On marriage these names remain the same. You are still the son (or daughter) of X and Y. Only the resulting children have a different name, taking the first surname of each parent. Thus a Vasquez Blanco, and a Perez Rodriguez would have children with the surnames Vasquez Perez. I quite like this system. It keeps the female line going that bit longer than in England and does away with all that 'woman being the chattels of

JUNE

a man' bit which is implied by changing one's name (in my very humble opinion). It can however cause some interesting problems.

A married English couple, who I shall call Peter and Barbara, had a female Spanish friend. One day this friend asked Barbara if she thought Peter might go out with her. Barbara, unsurprisingly, was unsure how to answer this question so went for the direct approach.

"You do know we're married don't you?" she said.

Apparently not. I'm told the friend went a most interesting shade of red before apologising repeatedly. It turned out that, as they shared a surname, the Spanish friend had assumed they were siblings rather than man and wife. Another good reason to stay a Wright.

Diary Friday 18th June
Number One chicken not laying. Had a good look at her and vaselined her rear end for her. Neither she nor I enjoyed that really! Sarah is now on 7 eggs. Due 5th July.
S finished making an unholy mess in the kitchen, cleaned up, then began to cement the new stove in place. I continued knocking plaster off the outside north wall. It's only 5ft high there so shouldn't take long to mortar.
Vodka festival at the Club Náutico this evening, so toddled over after our swim and cheese butties. Not really much of a fiesta but we had four games of pool (S won 3-1... think I've lost my touch) and we had free queimada and Gecko brand vodkas. They are running a promotion for the Gecko brand which come in a multitude of flavours. The toffee one was particularly scrumptious!

Diary Monday 21st June
Up rather late again. Spent the morning cleaning the kitchen cupboards of cement dust and soot. S

raised the worktop height around the cocina by creating a brick surround infilled with cement.
Sarah only on 5 eggs?? Looked everywhere then found two crushed. Not fertile so maybe it was deliberate? Left her on the others.
To town for a drink. I was reading some story in La Voz about Charles and Camilla except the newspaper kept calling him by the Spanish Carlos. Odd that. I mean we call their king Juan Carlos not John Charles. Seems rude to me!!

The Spanish do like to Hispanicise (is that a word? What is the equivalent of Anglicise?) names. I was intrigued early on by the fact that the British queen is Isabella, her son Carlos, and her grandson Guillermo. Oddly Camilla is Camilla and Harry is Harry. I queried this once with a newspaper chap I met at the University when I did my CELTA course but was met with blank looks.

Maybe it's to do with the Spanish not having a huge reservoir of names to work from in the past.

The *Instituto Nacional de Estatística,* or National Statistics Institute, publishes data regarding the incidence of names in Spain and their evolution during the previous century.

In Lugo province, prior to the 1930s, the top three boys' names were Francisco, Ramón and José Maria. Carmen, Maria and Josefa took almost all the options for girls. That is almost half of all newborns being called Mary, Joseph or a combination of the two. (Maria José or José Maria works for girls and boys).

For the next five decades, Carmen, Maria and Josefa or some combination of the above such as Maria del Carmen, Maria José or Ana Maria took the top spots year after year. For boys it was Manuel, José, Antonio or a combination of these (José Antonio, José Manuel, José Luis) which gained parental approval.

JUNE

The biggest difference during this time was the relegation of Francisco to oblivion. As the article I read in *La Voz de Galicia* stated *"¿Cómo se llamaba el anterior jefe del Estado?"* What was the boss called during that time? That well known dictator, Francisco Franco of course.

Suddenly, with the demise of the said dictator in the late 1970s names began to show a change. The mother and father of Jesus dropped out of favour as more secular names became popular. The top names in Lugo province in the 1980s were Iván, Diego and Javier for boys and Lucía, Maria and Marta for girls. This trend for the more unusual names continued through the 2000s. In 2011 the top spot for boys went to Hugo - a name the Spanish pronounce with a silent H. Top Girls' names were Sara and Noa. José didn't even make the charts and Maria was demoted to seventh place behind the upstarts Carla and Claudia.

The biggest difference in the 2010s though was not just the less usual names but the diversification of the names. During the last few years the sheer variety of names registered in Lugo has rocketed. Where in the past there were only Marias and Josés, now we have Iker and Brais, Nerea and Antia.

Thursday 24th June 5pm. Far far too hot on the terrace, 28°C in shade

Dear Mum,

As it is much too warm to do anything outside, and I have finished my inside jobs (cleaning and sanding wood surrounds below the kitchen island and cleaning up the new brass pole on the stove front) S says I can sit and write to you!!

We were going to go for a drink on Tuesday but by the time we had packed up and watered it was after 9pm so we said we would go for an early one on Wednesday. We went into Bar Mencia first but it was a new girl on and she didn't seem at all happy so we went up to Bar Gema as we haven't been in for a bit. On the way there I saw a poster saying 'sardine festival 23rd June 9pm'. I had forgotten it was San Juan again. By the time we got to the bar we had established between us, with more or less certainty, that it was probably the 23rd that very day.

After a drink (and tapa) in Gema we wandered up the street counting bars (there are 12) then headed up to the square and a nice warming bonfire. There weren't many people when we arrived but the sardines were already cooking so we got in first! I think we managed three plates full (about 9 or 10 sardines) before retiring to watch the crowds. One chap had at least six platefuls to himself and was still going when we left. Quite impressive!

It was all quite orderly, despite the numbers, until the bacon started coming out then… scrum! S battled to reach some bread then pushed forward with his arms outstretched until some bacon was plonked onto the bread in his hands. Think rummage sale in England and you have an idea.

Of course we were already full of sardines but couldn't resist so we brought the bacon

JUNE

butties home and had toasted sandwiches for breakfast! We did leave before the queimada this year and, to S' disappointment, the sponge cake. Not that we would have had room for that either.

The mayor was at the 'do' taking pictures. We actually managed to talk to him on Tuesday. I was beginning to think he was a figment of our imagination. Mind you, it was the briefest interview I've ever had. We were told 28th August was fine then sent downstairs to talk to Manuel in the justice of the peace office. Good job we went in again as we had to sign to say we wanted the use of the Casa Cultura (the building next door to the library we are using for the wedding) not the registry office (which has space for two sitting and two standing, providing everyone is on close terms, so wouldn't have been much use).

Apparently we can have the room the day before to set up so that's all sorted. Tell brother he can get his suit dry cleaned now - it's a go!! I do hope the mayor has something other than his trademark jeans to wear for the occasion though!

I have asked friends to bring some potted plants if they have them, to brighten the place up, and Steve and Cris are going to do the music for us.

Had our first lot of peas off today, about a pound so that's not bad. Have frozen some and had pea, mint, shallot, and bacon risotto for lunch. They really are so much better than bought. I think my veg enjoyed the rain you brought with you so thank you! I have pulled the remaining 3 or 4 shallots the mole/vole thing didn't eat. Don't think I will bother next year unless I can do something about it.

Have had a good crop of blackcurrants this year. I have frozen some of those and made a pie and some muffins, which are scrummy. I may have to make more. Think blueberry muffin but with more flavour.

The allotment is looking very dry already in this heat. The tomatoes in pots up here are much bigger than the ones on the allotment this year, and the sunflowers are tiny... except S' prize specimen on the compost heap. Just goes to show we need more compost over there.

The chickens meanwhile are systematically pulling down and eating all the vine leaves, naughty things! Sarah is still sitting on five eggs.

This Sunday there is a car boot sale near to John and Mike. We said we would go along though we don't have anything to sell as we reuse most of our junk (and other people's). I thought about taking some muffins but they are so good we may just eat them instead!

The kitchen stove is more or less cemented in place now and S has been levelling the floor in there for me so I can continue my floor tiling. We have raised the worktop around the cocina a bit which will be better for us tall people (over five foot), but it is still low enough that I can easily do my mixing. The marble goes back on next. Hopefully by August it will be done!

Thursday 9pm. Must try that trick again. Watered about 8pm. Clouds rolled over, thunder, lightning, and then when I had finished watering, rain! Heavy but only 10 minutes. Still hot. About 23°C in the sunroom. Certainly don't need a fire now! Can't believe the difference a week makes.

Hope you bring good weather in August, even if just for the weekend. Still looking for a parasol for my outfit. Carmen has offered me some of her lovely roses for a bouquet though I wasn't planning on having one.
Love you tons and tons
Xxxxxx
PS This mountain of pots and pans is getting dangerously close to avalanche stage... where is my washer upper?
Pumpkin time, night night xxx

I remember a Swiss friend telling us that in Switzerland one has to prove a name is in general usage, or genuinely historical, if it is not in the approved book of names. No entire football teams or Blue Murder Johnsons there. I was also once told that that delightful dictator, Francisco Franco, insisted everyone had either Maria or José in their name to butter himself up to the church. I don't know if that piece of hearsay (or heresy) is true but the older generation certainly have a few of them.

When 80% of the population turn to look if you shout 'José!' in the street (try it, it's such fun), diminutives are common. José is often Pepe, Pepito or Pepiño. Manuel is Manolo or Cholo or Manny. Jesús is Suso or Chus if a girl.

In our tiny parish we have at least five Carmens. There is our wonderful neighbour Carmucha (much Carmen). I'm not sure why. Carmucha is a small lady (one of the many things I love about Galicia is that at five foot two inches tall I can actually gaze down on so many of my friends) though she has a big heart.

There is also a Carmina, a Carmencita and a Carmenita in ever decreasing size... of title. This causes confusions even amongst the locals.

One day Isabel, our lovely cheese lady, arrived hooting her horn as she spun in a cloud of dust. This is normal driving for most Spaniards so nothing to cause alarm.

"*Hola Isabel. Un queixo piquante por favor.*" We like the mildly spicy, paprika flavoured cheese from our local dairy Diqueixa – which, you may have gathered, delivers.

"*¿Carmen no está aqui?*"

"No, sorry, Carmen isn't here." It wasn't my fault that Carmen wasn't here on cheese day but I felt (and still do feel) that the English need to apologise for everything.

"She rang to ask for four cheeses as the family are coming," continued Isabel.

"Oh, okay, I'll take them if you like."

"Good, tell her I'll collect the money next time." And she was off like Michael Schumacher on a fast day.

I stored the cheeses in the cool and continued what I was doing. Three hours later Isabel was back.

"Do you still have the cheeses?"

"Of course, why?"

"They were for Carmen in the lower village."

JUNE

Another dust cloud settled over our sleepy hamlet as she vanished once more.

Shortly afterwards we passed through the lower village on the way to the swimming pool. Isabel was driving towards us. S prudently pulled to the side of the road to allow her to pass. Instead she stopped.

"*Hola* Isabel, did Carmen get the cheeses?"

"No! They were not for this Carmen. Will you take them?"

We took delivery of the cheeses once more and treated them to a trip to Chantada. They had had a frustrating day!

The next morning I took them over to Carmucha, our Carmen.

"I didn't order cheese," she said. "But I'll ring Carmen in the lower village, her family is here."

"No, Isabel tried that."

"Maybe Carmen in the upper village. I'll ask Sonia to call in."

Later I saw Carmucha again. I asked about the cheeses. I was starting to feel like a foster parent for these soft round dairy delights.

"We tried the upper village, they weren't for Carmen there. But," she continued seeing my face fall. "They were for Carmen here, at number one."

As I wandered back, pleased my little orphans had found a home, I wondered briefly if telling Isabel on the 'phone that it was Carmen at number one who wanted them when the cheeses were ordered would have saved a lot of effort. But no, that would be far too simple.

Tuesday 29th June. V v hot
Dear Mum,
Thanks for your parcel. Tried the spatula today. It was quite good. A bit narrow for picking up tortilla, but thinner than the one we have.

S thanks Aunty Jean for the glasses case, we will try not to lose this one!

Sunday was John's boot sale. There were about 12 stalls and it was quite enjoyable. I made two dozen muffins and put them on a tray with a cord round my neck so I could wander about. I sold the lot at 50c each. Not sure I made a profit but good fun. We all went for lunch after, at a restaurant opposite.

The England-Germany football was on so we stayed to watch. Anne and I cheered when England lost. Not very patriotic are we?

We called at Jorge and Kath's on the way home to collect some more donkey muck so it was 9pm when we got home.

We have two of the pieces of marble worktop stuck on in the kitchen. Need to order a new piece for the far end on Friday. I have been tiling the floor. It is starting to look rather smart. I will be glad to be able to move the hob back indoors away from all the flies on the terrace!

Wednesday. Still red hot.

Sarah only has four eggs now. She must have Doc Martins on this year or is jumping about too much! They should start hatching next week.

The other chickens are failing dismally to keep the nettles and brambles at bay in there. Had to go in with secateurs and gloves yesterday to clear a path to the gate!

JUNE

Nasty with a short sleeved vest on! The hens enjoyed following me around giving advice! Love you tons
Xxxxxxxxxx

PS Aunty Jan will be pleasantly surprised at our tapas here at that price for a dish of olives! Must tell Luisa... then again, better not. My free albóndigas tapa would be a good eight quid I reckon! I told you Belle had agreed to be my best woman didn't I? So long as she doesn't have to wear layers of peach tulle and satin haha.

PPS Oh, funny story. I was in the chicken pen today looking for hidden eggs when I heard the cows coming by, and shouting. I didn't take much notice until I heard louder shouting and glimpsed Mr Grumpy running into our garden. A cow had wandered the wrong way. Mr Grumpy had a big stick and was not at all happy. The cow meanwhile was quite enjoying looking round at all the interesting weeds in our garden. Then she wandered straight into our Long Barn. Our poor neighbour was nearly apoplectic and I couldn't stop giggling. He must've heard me because he glared in my direction before shooing the poor cow back onto the lane... after chasing her round the barn three times!!!

Belle is not my niece's real name, but it is what we have always called her. And it suits my beautiful niece so well. Mr Grumpy is also not our neighbour's real name.

TOMATO, FIG & PUMPKIN JELLY

When we first arrived at *A Casa do Campo*, we tried to persuade Mr Grumpy to take the grass off my allotment-to-be. His '¡*No!*' was really quite grumpy and so the name stuck. In fairness to our helpful and kind neighbour I feel I have to state for the record that he is not grumpy at all. He always greets us with a hearty '*buenos dias*' but has what I call a Galician facial expression: a sort of frown, as of one peering closely as at an unknown specimen in a jar, willing to be convinced that it is harmless, but not about to be the first to test it.

This is normal for most *Galegos*. They are open and friendly people but you have to earn their trust and loyalty. The day Mr Grumpy, as he continues to be known in our very small circle, told me I was doing a good job of the mortaring was a day I will remember with pride for the rest of my life. Mum swears he smiled at her once, but then she does have a very vivid imagination.

JULY
Thermals in summer

Summer seemed to arrive on the stroke of July that year. It was hot and humid. Outdoor work was carried out during the occasionally misty mornings then suspended until dusk. The daylight hours were spent doing indoor jobs. Luckily, we had plenty of those to keep us busy

Monday 5th July 9.30pm. Very hot
Dear Mum,
  Another week of no rain. It poured in Chantada on Friday night but when we got home it was bone dry here.
  We have spent the afternoon trying to put the kitchen base units together. So far we have found one foot missing (that was the first pack we opened), and two of the three drawer fronts are the wrong size. Great! Don't know when we will get to Santiago again to change them. The kitchen therefore will NOT be finished for our visitors. You will have to imagine it instead. So frustrating!
  We have also had fun with the worktops for the cocina surround. As you know one piece

of the old marble broke. We went to the marble place to match it. The girl is very friendly and said she would give us a quote. The white marble, like the original tops, is very expensive because it is used for headstones. It is also very soft. The quote was 150€.

She then priced up for all three pieces of worktop in a local black and white granite and it was the same price. So for 150€ we get all new, properly finished, very smart and tougher worktops. The downside is that S had already cemented the two pieces of marble on, so more work to remove them. Oh well!

We think Sarah is sitting on a duff batch of eggs. They were due to hatch today but I found yet another broken one... no chick, just yolk. She has three eggs left but doesn't look a happy girl. Anne, fount of all knowledge about chickens, tells me that thunderstorms during the first week of brooding will addle the eggs. We did have all those thunderstorms the first week she was sitting, though surely that can't affect an egg... can it?

We went out to lunch on Saturday to Kath and Jorge who we met at Monterroso and at the rastrillo. Kath was brought up on Tenerife so of course her Spanish is impeccable. She has agreed to translate the wedding for the English contingent, as I don't think our mayor speaks much English.

JULY

She is also a fabulous cook and we had the most wonderful lunch at their house. Met lots of new people including a bear of a Galician chap who came dressed in a kilt (Galicia being one of the Celtic nations). He is very loud and jolly and rather uninhibited. He told me, very stridently, that I had the best breasts in Taboada! Not sure of the correct response to that 'compliment'!

It's getting to party time again now it's officially summer. This weekend is the Celtic folk festival in Ortigueira. Richard is driving up so we will make good time. He said our car was too slow. Cheek!

The weekend after is S' birthday. Anne is having a BBQ as it is their helper's birthday the same day. On the 8th August we have another car boot sale. Oh yes, and we thought we might have a party of our own at the end of August! Then it will be autumn again.

Wednesday 8.30pm. Sticky hot. Thermometer has reached the magical 30°C on the terrace (in the shade). The chickens are all walking about with their wings out to cool down. Not that they are bright enough to just go into the shade for a bit! Poor Sarah must be literally roasting in the hen house all day. She won't come off the nest, even though nothing has hatched.

Thankfully the rest of the kitchen units went together successfully, if not easily. Why do they have to make the hinges and everything so complicated and all the instructions in totally useless pictures you can't even see without a magnifying glass. So we are 'just' missing one leg and a pair of drawers. (Oh that sounds funny!)

S is sorting the electrics for the fridge so we can move it into the kitchen, and then we can look at fitting the wooden worktop, that he had fun collecting in March.

I am still tiling the floor. Unfortunately the bit behind the cocina works out at just less than three tiles wide so that's a full one in the middle and cut ones on each side all the way along. Pleased the lad has his angle grinder.

I have pulled my red onions up as they have flopped now. Very small sadly. I think they need lots more water. Anne says she waters twice a week but leaves the leaky hose on all night.

If I did that I would drain the 1000L tank twice over! Still, we are not short of land and small ones are tastier (so S tells me!) so I will just grow more.

Had a bumper crop of peas, and the peapods are flowering again. The broad beans have done well (eventually) but the shallots all vanished thanks to the monster. I have left some leeks in the root trainer pots to save them from being nibbled. May have to move on to large concrete walled raised beds with barbed wire tops next!

JULY

The French beans are flowering as are the runner beans, though the latter are not setting again despite watering. Maybe the bees don't like red? Mind you they love my giant (narcotic) poppies. The noise they make when you go near. Wonder if the honey will be narcotic too? Oops I can see the police raiding us!

Will post this tomorrow.
With all our love and see you soon
Xx
PS Just been texted for another party! 16th July so that's two that weekend.
PPS A little bird tells me there is another birthday on 14th July… who could that be?

July is birthday month in our house, with Mum and S having a birthday within four days of each other. In Galicia, July and August are *the* party months both amongst the international community and for *Galegos* themselves. It goes without saying that we enjoy the summer here.

Thursday 8th July
Woke to thunder in the early hours, no rain to accompany the noise though.
Finished putting the kitchen units together – other than the two missing drawers and the missing leg, leaving one unit sadly lop sided and toothless.
Lunch: Mixed grill of liver, kidney, sausage, egg, chips and our 'baked' beans.
S brought his grass in to dry as Jayne rang with a storm warning. They had hailstones the size of golf balls (she sent me a photo) which punched holes in the guttering. I stood on the terrace as the sky got darker and the lightning flashed around the valley and the thunder echoed, completely naked

enjoying the coolness of the breeze. As for rain...zilch!
Sarah still sitting on the nest.

Poor Sarah was determined to hatch some chicks. On the Friday I saw our neighbour Carmen and asked if she had any eggs I could put under our broody hen. She told me that she no longer had a cockerel after the vicious one met its end (even minus a head it had leapt over my allotment wall and tried to escape again.) but she would ask her sister. A while later she reappeared with six eggs which we popped under the patient Wyandotte.

On Sunday, Spain were playing the Netherlands in the FIFA World Cup final. Although neither of us follow football we felt we ought to be in our local bar to cheer on our adopted country. Us and the entire population of Taboada it seemed. Bar Scala was crammed, but the atmosphere was not one of great excitement. Some chairs had been drawn up in front of the large screen TV whilst games of dominoes and cards progressed on the outskirts. I was pleased to see our local priest was there and waved to him to pray for the Spanish side. He grinned and put his hands together in supplication. I can't help but feel that if all priests at home were like Don Pepe I may have erred toward religion after all.

Once the game began, the noise level rose as decisions were queried. As the match went into extra time the atmosphere became strained, and when Spain scored just four minutes before the end of extra time there was a huge cheer. The last minutes counted down slowly but the wine flowed, and the bacon sandwiches kept us going until the final whistle.

There was a ragged cheer before the serious business of cards and dominoes recommenced. Luis brought out bottles of cava to share with customers.

JULY

I helped distribute glasses of bubbly, but at least half of the card players declined. I felt like shouting 'but Spain won, and it's free!' We gamely helped finish the free bubbly before making our way home in the silence of a Taboadan evening.

Diary Tuesday 13th July Hot
No water last night. S opened up the switch to the electric pump this morning and found it full of small beetles. Obviously a good place to hide out but they had caused the switch to insulate itself. He cleared it out and reset the switch.
One of Brown Bunny's babies, a beautiful black rabbit, seems to be a girl so we decided to keep her for breeding.

Wednesday 14th July 9.30pm. Drizzled after I sang 'happy birthday to you' this morning but sadly not for long haha!
Dear Mum,
Top of my shopping list, new writing pad. Apologies for the paper, I had to raid the cupboard!
Hope you had a lovely birthday and liked your card. I did tell the postman the card was very important as it was for my mother's birthday. Did you get the letter too? I sent it separately.
We had a good time at Cris and Steve's. Richard drove, and actually followed S' instructions (he tends to do his own thing generally). It was only 1 hour 40 as the new motorway is open as far as the 'windmill' road now. We had a lovely seafood lunch at a bar on one of the beaches then a wander

along the beach. It was quite busy being a weekend with lots of people playing football. Steve and Cris didn't go to the festival but Steve volunteered to drive us there. It was enjoyable but very busy. A lot of people had had rather too much to drink, though there was no trouble. We finally gave up around 3am and 'dad' came and picked us up!

In the morning, Steve took us a ride to another lovely beach and the lighthouse at Cabo de Ortegal while Cris made us a super lunch. We left about 5pm. They are both coming to the wedding and bringing music, which they have downloaded, for both the ceremony and the party later.

We enjoyed watching the big match at Scala. They have decided that we are mascots. We had 3 vinos and a glass of champagne. I swear I floated home!

My courgettes are doing well this year, as are the squashes/pumpkins (though I have no idea what anything is as we mixed them up somehow between growing, potting up and planting). It's exciting seeing what the fruits look like! All the fruit trees are loaded too. This morning the Victoria plum tree cracked with the weight of plums. We had been enjoying our tea break when it went. Ever so loud!

Sarah is still sitting on her nine eggs. Three of ours and six from Carmen's sister. Some of those eggs are huge, I don't know how our little Wyandotte can sit on them

JULY

all. I wonder if she thinks they are taking a while to hatch or if chickens don't view time in the same way? (Or think at all?) These are due at the beginning of August. She deserves some babies for sheer patience.

S cut the last of the floor tiles today and amazingly they all seem to join up behind the stove. I AM impressed at myself!!

We also managed to carry one of the 8ft long wooden worktops in today and put it in place on top of the base cupboards. Boy is it heavy! It's not yet fastened or finished but it makes it look like a proper kitchen with the wall units above and the (unfinished) base units below.

S has also cut one of the old pieces of marble to fit into the cubbyhole in the kitchen. I remember the day we viewed the house - that cubbyhole was so mouldy and damp, with one door hanging off and the other propped up on the floor below. Looks a bit different now (as does rather a lot of the house thankfully). I will put my Clarice Cliff plates in there I think, once I've plastered the back wall.

We have moved the fridge into the kitchen. This means I now keep going into the storeroom and opening the freezer to get the milk out. I suppose I will get used to it eventually.

We also now have no door on the sunroom to be. As I said on the 'phone, I think we will be keeping the old wooden door after all! I *have started to clean it up. More jobs to finish before the end of August!*

We are out partying on Friday and again on Sunday (for the lad's birthday) so I will ring you on Saturday evening

We are watching Ashes to Ashes tonight. Had Dr Who last week – good stories but I'm not keen on the new doctor, Matt Smith.
Love you tons and tons
xxxxxxxxxxxxx
Happy birthday again...79. Wow!

We had thought that a glass door to the sunroom-to-be would let more light into the darker central living area. Unsurprisingly, given our record with window people, no quote was ever forthcoming from either firm we contacted. I had chased them both half-heartedly a couple of times – then we went to a glass place in Lugo. In the showroom they had exactly the door we wanted: one huge sheet of etched glass with no surround, just discreet hinges in a satin steel finish. Its price tag? Eight hundred euros.

Time to rethink.

After three years that ugly old door was starting to grow on us. We went from '*we are definitely getting rid of that monstrosity*' to '*well, maybe we could do something with it.*' The price tag of the alternative helped. We sat down and looked at what we disliked about the door... It hinged on the wrong side for a start, opening into the room so you had to do a dance around it when the sofa was in position. Then there was the peeling off-white paintwork and the woodwormy panels, the cracked bubble glass and the wooden cat flap.

Actually I rather liked the cat flap, it told a story. And the paint would come off with some sanding and elbow grease. Now we came to look at it, there was only one woodwormy panel: the end one had been replaced at some point with a cheap pine board. The rest were solid, sweet chestnut. S could replace the rotten one from our stockpile of wood. And, if we removed the two cracked pieces of glass and the narrow fillet between, we could fit a large, double glazed unit in there allowing the light to pour in to the hall from the sunroom. We would also keep just a little more of the history of the house.

That ugly old door is now my pride and joy. We cleaned it and repaired it. S rehinged it so it opened against the wall instead of into the room. He found a heavy iron handle from another old door. He even kept that wooden cat flap and the oddly carved figures in the wood. The new glass has an etching in the corner and the sun shines through it.

It looks perfect.

Diary Friday 16th July Hot at home
S propped up the cracked plum tree. I made chocolate fudge topping for someone's birthday cake.
Called for fuel on the way to the party. Got to the top of town before we realised neither of us had paid for said fuel! As we screeched to a halt back on the forecourt, Luis was standing, hands on hips, laughing at us. I was mortified, but he said he knew we would come back. Thank goodness for Galicia. Sure we would be in jail now in England!
Enjoyed the first of our weekend parties. Home 11.30pm

It was also S' birthday that weekend and we had been invited by Anne and Simon to a barbecue at their house, our 'other' choice house out beyond Lugo on the Madrid road.

The year before had been a 'big' birthday for my beloved. We had been at Ortigueira for the festival again when his brother rang to say they were coming over for his 60th birthday… for two weeks!

If we were going to have visitors, I decided we may as well have a party. I started on my preparations, totally ignoring S' pleas for no fuss. We collected Bob and Glenis on the Friday, stopping for supplies at a supermarket in Santiago on our way home. Once I had explained my plan to Glenis she was more than happy to help prepare everything.

Back at home Glenis and I made a casserole dish full of dolmades using our own fresh vine leaves, bowls full of dips, and the obligatory jellies. I still maintain you can't have a party without jelly!

My plan was to light our outside oven or *horno* and make pizzas to feed the masses.

S and his brother spent the morning collecting firewood and lighting the fire. This was so much more fun than a simple barbecue. Our stone bread oven is four feet across and three feet high in a domed shape. At the front is an opening with a thick metal 'door' to place in front. Below is a space for ashes to be raked out.

The lads lit the fire and fed it piece after piece of wood. They were enjoying themselves so much that by the time people started to arrive for the festivities, we were already getting low on brushwood.

Glenis and I, with the help of most of the females from the 23 strong group of party goers, spent our time in the kitchen, shaping pizzas and arranging toppings whilst the men tended the fire and drank beer.

A Californian relative of one of our friends wandered into the kitchen, momentarily bored with the male company. S said he came back outside quite excited.

"The girls are having a ball in there, they have nibbles and everything!" He shouted.

Our 'nibbles' were the pizza toppings but yes, we were having a ball.

JULY

Sadly, despite the boys' best efforts, the *horno* had cooled too much to cook all our pizzas so the tail end had to be done in the oven. But the day was a success and Bob declared the pizzas to be the best he had ever tasted. Praise indeed!

Monday 19th July. Extremely warm
Dear Mum,
Thought the weather had changed this morning, cloudy and pleasantly cool. But just as I decided to go on the allotment to do some digging, the sun came out in all its glory!

I am making a collection of pumpkins and marrows at the moment. I seem to have quite a mixture of colours, shapes and sizes. They are piled artfully on the terrace.

Last night I was just going to bed when there was the biggest rumble. It wasn't thunder as the sky was clear. S said it was a low flying aeroplane but a few moments later it did it again. I have just rung Kath, and she asked if we were okay after the earthquake! Apparently it was centred on Taboada and registered 3.5 on the Richter scale. Their dogs were going mad trying to get them out of the house.

We are going to the hot springs in Ourense tomorrow 'en masse'. Jorge is taking his minibus, and Mike and John are showing us the way. Hopefully we will learn the route so we can take you three ladies in September.

TOMATO, FIG & PUMPKIN JELLY

Anne had done a fabulous spread for the 'birthday' party on Sunday. She asked people to bring dips and cheeses but had obviously bought tons herself. Poor Simon had been running round all day setting up tables, sorting the BBQ and making dips (Anne's leg was playing up so she had gone to bed leaving him instructions.) There were over 20 people there. Very enjoyable and very hot. We were under the barn overhang which was in the shade but as it's a tin roof it was radiating the heat downwards on to us. I was still sweating when we left after 10pm!

Weds: Had a lovely day yesterday at the thermals. Mike managed to direct us back and forwards over the river... very complicated. It is a lovely setting with shallow stone pools of different temperatures set in a grassy 'park' alongside the river Miño. There are some private pools you have to pay for but, being Galicia, the public ones are free. It's like sitting in a big hot bath. Very relaxing. Will definitely have to take you, though we may need to invite Mike to show us the way again!

Kath did us supper when we got back while S shovelled more donkey muck for our compost.

Sadly we brought a car full of flies back with us too. The muck was a bit fresh so we had to drive back with the windows open and our eyes stinging!

JULY

We did manage to get the last piece of granite onto the cocina surround in between socialising. It looks very smart.

Thursday. That was a nice surprise, I got your letter today. I'm glad you liked the rose petals, I meant to ask if they were still scented when your birthday card arrived. They were from the pink rambler which is growing wild under the walnut tree. The perfume is incredible so I'm pleased it lasted for you.

CJ says his op looks like being mid to late August which is great for him but means he may miss the wedding sadly.

I am compiling a list of things people can bring between them in August. So far I have: two jars basic peanut butter (crunchy); Yorkshire tea (for those with hand luggage only); a packet of lemon grass from Tesco, as it will apparently grow if put in water; and 3 packs of Tesco tampons (regular).

What a mixture eh?

Off to watch the last Ashes to Ashes. Hope you got it all or you may hear the mutters all the way across the sea.

Love you tons and tons

Xxxxxxx

…did you hear the rude words? Thought it was odd that the last episode was only a half hour long. We will never know the end now! If anyone happens to have all of it, it would be nice to know if she got back.

Carry on taping, we love you anyway! Xxxx

TOMATO, FIG & PUMPKIN JELLY

This was the first time we had been to the thermal springs in Ourense, though we were to visit them many times afterwards.

Ourense is a city of bridges. From the futurist looking Millennium bridge, with far reaching views from its highest walkways, to the ancient stone Roman bridge (Ponte Vella, or old bridge), and from the tall stone Ponte Nova (new bridge, built in 1918) to the pedestrian only Pasarela de Outariz, near to the hot water pools, each one is different.

There are eleven bridges in total crossing the river Miño in Ourense, and I think we crossed and re-crossed every one of them that day, following Mike on a complex and convoluted route to the thermal pools at Outariz.

The river Miño lies along one of the fault systems of the Iberian Massif. The northwest trending fault system here is permeable, allowing rain to seep through the fractured granite to some several kilometres deep. Far below the surface, the water is heated and forced back to the surface under pressure, acquiring many of the mineral properties of the rocks on its way to heat the some 70 thermal springs which litter the Miño valley.

Our fairly frequent, but thankfully minor, earthquakes are due to the movement of the various tectonic zones of the Iberian Massif and are often centred on the river Miño. The presence of bubbling, mineralised, sulphurous, and slightly radioactive, hot water which forces its way to the surface at 75°C is another, rather more pleasant, manifestation of the fault system.

Ourense is the third most populous city in Galicia with 110,000 inhabitants (I know, I know, massive.) It is also the capital of the province which shares its name: the only one of the four Galician provinces without a maritime coastline. Despite this, Ourense is known as the city of water. The Romans called it aquae urente (hot water) or aquis auriensis (golden waters) for the local gold and the hot water springs.

The modern city of Ourense sits along the confluences of the river Miño and its smaller tributaries the Loña and the Barbaño, in a basin formed by the action of the rivers themselves: actions which also left behind many rocks, still used to pave the streets in the old town.

Due to its topography, Ourense has one of the most extreme climates in the whole of Galicia. In summer the intense heat and humidity are energy sapping whilst in winter the all-consuming fog can remain for days, with the city shivering beneath its cold blanket embrace. Often, driving down to Ourense, we would leave the sunshine behind at the village of Cambios and descend into greyness. Oddly, bananas and lemons seem to thrive in Ourense, near to the river at Reza, where the heat from the thermal springs warms the area.

Despite its weather, Ourense is a lively and well-dressed town, with many clothes shops, eateries and a lively student population due to the University campus here. The Rua Paseo has many big name clothes shops and the Plaza Mayor is a great place to hang out with a *café solo*, a waffle, or an ice cream.

There are many myths and legends about the founding of Ourense. What is known for certain is that the Ourense basin was a crossroads from early Neolithic times and there was a primitive settlement at what is now the thermal springs at As Burgas Abaixo, close to the city centre.

A Roman era carved stone proclaims the legend of Calpurnia Abana Aeboso who, a thousand years previously: "*completed with thanks, the vow that she had made through the inspiration of a dream to the nymphs of these waters.*" (My translation). This is the first known documentation of the area which became the city of Ourense.

TOMATO, FIG & PUMPKIN JELLY

The fountain now situated at As Burgas Abaixo was built in the 19th century by the architect Trillo. But the Romans are known to have used the springs here. In the first century AD they built a stone bridge, the Ponte Vella, at a strategic point on the river to both control the area and facilitate access to the thermal waters at As Burgas.

The mineral rich water at the fountain pours in a constant stream of 300 litres a minute and at 67°C. It is said to be particularly good for skin conditions. The high temperature also means I have personally seen a number of visitors coming away with a burnt skin condition after putting their hand directly, and inadvisably, into the flow.

The Romans enjoyed thermal waters and often built their cities near to hot springs. The Roman spa we tried to visit in Lugo some years earlier was one such, but in Ourense the art of hot water bathing has been taken to new heights.

In 2007, Ourense was proclaimed the thermal capital of Galicia: the second major thermal area in Europe after Budapest, with a flow rate of three million litres a day. In 2009, it became one of the founding members of the European Association of Historic Thermal Cities. The city council has developed the area along the north bank of the river Miño into a string of mainly free thermal baths for the use of residents and visitors alike.

These pools sit at points along a well-maintained pathway, A Rota das Termas (The Thermal Route), a 14 kilometre pleasant, pedestrian loop along the north and south side of the river. Our favourite walk involves doing half the loop then stopping for a huge lunch at an Italian restaurant, Romantica, near to the Ponte Nova, before wobbling the last few kilometres to the car park and a relax in the thermal pools at Outariz. There is also the option of a small road train which drives from Outariz into the city centre in time for lunch.

JULY

Nearest to the city are the pools at Chavasqueira. Three tiny stone lined hot water pools sit near to the edge of the river, making this a cosy place to sit and enjoy the warmth. A little way further along the paved walkway there is a small fountain O Tinteiro (the dyers) where people are often found soaking their feet in the mineral rich waters. The pools at Muiño da Veiga are grouped around a restored water mill or Muiño and are the first to flood after heavy rains.

The largest of the free pools are at Outariz and Canedo where pools of differing temperatures are controlled by the judicious use of a stone to channel water in one direction or another. All of the pools are built of granite and slate, providing a comfortable place to sit and contemplate the beauty of the Miño valley.

There is even one part of the actual river Miño where water bubbles out at over 70°C. It is odd to see the river steaming in the chill of an evening, though not so funny if one walks into the river here.

If I sound like a tour guide at this point it's because sitting, contemplating the beauty of Galicia is something I do frequently, and to do so in a warm, bath-like pool is close to paradise. We usually take the 40 minute trip to Ourense in winter. There is something extremely satisfying about soaking in hot water watching the steam mingle with the mist overhead, then keeping warm long enough to get dressed and glowing all the way home. We really didn't need our thermals in summer though.

Diary Thursday 22nd July Hot. Black clouds, no rain Posted Mum's letter while S stacked firewood. Good summer job! Still, we need it dry for winter.
Plastered inside the new cubbyhole. Nice and bright now.
Lunch: Stuffed squash with rice, cheese, beetroot and onion. Very tasty.

TOMATO, FIG & PUMPKIN JELLY

Black bunny found humping mummy rabbit so not a girl then? Dispatched forthwith.

Wednesday 28*th* July. Ridiculously hot and very dry and brown... the grass that is, and me!

Dear Mum,

And no rain forecast this week either. That will be NO rain at all in July this year despite the thunder and lightning. Oh well, we are getting good tans, despite hiding indoors as much as possible.

The heat means the kitchen is coming on as it's nice and cool in there. All the granite tops are on and I have plastered the front and sides of the central unit around the cocina. Just the back to go. My arms ache.

S has cut the pieces of floor tiles we had left to make a very neat upstand around the walls. The wooden worktop/draining board for either side of the sink is cut and varnished. We need some wooden edging now so I can tile the walls. S has the electrics to finish and a lid to make for the base of the chimney (the rodding plate which the chimney 'experts' broke the first year we were here). Then we just need the correct drawers from Leroy Merlin and our missing leg. Oh, and a new electric cooker for summer use.

S cut his hair today in preparation for the big day. He was also my 'hero' last week when I managed to pop one of my contact lenses out whilst mowing the back lawn. I

JULY

couldn't see it anywhere but we did a fingertip search and old eagle blue eyes found it. Phew! Thought I would have to get wed winking haha.

Sarah is still sitting on her eggs. She must be keeping them cool rather than warm I would think. We will see this weekend if any hatch.

Despite that branch splitting, our plums are starting to ripen. Propping it up must have worked. Reckon the figs will be ready for our wedding guests to enjoy too. The tree is loaded (if we can keep the blackbirds off!).

Also have lots and lots of French beans. The ones I sowed late have caught up with the early ones so they are all ready together. I think the leaky hose in that bed is helping though I'm in two minds about the mulching. It keeps in the moisture but also is a perfect hiding spot for the slugs and for the beast... The runner beans are also setting well now. There should be some of those for you to try. I can't give the marrows away! I did give Dasha, the lady we met at the swimming baths, one yesterday. She visited with her two boys. The youngest was fascinated by the chickens. At first he was throwing stones for them to 'eat' but once S showed him that they liked grass he was stuffing it through the mesh as quick as his little hands could. Her eldest sat cuddling the marrow in the car!

TOMATO, FIG & PUMPKIN JELLY

Why can't you find shoes? What about those green summer canvas ones you bought here? They would look okay and I can clean them for you.

Just watched one of your films... Ian McKellen and Lynn Redgrave. Very good, and taped all through - mind you it was 1H 39 and you have written that the second film is 1H 45 on a 3 hour tape, so I think we might have a problem! I suggested to S that we fast forward to see if the end is missing on the second one but he says that spoils the surprise and anyway he enjoys making up the endings. We shall let you know next Wednesday night.

Thursday: Hot already at 9.30am.

STOP PRESS: Went to see Sarah this morning and I heard a squeak. I was going to look closer but I swear she growled at me. Looks like we may have chicks.

Love you tons and tons
See you in a month.
Xxx
PS. Richard has agreed to collect a cooker from the UK for us. I saw a Hotpoint one I like online so providing they can do the bottled gas conversion kit I will order it.

Although I love my *cocina*, in the heat of a Galician summer it is impossible to keep it lit. By May, I am sweating in my lovely kitchen and wishing it was off. This meant that we needed a cooker for the summer months. I wanted an electric double oven and a gas hob but had failed to find anything suitable here.

JULY

There were no double ovens, the quality was poor, with no insulation, and there were no mixed fuel stoves to be seen. Sadly, I decided this was one occasion when I had to resort to the good old UK.

Diary Friday 30th July Very hot again
S cleared the top of the driveway for the next load of gravel. It is looking very smart.
I laid the pre-cut tiles onto the metal plate S made to cover the rodding hole in the kitchen floor. Once in place it should match the rest of the tiling and be invisible.
Bathnight. Bought wood edging for around the wooden worktop plus red gloss paint for around the cocina, on the way to the swimming baths.
2 vinos 1€.
Sarah has at least four chicks.

Diary Saturday 31st July Hot
That's it! No significant rain in July.
Figs starting to ripen. They are the most delicious things I've ever eaten, now I know they have to be really soft and ripe. Augusta told us off for picking them too early last year as Jen had told us to pick them while they were woolly inside. No, you wait until they start to sag off the tree then stand, preferably naked in a bath, to suck the honey sweet juice out. Scrummy!
Five chicks hatched. Poor Sarah, she has spent the best part of two months brooding eggs so I'm pleased she has something to show for it at last.

AUGUST
Consiento

It was finally August and our wedding was fast approaching. Despite all that Spanish bureaucracy could throw at us we had made it - almost.

Monday 2nd August. Quite windy and occasional bits of cloud but no rain forecast all week again.

Dear Mum,

  We had a lovely picnic and lazy afternoon down at the swimming pools and river at Monterroso yesterday. Mike and a couple of youngsters even braved the river for a swim. Mike said they had to crack the ice to get in but I'm (reasonably) sure it wasn't that bad, though thermal spa it wasn't.

  Looks like we have two campers for the end of month party. Graham (who you still haven't met) and Steve are camping out on our first tee for the duration of the festivities. We had better get the tent out and check it's not rotted.

  The kitchen is coming on. I started tiling the wall today. My cockerel tiles look good. S has cemented the backs of the electrical

AUGUST

sockets into the wall. They will look much neater than the ugly external boxes the electricians put on. The big island unit around the cocina is all plastered and I have the paint for it. Same colour as our external doors. The burgundy matches the new tiles lovely, and I am going to use it for the kitchen door too. We have also ordered the new dual-fuel cooker. Richard will collect it in the autumn from the UK.

The lad has finished gravelling the top part of the driveway, and we have bought some more floor tiles for the 'horno' eating area (same as the indoor ones). Will try to get that done next.

Anne is coming for an inspection tomorrow so we will have to have a quick tidy round. She is bringing Lauren - the girl who walked past our loo when it was hiding behind the sofa in the living room all that time ago! She should see a difference.

Sarah has five beautiful chicks. Two brown, one of which has a black Mohican stripe and three paler/white ones. Yesterday one must have fell out of the doorway and couldn't find its way back up the ramp so I had to lift it in... Sarah didn't like that one bit. Today they were all out but again couldn't find their way back up. This time I sent S, as Sarah likes him better than me. She flew at him as he popped them all back inside. 'I only put them to bed!' he shouted at her. Brave lad! The other chickens are

TOMATO, FIG & PUMPKIN JELLY

skirting around the pen very warily even though she is shut in.

I have a set of steps full of marrows and pumpkins up to the utility room. Must find a few more recipes other than stuffing and pickling! They look very pretty drying. Sadly most of them are not that tasty, though I have a couple of butternut squash coming on and a record sized orange pumpkin.

The chickens like them roasted and split in two.

Tomorrow's lunch for our guests will have to include squash/marrow, french beans (100s of) and plums… of course. I have made a plum tart already.

Tuesday. Scorcher! Bit of wet would be useful for the veg.

Well, we got the royal seal of approval for the kitchen. Anne said it was perfect. And Lauren, who hadn't been for two years, was amazed at the differences. She said we hadn't even done the guest bedroom or the bathroom (and of course the loo was still in the living room.)

We had pork casserole with butternut squash and plums in it, with rice and french beans for lunch and a plum tart. The tart was huge but it all disappeared. There were seven of us altogether. S had put the big trestle table on the terrace. It all looked very nice.

Do you have shoes yet? If not it will have to be the wellies!

AUGUST

Wednesday: Still hot and muggy. Maybe thunderstorm due?

Sarah is doing a fine job with her brood. They are managing to get up the ramp to bed themselves now. We caught some crickets earlier which they enjoyed, but when S accidentally dropped his catching tub Sarah flew at it in a temper. She is so protective. The one with the black Mohican stripe is very independent so I think it is a boy.

Had the first of our tomatoes yesterday. It's so nice having fresh tomatoes after so long. Though I'd rather wait than buy tasteless supermarket ones. And it's nice having things seasonally. I was looking at a Christmas edition of Sainsbury's magazine the other day (just for ideas) and they had a strawberry tart - in December!

Should have plenty of veg and fruit still for you all. And Aunty Jean's faggots of course, though S ate the tripe while I was in the UK (thankfully!)

Anyway, we are all ready for you. Dawn has finally got the marzipan off Anne (who wanted to make it) so she can do the icing on the cake. I think they almost came to blows over the delay. My cake has had so much alcohol poured over it that it may self-ignite near a naked flame!

We almost have our final numbers. Just need to book restaurants for our meals on

TOMATO, FIG & PUMPKIN JELLY

Thursday and Friday and sort transport for the hen do.
See you very soon
Love to the three abuelas (grannies). Can't wait to see you all
Love you tons and tons
Xxxxxxx
PS Weds film night... had to make up our own happy ending again! Xx

Diary Friday 6th August Still hot
S started on the electrics for the kitchen, unravelling the electricians' mess. They had used four core wires, somehow using two of the wires for one socket, the other two for the second, and there was no consensus as to which side the live wire was. And of course the sockets were all skewed... probably that big hammer used to put them in with. Prefer my electrician.
I tiled the kitchen wall. Not enough for the last row above where the cooker will go due to some poor measuring on my part. Laid the floor tiles in front of the horno together and S cut the edge tiles.
No buses available for our hen do. Last bus back here is 7.30pm! Jayne offered to be a driver and I will drive too so we should be okay.

Unfortunately, our wall tiles had come from France. Matching them in Galicia proved to be impossible. The French DIY store had stopped selling that line of tiles so that was also a dead end, despite CJ's sister begging the store to sell the last half dozen on display. In the end we found some similar, but not identical, tiles in a large discount tile store in England over a year later. Those half dozen tiles are all but invisible to anyone – except me.

AUGUST

Sunday 8th August 10pm. 25°C in the Sunroom!

Dear Mum,

  Thank you for your text. That is very kind of Aunt Irene though we really don't want people to send us money as we have enough, honest!

  Can you give me her address so I can thank her please? And would you mind paying the cheque into the bank there as it is difficult for us to cash UK cheques here. Also, S says he doesn't need the 'black sheep' booklet. You can keep it with our other paperwork! Our secretary will be wanting a pay rise haha.

  We have had a nice day out at the second bring and buy/car boot fair arranged by Mike and John. We sold some of the junk/antiques from the house and bought a jumper and a DVD. Overall a princely 3€ profit! I even sold some plums but still couldn't find any takers for the marrows. I have so many they are in danger of taking over the terrace entirely.

  There were lots of people at the sale and more Spanish this time, which was good. It's nice to see people we don't have chance to meet up with so often.

  We needed a rest! Last Thursday evening, 8pm, the man arrived with our second tractor load of firewood. He hadn't rung but we are used to that. He tipped the whole load in front of the drive as usual but unfortunately neither of us had remembered to move the car which was in the garage. This meant that if we wanted to go swimming on Friday, we had a large stack of wood to barrow and stack in a day. We got it done by 5pm on Friday. I'm sure we enjoyed our swim all the more.

Thursday am. Big black clouds passing overhead. S has tried saying 'I bet it won't rain' to provoke it but no luck so far!

We seem to have had a busy couple of days doing nothing. On Tuesday we were in the kitchen, painting the door and cocina surround, and trying to get done so we could go to Taboada pool for a swim, when I saw Maribel, our Spanish estate agent, coming down the path looking very smart as always. I was terrified of her brushing past the wet gloss paint with her elegant clothes on! She had brought us a wedding gift and insisted on paying her money for the meal. She asked if she has to wear a long dress. I said no, she always looks lovely but told her my aunty was bringing 6 or 7 new outfits. Maribel said she would need her own plane. Do tell Aunty Jan! She also thought the house was wonderful and asked why we didn't design houses for a living. I said I thought one was enough!

We did manage to get the painting finished in time and took a picnic down to the pool. We had a swim and stayed until about 8pm then had a drink at Bar Mencia

AUGUST

on the way home. Being the last night of the town fiesta we decided to walk back in later to hear the band (around midnight). Luckily, our neighbours caught us as we left the village so we got a lift in. The band weren't as good as Panorama. Too much talking, which of course I didn't understand anyway. The oldies were drifting away too as they wanted to dance. We met up with Geni and Paco and had a coffee with them, so it was 3am when we got home.

Yesterday we visited a local organic cheese-maker near to John and Fiona. He has a lovely place and lets three houses on the land too. They do cheese, yoghurt and milk (pasteurised rather than UHT). The houses are renovated using no artificial fibres, cements or paints. Puts us to shame, though goodness knows what it all cost.

We had lunch back at John and Fiona's then came home in time for tea. By the time we had watered that was another day gone.

I am off to post this. Jorge has rung to ask if we will meet him in town for a coffee so we are both going in.
Love you tons and tons
And see you very soon... must get my fingers out and finish this kitchen!
Xxx
Black clouds gone at 10am...oh well!

We were determined to get the kitchen, and the eating space by the outside oven (*horno*), finished for the arrival of our guests. The outside space in particular would be a lovely place to sit in the shade of another hot, August day. And, I have to admit, I was looking forward to showing off our hard work.

Diary Saturday 14th August Breezy but hot
S levelled the wooden draining boards around the sink. I finished laying the edge tiles in the horno and started grouting.
Lunch: Lasagne with spinach, marrow and cheese. Fresh figs for afters.
Made tomato chutney and plum ketchup. Mated white bunny with Carmen's buck.

Sunday 15th August 10pm. Last letter before you arrive. Still hot at the moment but probability of rain slightly higher for next weekend.
Dear Mum,
We seem to have another busy week ahead. On Tuesday, if it's nice, we are going to the outdoor swimming pool in Taboada again, then on to the Club Náutico to chase them about the lad's stag do.
On Wednesday we are going to a bar near Mike and John, and S is having a Spanish lesson with a friend of ours who is Spanish and used to be a teacher. And on Friday, we are meeting Cris and Steve, from Ortigueira, in Lugo to sort out the music for the big day.
Phew!
In between we plan to get the kitchen walls painted and then we will have to clean up for the grand visit.

AUGUST

You will be pleased to know that there is now a new brass handrail going up the steps, for the abuelas (not yet tested), and the wellies will be cleaned ready for you to use... they may be a good wedding attire choice if the goddess of the rainbow strikes again!

Last week was busy too, as I said in my letter, then on Friday Anne decided she was bringing a couple over who wanted to see CJ's friend Pete's house (he is selling it). I said I wasn't doing lunch again as we were too busy. They were supposed to arrive at 12.30pm but it was 2.30pm by the time they got here. I had told Gala we would be there for the key at 1pm so that wasn't good as she likes to be punctual.

We went to Bar Mencia for lunch. Anne was very pleased as Luisa had done a salad with carrots and veg in it... very unusual for Galicia. Luisa said it was a new recipe. We visited the house after lunch (having rung Gala to apologise) and that was the afternoon gone. Don't think the couple were interested in the house, but a cat and four kittens were hanging about and Anne was all for taking them home with her.

Today was our parish fiesta. The village has been busy with visitors all day. We had just sat down to lunch when Pepe (son of the lady we bought from) and his nephew arrived. We gave them a tour and he said 'we will buy it!' They said they were

TOMATO, FIG & PUMPKIN JELLY

impressed with what we have done, which was nice. Pepe told us he used to sleep in our bedroom. He loved the vaulted ceiling and the mirrored wardrobes.

We are still picking plums! The greengages are just starting to ripen so Aunty Jean may be in luck. I made some fig ice cream (very good) and have tried bottling some figs too. They go off so quickly once picked but are delicious, like pure honey. They are called honey figs and are yellow when ripe with a pale centre. Dawn has crystallised some of hers so I'll have a go at that too. I've also done a couple of jars of chutney.

Monday 9pm. Sunny. I have been making jam. Greengage today, and fig. Forgot to say how useful that jam funnel is that you bought me. Much less messy than spooning it into the jars and it cleans easily too. A good buy. Thank you.

I missed out our other visitors this week. A German couple who run a B&B and a plant nursery. They have offered to loan us some plants to brighten up the cultural centre, where we are getting married, and wanted to have a look at the room beforehand. Our Spanish friend, Clara, also rang today to say she is coming to the wedding.

I have started giving the invites to the neighbours. Pepe told us yesterday he had another wedding to go to that day. Concha said the same this morning. Must be a popular weekend.

AUGUST

Tuesday 10pm: Just finished watering in the dark.

We went to Taboada pool this evening. I had a swim, but someone wimped out and sat on the edge saying it was too cold. I said it was refreshing, though I admit I was a bit blue around the edges when I got out. We went to the boat club afterwards to confirm his table for the stag do, so he is sorted too.

The lad has been busy cleaning down the kitchen walls so we can paint them. They were filthy with years of smoke from the cocina.

I've made some plum cordial. Thought the non-drinkers might appreciate that. I think all the remaining plums fell off together this morning - had a full bucket of purple ones so I will have to think of something else to do with them.

Any recipes for plums, tomatoes, figs or pumpkin welcome. I am hanging marrows in the bottom barn to keep but have to contend with the bats flying around every time I go in there. Tell Belle she should get her wish to see some this time.

Tomorrow will be tomato sauce day (fantastic this year), and podding the older French beans (haricots) for casseroles. Our freezers are full already. I think this has been our driest year so far.

Worry not, we have transport arrangements sorted for your visit! Door to door service guaranteed. Tell Aunty Jean,

TOMATO, FIG & PUMPKIN JELLY

NO ONE rushes anywhere over here so she certainly won't hold anyone up. Though S says she can hold him up (i.e prop him up) on the day if she likes!
SEE YOU SOOOOON
Xxxxxxxxxxxx

The transport from the airport had been arranged, as I said. But, unbeknown to Mum we had a surprise awaiting them.

Worried about fitting everyone into the ageing Escort, I had asked Jorge if he would be able to collect our guests in his minibus. Not only did he happily agree, but he decided he would do a bit of ad-libbing too.

That week we managed to finish painting the kitchen and even persuaded some friends, who were flying back to Santiago, to collect our missing drawers and leg so we could actually complete our kitchen units before our visitors arrived.

Diary Sunday 22nd August Cloudy but very hot
Spent the day cleaning in preparation for our guests. Got the long table back out of the barn and onto the terrace. Made my special chocolate and walnut cake for the evening do.
Mopped floors, swept the kitchen and utility. All tidy.

Diary Monday 23rd. August Hot again, whole one millimetre of rain overnight!
Confirmed numbers to Luisa. Still not entirely sure what we are getting for the wedding breakfast but I am sure it will be fabulous! Booked Restaurant Anduriña for Friday lunch and ordered two empanadas from the bakery for Saturday evening. Carmen came round with Daniel, carrying another box of wine for us and a wedding present. It is a

AUGUST

reproduction water carrier in gleaming brass and wood with our initials on the front (so she does know what his name begins with then lol) and comes complete with a brass scoop. Carmen explained that these conical wooden containers were used to store water and keep it cool. They were often carried on the head from the nearest spring. It is quite beautiful... and the wine was very welcome too with so many guests coming.

Concha turned up later carrying a huge flat box. Another present. She says it is bedding. I am incredibly touched, but embarrassed as we don't expect people to spend money on us. Kath says it is how the Spanish are.

Mum, along with her sister Aunty Jan, my godmother Aunty Jean, and my beautiful niece Belle, were the first of the wedding guests to arrive.

Their flight was mid-morning on the Wednesday, but Jorge appeared at 9.15am with the minibus and wearing a rather fetching chauffeur's cap. As requested, I had made a board with the names of the four arrivals on it. Once at the airport, S and I hid behind the potted plants whilst Jorge, resplendent in cap, stood by the metal barriers, name board in hand.

I heard our party arrive. Aunty Jan was chattering away but was still the first to spot our friend.

"That's us! That's us!" She announced, pointing to the board.

Jorge moved into actor mode.

"I am to collect you but my English, she is not very good. I am told the one called Irish knows the way, yes?" He asked in an execrable accent.

"Oh, yes," said Aunty Jan. "Our Iris knows the way."

Poor Mum was cringing and trying to step away, but Aunty Jan was happily organising the party.

"Belle speaks Spanish," she said, this time pushing my niece into the firing line.

By this point I was almost wetting myself with laughter and had to come out of hiding.

"This is Jorge," I told everyone. "He's rather a good actor. Oh, sorry, you should see your faces."

"It's my sister," said Mum. "Look at her, telling him I know the way."

"Well, you should," said Aunty Jan, unrepentant. "You've been often enough."

"Yes, but I don't take that much notice."

"You should do then, what if you had to find your own way?"

I intervened before a full blown row started, and blame for that vase which was knocked off grandma's table some 60 years previously was laid at someone's door. Once these two got together they reverted to childhood. Belle also looked pleased to be let off the hook.

I escorted everyone outside, then sat on the front seat of the minibus giving them my tour guide routine as Jorge drove us home.

Thursday 26th August Actual drizzle!
Probably because more guests are arriving. Collected Mum et al for breakfast casa nosotros. Aunty Jean was still going on about how perfectly mashed the potatoes were yesterday. S' head will be fit to burst. She enjoyed her faggots too.

S' friends, known collectively as 'The Last of the Summer Wine', were due to arrive at midday. The four of them arrived in a tiny hire car. Steve was spitting feathers as he hauled himself out of the driver's seat.

"I asked for a bigger car, I mean, look at it. And some idiot nearly drove into us up the road. The lights were for us but he drove out of nowhere."

AUGUST

Oops. The junction at Monterroso is admittedly awkward for newcomers as all directions have a flashing orange 'proceed with caution' traffic light, which can be confusing.

Steve calmed down after a beer at one of the café tables while we waited for Judith and Les, S' best man and building buddy, to appear with the final Rochdale couple, Pete and Jeanine.

We had booked lunch at the Parillada San Martiño, just out of town, trying to ensure we distributed our business fairly over the wedding weekend. This grill-restaurant specialises in local *churrasco* and does a substantial *menú del dia* for an insubstantial price. They had seated us at a long table within easy viewing of the vast *parillada* grill which kept our guests fascinated whilst they ate their lunch.

Friday 27th August Back to Sunshine for brother's arrival
Invited the LoTSW over to us for breakfast, so long as they like eggs. They turned up carrying a dozen eggs they had bought that morning! Coals to Newcastle comes to mind.

The town was becoming a mini-England by the time my brother arrived on the Friday, in time for yet another 'Galician light lunch' as he dubbed the 3 hour *menus del dia* we inevitably had. We were worried whether Pip and Steve would get on. They were both outgoing, strong characters who tended to take charge. They would either love or hate each other. Luckily for the party, it was the former and they became firm friends.

Our evenings were spent in Bar Scala, where they possibly had their largest turnover ever in a single week.

The first night, Mike insisted on asking for the bill. We'd had four rounds of drinks for 16 people, each round coming with platters of ham, cheese, and bread. All the lads were drinkers and the golden girls, as Mum and my two aunties became known, enjoyed a post-tipple brandy.

"*¿Cuanto costa?*" asked Mike.

Sandra, the waitress, told him it was 40€.

"No! Up!" said Mike, raising his palm in the air.

Sandra looked bemused.

"Sit down," said Mike. "Now, how much?"

"45 euros?" she stammered.

"No! More!" he said again.

This continued in the same vein until we told him to put the poor girl out of her misery and pay her. The wedding guests could not believe the prices here and the townsfolk still mention how generous the 'English' are.

The three golden girls also enjoyed the attention of more than a few of the elderly male population of the town. At times, there appeared to be more suitors than there were ladies... and I'm sure most of the gents had wives. That, of course, has never stopped a Spaniard flirting, and it was all taken in good fun.

Friday evening were to be the stag and hen dos. Friday morning, however, almost began with a disaster.

The 'phone rang early, as we were in the garden chatting following the shared breakfast *casa nosotros*. Over the usual crackly line I caught the odd phrase. '*boda*' and '*no se puede*' were enough to have my heart racing.

I ran to the wall above the track where there is a mildly better signal.

"What!" I yelled.

"The mayor is not available, he cannot do your wedding," the disembodied voice repeated.

Trying not to scream, I said I would be down to the town hall immediately. I loathe talking on the 'phone in Spanish. Especially when a catastrophe is looming.

AUGUST

At the town hall I paced the floor waiting for someone to be free. It was Pilar.

"What's happening?" I rabbited.

"Don't worry," she replied. "The mayor is double booked. Did you know that there is also another wedding in your village?"

Our tiny village of six houses? Another...? What was the chance of that happening? No, I didn't know. But now it made sense why Pepe and the others couldn't attend. What were we to do? Pilar calmed me by waving her hands.

"Isabel will marry you."

Isabel was the deputy or assistant mayor and very friendly. She is also tall, elegant, and beautiful. S was most happy with the swap.

That evening, we once more met in Taboada, at the Café Santa Lucia, before dispersing for our respective hen and stag dos. The agreement was for us all to meet back at Bar Scala at 11pm.

The 12 hens set off to Chantada in three cars. I was leading, but had inadvertently forgotten that it was fiesta weekend in Chantada. The main road through town was closed for the festivities. After living in Galicia for three years, closed roads no longer held any power over me. This is a snippet from our friend Linda's diary entry:

'Apart from a slight diversion where a road was closed, which Lisa ignored, we made it and parked.'

Me, ignore a closed road? Well, yes. I am a local, road closures don't count.

We did however have to walk along the river some little way to reach our destination. The golden girls managed admirably with the walk, though Anne complained bitterly most of the way.

By the time we reached the swimming baths, I was ready for my swim.

Half of our party settled for drinks in the bar whilst the rest of us dived into the gleaming, cool swimming pool. As I half-expected, my *abono* was only clipped for my swim. The others were magnanimously waved through for free.

Angela had gone to town for us. The buffet she produced was enormous. There were sandwiches, pizza and tortilla, *croquetas* and cold meats, breads and cheeses. In the background was some Spanish radio station.

Suddenly, there came the distinctive chords of the intro to my favourite ever album. I looked up in surprise as Jayne came back to the table.

"Your intended gave it to me as we left," she said. "He thought you might appreciate it!"

My wonderful spouse-to-be was still thinking of me.

We sat on the raised terrace outside the café and sang. We watched the darkness fall, and ate and drank. Each time we got near to finishing a platter or a bottle of wine, Angela was at our side filling them up. Linda's diary again:

'Some of us tried to dispose of the wine by spilling it over themselves! I tipped over my white wine but this was refilled. Unfortunately Jeanine spilt red wine onto her trousers. And ran with her towel between her legs to the toilet to wash it out. She returned in wholly wet trousers and had to change before going to Scala'

The photos of Jeanine in the toilets wringing out her trousers, kindly snapped by Linda, are wonderfully funny. As are those of me singing, rather passionately. Thanks Linda!

Things became a little raucous. My singing got louder and no one complained – which only goes to show that everyone must have been very drunk by that point.

It was way after 11pm when I looked at the time.

We decided, for some inexplicable reason, to take the remains of our feast back to the boys. Judith had a quarter bottle of wine tucked under her arm when

AUGUST

Angela called her back. She looked like a schoolgirl caught in the act of pilfering so I wandered back with her.

"I didn't think she'd mind," Judith said, waving her prize.

"I don't think she does, look!"

Angela had a five litre plastic container of wine in her hand. "I bought all this for you and you have not drunk any," she complained as we reached her, topping up Judith's bottle.

Now we had wine, and food, to try and give away.

The stags had apparently eaten a huge *churrasco* meal so were not in the least interested in yet more food. It seemed like more coals to Newcastle to take the stuff into Bar Scala, but that is what we did.

Saturday 28th August Glorious sunshine for our wedding day!
Took our witnesses into the town hall to sign in and show their passports. Belle was her usually calm and serene self. Les was nervous and already panicking about his speech.

S was to get changed in the hotel whilst Belle came to help me get into my wedding frock and do best woman type things. She turned up early carrying a bottle of cava.

"You have to have champagne for a wedding," she announced, looking stunning in a simple black and white polka dot dress.

Who am I to argue with my best woman? I did decline Belle's suggestion that she help me put on some makeup. S has never seen me with my face painted, and I wasn't about to shock him on our wedding day. She did do my hair though. My long hair almost reached my waist and was one of my best features. I wanted the sides plaited and fastened at the back with the rest flowing loosely.

TOMATO, FIG & PUMPKIN JELLY

We were just enjoying our second glass of bubbly when Carmen appeared carrying a bouquet of roses wrapped in foil. We offered her a cava but she declined. Maybe 11am was a little early.

We had just restarted when Judith came bursting in. It seemed S had forgotten to take the ring with him, and Les was in a tizzy about not being able to perform his duties as best man. S had been banned from returning to collect the ring by Judith. I pointed out that I would have brought it with me to the *casa de cultura* but she was insistent that things were done right.

By then I was happy to agree to anything, and by the time my brother arrived to collect us with Mike, one of the Last of the Summer Wine gang, riding shotgun, I was even happier.

I ordered the men to drop us off at the bottom of the main street in Taboada. I'd promised a number of our local friendly shopkeepers that I would walk through town in my dress and didn't want to disappoint. It felt like the entire population was watching us as we walked in the sunshine: me below my parasol, Belle carrying the roses. I held my brother's arm as I wobbled in the unaccustomed high heels.

Mike, meanwhile, walked backwards the whole way taking photographs.

As we entered the coolness of the hall, the wedding march from Aida began and I grinned inanely at our friends and relatives lining the 'aisle'. S was slumped in a chair at the front. He told me afterwards that we were a good 40 minutes late, and his mates were ribbing him that I'd got cold feet.

"Did you think that?" I asked.

"Of course not. I knew you'd be late."

Isabel was lovely. She had prepared a story about not rocking the boat which Kath translated beautifully, though by that point the cava was kicking in. I managed my '*consiento*' at the right

AUGUST

point whilst S settled for a '*si*, yes, *consiento*' which I think amounts to saying 'I do' three times.

"And now, we are married," announced Isabel in heavily accented English.

S grinned. "Ooo, that's nice!"

To this day he maintains that Isabel is his 'other' wife.

To celebrate our union, and I think being the first foreigners to marry in the *concello*, Isabel presented us with a ceramic plaque of the coat of arms of Taboada town council. It has pride of place on our bookshelf.

Steve and Cris continued the music they had prepared, and I, at last, took a look around the hall. The normally barren space looked wonderfully festive. Our German friends, Barbara and Martin had brought two large standard box trees trimmed with bright ribbons. Others had brought daisies and begonias, pansies and roses. More cava flowed freely at the back of the hall and everyone mingled, chatting, until it was time for lunch.

We walked outside the hall to be met with a hailstorm of rice hitting us smack in the face. It appeared that Luis, from Bar Scala, had asked some of the wedding guests whether they had rice. On receiving a negative reply, he had kindly (or not, depending on if one was on the receiving end) produced a couple of one kilo bags. I am still planning my revenge for that particular act.

My sister-in-law was particularly violent in her throwing as evidenced from a couple of photos which show her, arm pulled back, wicked grin on her face, ready to hurl the grains as we duck and cringe. Within minutes the road had turned white, and thankfully the rice had run out. We left the pigeons to their feast and walked down the street to Bar Mencia.

Luisa had done us proud. The upstairs dining room was transformed with a long top table and two 'arms' running the length of the floor, making a large 'U' shape. She had hired a girl and a boy to wait on, and the tables were decorated with ribbons and snowy cloths. There were platters of hors d'oeuvres lined up along the tables; seafood salad, Russian salad, the 'new' carrot salad, olives and other nibbles. The cake sat behind us, decorated with satin and beads. Our two plastic frogs, symbol of our old jobs, and of our union, sat astride it.

Wine was poured and more food arrived. Luisa's homemade *Albóndigas* in the *Galego piquante* sauce.

Once that was finished, our two young servers came bearing platters of pork which they freely distributed. The non-meat eaters had salmon or hake.

As we ground to a halt, someone pointed out that they still had their knife and fork.

"Is there more to come?" they asked.

I had to admit that I didn't actually know. Our agreements over food had been vague to say the least, beyond my argument that ten euro a head was not enough and that I would pay her 15. I think I may have said something along the lines of 'do what you can with that'. To a *Galega* that is tantamount to a challenge.

More meat arrived, this time lamb. A few people were declining and the young waiter was looking worried. I was talking when he arrived by my side so he triumphantly lowered the biggest piece of meat he could find onto my plate.

After dessert I threw my bouquet towards our friend Mike. He happily caught it and placed it in his top pocket. Just three months later he and his long term partner, John, also said '*consiento*' here in Galicia.

S and I cut the cake together, tangling the knife in the beads strung over the icing and giggling like five year olds, but no one had space to manage a piece so it went home for later.

AUGUST

There was not a dry eye in the house as S gave his speech...

"I know I have made one woman very happy today." He paused, infinitesimally, "Lisa's mum."

Les managed his speech, although his nervousness showed. Mike, never nervous of public speaking, helped out by making a long rambling speech on behalf of the Last of the Summer Wine group.

That evening we had organised a shared picnic back at *A Casa do Campo* – or rather Anne had organised it. My plan had been for people just to turn up with whatever they wished to bring. Anne was more organised – telling each guest what they were expected to contribute. She was also more than a little stressed by that point, which was not the idea at all.

All our guests went back to their hotel, or home, or hung around in Taboada drinking coffee for a couple of hours so the newlyweds could, well, relax. All that is except Anne, who had things to prepare for the evening buffet. Despite the 30°C heat, Anne plated up her prawns and fish bites. I spent most of the evening warning guests not to eat them for fear of causing an outbreak of botulism poisoning.

Despite, or because of, Anne's organisational skills, the evening was a lovely extension of the day, with music, eating and drinking, and laughter. When Aunty Jean asked if she could possibly have a cup of tea it sparked requests from a whole section of party goers.

The end of the day brought a magnificent sunset over the house. The perfect end to a surprisingly perfect day.

§

This wasn't the end of the festivities though. Our wedding celebration was to carry on for the next few days.

TOMATO, FIG & PUMPKIN JELLY

On the Sunday, we had booked the party in for lunch at Maribel's beautiful *bodega* overlooking the river Miño. The sun was blinding as we set off in four cars along the winding roads towards lunch. The three hire cars (all tiny Peugeots) were red, white and blue. We looked like a procession from the Italian Job, winding our way ever onwards.

Maribel had laid out a wedding table inside the *bodega*. But there was no way the Brits were going to eat indoors on a beautiful sunny Sunday afternoon, so everything had to be transferred to the picnic tables outside.

In the *bodega*, José's *jamones* hanging from the rafters, and the soot blackened walls, fascinated the visitors. Beer and sunshine, *churrasco* and *queimada*, all helped encourage our guests to fall in love with this beautiful area.

I gave my wedding speech that day, in which I thanked Ryanair for allowing everyone to arrive on time, and S for allowing me to do the talking for a change. That drew a laugh from those who know us – can't think why!

My brother made a return speech, praising the golden girls and praising Galician light lunches and light dinners. He also praised me for wearing a dress.

My aunty then sang. Aunty Jan was, many years ago, a professional singer and has the most beautiful soprano voice. (What is it with this family and singing – why did I not inherit this trait?) Aunty Jan sang *This is My Lovely Day* which was absolutely stunning with the backdrop of the Miño behind and her voice soaring into the sunshine.

Not to be outdone, Maribel and her son, Pablo treated us to a number of Spanish songs and we ended appropriately with a rousing rendition of *Land of Hope and Glory*.

From the *bodega* we wound our, rather longer than I had envisaged, way to the local river beach.

AUGUST

My brother, having a short attention span, got bored well before we arrived at *A Cova* and started to blow his horn in time to some internal music. This of course set off everyone else. By the time we arrived, the cacophony was horrendous.

Thankfully there was no one to complain. We swam and paddled in the cool clear water of the Miño, ate ice creams and pondered on another 'lovely day'.

§

"That was the best week," I murmured sleepily.
"Mmm," replied Stewart, my husband.
"They said we couldn't do it."
"Mmm."
"We showed the Spanish bureaucracy didn't we?"
"Mmm."
He was waking up, I could tell.
"I wonder what we should do next?" I continued.
"Mmm, sleep?"
"Mum loves it here you know."
"But she won't move over, she's said so." He had given up trying to sleep.
"Well..."
"Oho!" My wonderful blue-eyed husband knew well that click of cogs whirring. "Just leave it, eh?"
"Maybe if we found her a house?"
"She's said she won't leave Aunty Jean."
Too late. My mind was busily planning how we could persuade Mum to maybe, just maybe change her mind. I knew she would really, really enjoy it here in our little bit of paradise, if she only gave it a chance!

The story continues in…

Chestnut, Cherry & Kiwi Fruit Sponge
A final year to write home about
– & Mother makes 3 in Galicia

Tuesday 23rd June 10pm. Cloudy. Huge thunderstorms, Sat/Sun/Mon and electric off overnight.

Dear Mum,

What a busy week we are having!

Saturday, we had that thunderstorm whilst I was talking to you then unexpected visitors later on – but more on that in a bit.

On Sunday, we had friends over for dinner, lovely afternoon, they didn't leave until 7pm. Then we had another big storm. Monday, CJ came over for tea and cake.

Then, this morning, we met Leo and Margaret in Melide. They had kindly agreed to act as translators for us. We all met Pepe and Mercedes, our visitors from Saturday, at their house, and after we had sorted everything out, they took us for lunch. We didn't get home until 5pm but no thunderstorm tonight as yet.

Oh, yes, I haven't told you what we were actually doing today yet have I? Must be getting forgetful…

We bought a house. In this village to be exact.

The story continues in...

Now we are the proud owners of not only A Casa do Campo but A Casita do Campo too! The neighbours think we are crazy but that is nothing new.

The house has been empty a while and the garden looks like something out of sleeping beauty after the 100 years but it has a lovely view down the valley and will be a nice two bed cottage... eventually.

Now we just need a tenant.

Look forward to speaking with you on Saturday, as I say it's been a busy week and it's still only Tuesday!
Love you tons and tons
Merry Christmas! Hope you like your present!
XXXXXXXXXx

What do you do when you have almost, but not quite, finished renovating one ruin?... Buy another one of course!

After seven years living in the remote northwest of Spain, Lisa and husband S are finally getting near to completing the renovations of their stone farmhouse. They have no intentions whatsoever of buying another house, never mind another ruin, but that is exactly what they do.

It's all in a good cause – Lisa's mum, Iris, has finally agreed to move to Galicia. Now they have a year to make this ruin habitable before *La Jefa* arrives, with 63 years' worth of household possessions in tow.

TOMATO, FIG & PUMPKIN JELLY

The bumper third book of the *Writing Home* series, *Chestnut, Cherry & Kiwi Fruit Sponge*, follows two more wonderfully witty and food-filled years in Galicia:

Join us for more building, more bureaucracy, and much more fun, when Mother makes three in Galicia.

Coming soon...

For updates and free offers follow me at

http://www.facebook.com/lisarosewright.author
http://www.lisarosewright.wixsite.com/author
http://www.twitter.com/galauthor_lisa
http://www.goodreads.com/author/show/20423710.Lisa_Rose_Wright

If you enjoyed this book, please consider leaving me a review on Amazon or Goodreads. Reader support is important to indie authors and I really appreciate your feedback.

Thank you,
Lisa

https://www.goodreads.com/book/show/55026981-tomato-fig-pumpkin-jelly
https://www.smarturl.it/TomatoFigPumpkin

To download your free photo album which accompanies the stories in this book month by month just follow the link below:

https://www.flipsnack.com/65E9E6B9E8C/tomato-fig-pumpkin-jelly-the-album.html

THE RECIPES

August: *Empanada*

We may not have eaten any of these Galician flat pies at our aborted *empanada* festival but they are easily found in any bread shop (*panaderia*) in Galicia. This recipe makes an 8" (20cm) round pie with plenty of filling and uses a lighter pastry which is still robust enough to be eaten by hand. I have used rabbit and *chorizo* as the filling here. Also popular is tuna, bacon and *chorizo*, or any seafood. You could even make a vegetable *empanada*... just don't tell a *Galego*!

For the filling: (Make the day before)
1 large onion, sliced thinly
1 red pepper, diced
1 green pepper, diced
1 clove garlic, minced
Olive oil
4 cocktail sized cooking *chorizos* diced
500g jar of tomato sauce or a tin of plum tomatoes*
2 boned rabbit loins or a boned chicken breast, cooked and cooled

Put the onions, peppers, and garlic in a heavy pan and fry very slowly in two tablespoons of olive oil until soft but not coloured. Add the *chorizo* pieces and fry until the paprika flavoured oil begins to run. Add the tomatoes and continue cooking on a very low heat, uncovered, for up to four hours until very thick and dark.
Cool, then place in the fridge overnight.
Note: You will probably have more filling than you need but any excess makes a wonderful snack on toast or with pasta.

TOMATO, FIG & PUMPKIN JELLY

For the dough:
30g butter
20g lard or solid vegetable fat
75ml white wine
75ml water
300g plain flour
A pinch of salt

Put the two fats in a pan with the wine and water. Heat until the fats are just melted.
Put the flour and salt in a large bowl. Make a well in the centre and pour in the melted liquid. Stir to form a soft dough then tip out and knead lightly until the dough forms a smooth ball. Wrap in cling film and leave in a cool place for an hour or more.
Cut the dough in half and roll each piece into an 8in (20cm) diameter round.
Add the thickened tomato filling to one round, leaving a half centimetre gap around the edge. Chop the rabbit or chicken meat and sprinkle evenly over the sauce filling. Cover with the second half of dough and pinch or crimp the edges to seal. Brush the top with beaten egg and cook at 180°C for 45 minutes.
Traditionally, *empanadas* are baked on the floor of the stone-built, wood-fired bread ovens found throughout Galicia. This gives the base a nice crisp texture. If you have a pizza stone this is ideal to cook the *empanada* on, or heat a baking sheet in the oven whilst preparing the pie and slide it onto that to cook.
Best eaten hot or warm. Allow the pie to cool for five minutes before slicing. This will feed eight as part of a buffet or far more as a mixed *tapas* plate.

*I use my homemade tomato sauce in this recipe but since the cooking time is so long a tin of plum tomatoes will cook down to the same rich flavour if you don't happen to have your own handy.

THE RECIPES

September: *Carne ó caldeiro*

This is the dish Don Pepe served us in his *bodega* many years after the events in this book. It is such a traditional *Galego* dish: typically simple to make, *carne ó caldeiro* relies on good ingredients, long cooking and the important accompaniments of sweet paprika, olive oil and earthy Galician IGP (*Indicación Geographical Protectado*) potatoes, to turn it into a real winner.

Ingredients for four people:
1kg veal skirt, with the bone attached, cut into serving sized pieces
500g firm but floury potatoes. The Galician grown Kennebec are excellent for this dish
A piece of *unto* (the fat from a pig, or use lard)
Sweet or hot paprika, olive oil, and salt to taste

Bring a large pan of water to the boil. Add the meat and the *unto* or fat, together with a good pinch of sea salt. Reduce the heat to a slow simmer and cook for one to two hours (it won't hurt being left longer) until the meat is silky soft and falling from the bone. Add the potatoes to the pan and cook for 15 to 20 minutes until soft but not falling apart.
Place the beef and the potatoes (called *cachelos*) on a serving platter with a little of the broth poured over. (Save the rest of the cooking broth for a flavourful stock.) Sprinkle with paprika and a little sea salt and pour over a good glug of olive oil.
Put the condiments on the table for guests to add more to their taste.

By the way, *Galegos* are not big on vegetables but Padrón peppers (April) go wonderfully with this dish.

TOMATO, FIG & PUMPKIN JELLY

October: *Paella*

I enjoyed the *paella* at the *Anduriña* restaurant in Taboada so much that José Manuel, the chef, invited me back to see how it was made. I had a lovely morning watching José at work and got to bring a portion of *paella* home.
This recipe makes enough for ten people but the sums are easy. 100g rice per person and 300 millilitres of stock.

20 short pork ribs
20 chicken wings
2 cloves of garlic and 2 large onions, sliced
¼ litre olive oil
1kg short grain rice
20 baby squid or squid rings
40 mussels (cleaned)
1 large tomato grated or chopped finely
A pinch of saffron strands or ¼ tsp turmeric
200g peas
3 litres fish stock
1 lemon

Fry the ribs until the fat runs. Tip off any excess fat leaving a tablespoonful in the pan then add the chicken wings, onion and garlic. Fry gently. Remove the meats once browned and keep warm. Add the chipirones or squid rings to the pan. Fry until coloured then remove. Keep warm.
Add the olive oil, rice, grated tomato and saffron liquid. Stir so the rice is completely coated in the oil then add the stock.
Cook slowly without stirring until the stock is almost used up. Add the juice of a lemon, the mussels and the peas. Put the meat and squid back in. Cook until everything is piping hot.
Cover loosely with foil and keep warm until ready to eat.

THE RECIPES

November: *Tarta de castañas*

November is chestnut month here in Galicia. There are plenty of chestnut based festivals going on and locally the 11th November is *Magosto*, the Galician equivalent of the Celtic festival of Samhain. This chestnut cake is similar to ones served across Galicia at this time of year. It is delicious with ice cream, cream, or on its own.

For a 20cm (8in) deep cake:
250g chestnuts cooked and peeled, or use unsweetened chestnut puree
200ml whole milk
150g ground almonds
4 eggs, separated
180g butter, softened
200g sugar
100g plain flour
1½ tsp bicarbonate of soda
Cocoa and icing sugar to dust

If using fresh cooked chestnuts, simmer them in the milk for 15 minutes then blend until you get a smooth cream. If using chestnut puree, simply blend with the milk. Cool.
Beat the egg yolks, butter and 170g sugar until well blended. Stir in the chestnut cream.
In a large bowl mix the flour, ground almonds and bicarbonate of soda then beat in the chestnut cream mixture.
Beat the egg whites until stiff. Add the remaining 30g sugar, a tablespoon at a time, beating between each addition until they are stiff and white. Fold into the cake mixture then spoon into a deep 20cm round springform cake tin. Bake at 180°C for 30 minutes or until set in the middle.
Sprinkle with cocoa powder and icing sugar.

TOMATO, FIG & PUMPKIN JELLY

December: *Lentejas*

This is the *Galego* equivalent of chicken soup and is a standard *menú* option in many restaurants. You can't beat a good thick warming bowl of lentil soup when it's cold outside.

Ingredients for 2 people:
250g green or brown lentils
1 onion, peeled, whole
1 carrot, peeled, whole
4 cloves of garlic, peeled, whole
1 bay leaf
750ml cold water
100g cured *chorizo*, sliced
50g cooked ham, in small chunks
50g bacon, cooked and sliced

Put the lentils, onion, carrot, garlic and bay leaf into a large pan and add the water. Bring to the boil, skimming off any froth. Cook slowly until all the vegetables are very soft.
Remove the bay leaf then blend the vegetables to a puree with a little of the water and half the lentils. Mix the puree back into the pan, add the cooked meats and *chorizo* and reheat until piping hot.
Serve with chunks of fresh *Galego* bread.

THE RECIPES

January: *Pinchos morunos*

This staple of *tapa* menus throughout Galicia, is delicious. Think mini kebab skewers of pork, bacon, *chorizo* and onion. Traditionally a Moorish dish, pork would definitely not have been an original ingredient though it is a favourite here in the land of the pig. You could use chicken or lamb, or even make a vegetarian kebab with chunks of onion, peppers, aubergine and courgette, though I don't believe I've ever seen such a thing in Galicia!

Ingredients for 24 mini skewers:
1kg lean pork (fillet or loin) cut in to centimetre cubes
12 mini cooking *chorizos*, sliced thickly
12 rashers of bacon, rolled and cut in halves
1 onion par boiled whole then cut into 8
24 short wooden skewers, soaked

For the marinade:
125ml olive oil
Juice of one lemon
3 cloves of garlic, minced
2tbsp sweet paprika (or use a mix of sweet and hot paprika)
2tbsp cumin
Pinch of saffron threads
Salt and pepper

Mix the marinade ingredients in a glass dish. Add the pork cubes and refrigerate overnight.
Thread the pork on to 24 small skewers interspersing with the *chorizos*, onion slices, and bacon rolls. Brush with the leftover marinade and grill or barbecue for five minutes until cooked through. Turn regularly, brushing with more marinade as necessary.
Serve hot as part of a mixed *tapas* plate.

TOMATO, FIG & PUMPKIN JELLY

February: Rabbit stew

Many people have an aversion to eating rabbit. This is a shame because rabbit is one of our best lean meats with a delicious, slightly sweet taste. Commercial breeds also grow remarkably quickly, meaning we have food for the table in less than three months. Many rural *Galegos* keep rabbits at home along with pigs and chickens.
If you really can't face eating a bunny this recipe can be made with chicken, though the flavour is different.

For four people (with leftovers):
2 rabbits, skinned and jointed*
Offal from the rabbits – liver, kidneys and heart
A bunch of thyme
1 large onion sliced
2 cloves garlic, chopped finely
Olive oil
Sweet paprika to taste
2 carrots, sliced
1 large beefsteak tomato
Three thick rashers of bacon each cut in to four
A bottle of fruity white wine.

First make up the offal skewers. On four wooden skewers put a piece of liver, a kidney, three pieces of fat bacon, two pieces of rolled up belly with a sprig of thyme inside and half a heart.
Fry the skewers in a little olive oil until the bacon fat begins to run. Continue to fry for a further two minutes then remove to a large heavy bottomed casserole dish (I use my Le Cruset Marmitout which I couldn't live without).
In the same frying pan, fry the rabbit joints in a little more olive oil until golden brown all over. This will

take ten minutes or so. Don't rush the process. Place the rabbit joints on top of the offal skewers.

In the same pan, fry the onion and garlic, together with a teaspoonful of sweet paprika (or to taste), until soft.

Spoon the onion mixture on top of the rabbit joints. Add the sliced carrots, pour over a bottle of white wine (Galician if possible) and add a bunch of thyme. Grate a large tomato into the casserole, leaving behind the skin, cover tightly and cook for 2 hours in a moderate oven.

Serve the stew with fried potatoes and a Galician Albariño wine.

*Either get your butcher to joint each rabbit into eight pieces or do it yourself. Remove the two back legs at the hip. Remove the front legs at the shoulder, taking a portion of meat with them. Remove the belly flaps and cut each flap into two. Cut the saddle into 2-3 pieces depending on size.

TOMATO, FIG & PUMPKIN JELLY

March: *Torrijas*

This is the *Galego* equivalent of eggy bread or French toast. Maria at Bar Gema was frying these up as additional *tapas* when we visited one night. Delicious and simple.

Ingredients for 4 people:
2 eggs beaten
100ml red wine or sherry
4 tablespoons of cooking oil
4 thick slices of bread
Sugar
Cinnamon

Pour the beaten eggs into a shallow dish. Pour the wine or sherry into a second dish. Heat the oil in a non-stick frying pan until a crumb of bread sizzles when added.
Pass each slice of bread firstly through the wine and then through the beaten egg.
Fry each slice, turning once, until crisp, and golden on both sides.
Lay each slice onto a piece of kitchen paper to remove the excess oil, cut in half and pile onto a warm platter. Sprinkle with sugar and cinnamon.
Serve with a glass of Ribeira Sacra red wine!

THE RECIPES

April: *Pimientos de Padrón*

I'm not sure this can be classed as a recipe, it is so simple. But Padrón peppers (*pimientos de Padrón*) are such a classic Galician accompaniment or *tapa* that I had to include them here. The very best Padrón peppers are grown in Herbón which has a festival dedicated to them each August. Often called the Russian roulette of peppers, these small green delights are at their best from April onwards. Generally innocuous and sweet, the occasional one has a real hot kick! They go well as an accompaniment to *Carne ó Caldeiro* (September).

Ingredients for 2-6 people:
1Kg *pimientos de Padrón*
300ml olive oil for frying
Sea salt

Wash the peppers but leave the stalk intact. Dry thoroughly on paper towels.
Heat the olive oil in a heavy based deep pan or wok. It is ready when a cube of bread dropped in immediately starts to fizz.
Cook the peppers in batches until starting to blister. They only take a few seconds. Do not overfill the pan as this will make them soggy.
Drain on more kitchen paper then sprinkle with sea salt and serve immediately.

TOMATO, FIG & PUMPKIN JELLY

May: Rich Fruit Cake

Galicians don't seem to make cakes with dried fruit. Luisa was not at all sure what to make of our heavy, rich wedding cake. That seems a pity as Spain produces such a lot of excellent dried fruits.

This is Mum's Christmas cake recipe so it is in imperial measurements. It is full of dried fruits and brandy, keeps wonderfully moist for a long time, and tastes delicious. The brandy of course helps to preserve it. Traditionally the top tier of the wedding cake was kept for the couple's first christening. We ate all ours.

This recipe makes a 7" round cake but can easily be scaled up for weddings or parties.

1½lb mixed dried fruits such as raisins, currants, sultanas
6oz glacé cherries, halved
2oz nuts chopped. Almonds or walnuts are good
1 tbsp brandy or sherry plus extra for 'feeding' the cake
6oz plain flour
¼ tsp each cinnamon and mixed spice
6oz butter, softened
6oz brown sugar
Grated rind of half a lemon and half an orange, or use mixed peel finely cut if you prefer
6 medium eggs
1 tbsp black treacle

Grease a 7" deep cake tin then line with a double layer of greaseproof paper, leaving the paper slightly proud of the tin to form a collar. Use a piece of strong brown paper to form a second collar around the outside of the tin. This should stand an inch above the rim of the tin and helps prevent the cake darkening too much during its long cooking time.

THE RECIPES

Put the dried fruit in a large bowl and pour over the tablespoon of brandy or sherry. Leave to plump up while you continue.

Cream the butter, sugar, citrus rinds and black treacle in a large bowl.

Beat in the eggs, one at a time adding a little sifted flour after each addition.

Stir in the remainder of the flour and the spices then the fruit and any remaining soaking alcohol.

Spoon the cake mixture into the prepared tin and place in a cool oven for 2¾ to 3hours, testing after 2½ hours.

Mum always used to say this cake 'sings' in the oven. It does too! When it is cooked it stops singing and is silent. An easier way to check is to insert a metal skewer into the centre of the cake. It is ready when the skewer comes out clean.

Leave to cool on a wire rack then prick all over with a skewer. Pour a tablespoon of brandy or sherry over the cake then wrap tightly in muslin and put in a cake tin.

This cake will keep for a very long time. Feed it a tablespoon of brandy or sherry at two weekly intervals to keep it moist. And definitely don't drive after eating it.

TOMATO, FIG & PUMPKIN JELLY

June: *Albóndigas*

Tapas in Galicia are legendary, and large. These pork and beef meatballs form a staple *tapa* locally and are also often presented as a starter, when they come as a clutch with chips!

Ingredients for 60 small *albóndigas*:
2 eggs
2tbsp white wine
2tbsp milk
1 clove garlic, minced
2tbsp breadcrumbs
100g lean pork minced
750g beef minced
Salt and pepper
Flour to dust

Mix the ingredients (except the flour) in a bowl until well amalgamated. Leave to set in the fridge for 30 minutes then form into walnut sized meatballs using damp hands to prevent sticking.
Dust with flour and fry in batches until golden all over.
Set aside whilst you make the sauce.

Ingredients for the Galician sauce:
2 onions
4 carrots
1 green pepper
200ml white wine
1 tomato, skinned and chopped
1 clove garlic, minced
350ml good brown stock
200g peas

Chop the onions, carrots and green pepper into small pieces. Fry in a little olive oil until soft. Add the wine, tomato and garlic. Cook to reduce and thicken, then add the stock and peas.

Poach the meatballs in the sauce for 5 minutes until heated through.

Note: If you prefer a thicker sauce, the vegetables can be pureed with the stock before adding the peas. Add a tablespoon of cornflour mixed in a little cold water to thicken further.

TOMATO, FIG & PUMPKIN JELLY

July: Tomato, Fig & Pumpkin Jelly

I always maintain you can't have a party without jelly. Unsurprisingly, I had never made the cover recipe when I chose the title for this book. But I have set myself a challenge: to make an edible version of each cover recipe in this series (the titles by the way come from whichever produce we had the most of in the year in question – it makes for some interesting combinations!)
This is a highly-flavoured savoury, layered jelly with the figs giving an unexpected sweet note.

Ingredients for two individual jellies:
2 tsps of powdered gelatine
1 tin of plum tomatoes or use a good tomato soup
1 red birds' eye chilli (1 gives a nice kick but feel free to add more if you like heat!)
Confit figs or fresh figs, sliced
4oz cooked pumpkin. Or use unsweetened pumpkin puree
2 tbsps creamed coconut
½ tsp each ginger, cumin, allspice
2 small ramekins lined with clingfilm

For the tomato layer:
Chop the tomatoes and cook slowly, together with the whole red, birds' eye chilli until very soft and thick. Puree then pass through a sieve to remove the seeds. Set aside 4oz and keep the rest for another use. If using a tomato soup, simply heat 4oz of soup with the chilli until the latter is soft then blitz.
Keep the pureed tomato mixture warm while you dissolve the gelatine.

To dissolve the gelatine:
Put 2 tbsp of cold water into a bowl and sprinkle on 1 tsp of powdered gelatine.

THE RECIPES

Leave to swell without stirring then warm gently until the gelatine is completely dissolved and no crystals remain (over a bain marie is best). Do not stir as this can make the gelatine stringy. Test it has dissolved by swirling gently.

Mix the dissolved gelatine into the 4oz of still warm tomato mixture and stir until it begins to thicken.

Pour into two ramekins to fill halfway. Place in the fridge to set (approx. one hour)

For the pumpkin layer:
Any pumpkin can be used for this recipe though a bright orange one looks pretty.

Mash the cooked pumpkin flesh with 2 tbsps of creamed coconut and the spices. If using pumpkin puree, heat gently with the creamed coconut and the spices.

Remember a cold dish needs more spice than a hot one so adjust the spices accordingly.

Set aside 4oz of pumpkin mixture in a warm spot whilst you dissolve the other teaspoon of gelatine as above.

Once the tomato layer has set, pour the pumpkin layer on top. (Alternatively, you can make the jellies in separate shallow dishes and sit one on top of the other once they have set.)

Turn out onto a plate and decorate with sliced confit or fresh figs.

This makes a surprisingly tasty starter, or increase the amounts and use as a centrepiece in a mixed buffet.

Enjoy eating this book!

TOMATO, FIG & PUMPKIN JELLY

August: Chocolate and Walnut cake

This is not a Galician recipe but it is one of my favourite gluten free cakes. I once made it as a birthday cake for a friend who is a coeliac and was bemoaning the quality and price of supermarket gluten free baking. She declared it the best cake she had ever eaten. I hope you agree!

Makes a 9in (23cm) cake:
8oz (200g) walnuts, shelled
8oz (200g) dark chocolate
8oz (200g) unsalted butter
8oz (200g) sugar
4 eggs, separated

Grease a 9"/23cm diameter springform, deep, cake tin and line with baking paper.
Grind the walnuts and the chocolate together in an electric nut grinder or food processor. They can be ground coarsely or finely according to preference.
Cream the butter and 6oz (150g) of the sugar together. Beat in the egg yolks one at a time then stir in the ground chocolate and nuts.
Whisk the egg whites until stiff. Add the remaining 2oz (50g) of sugar and continue to whisk until thick and white.
Fold the egg whites into the chocolate mixture.
Spoon carefully into the prepared tin and bake for 45 minutes in a cool oven (150°C) or until a skewer poked into the centre comes out clean.
Leave to cool in the tin.
Serve alone or with cream. Either way it won't last long!

And in case you are wondering, yes, it's fattening!

A GLOSSARY OF ENGLISH WORDS

I write in British English, and at times, to Mum, in Midland's slang.

I soon realised, about three days after I published *Plum, Courgette & Green Bean Tart*, that not everyone speaks like what I do and that some folk don't therefore understand all of my utterances. I should have already known that, as I have a wide circle of friends here in Galicia of many nationalities with whom I sometimes have fun 'discussing' the meaning of certain words.

I should also have realised that putting a courgette (zucchini) on the front cover of my 'international best seller' may have caused misunderstanding. In my defence I had no idea the book would become an international best seller, nor in fact a best seller at all, when I devised the title.

I have had emails from a number of confused, and one or two irate, folk looking for answers. Luckily one of those very nice people agreed to help me compile a glossary for this, my second memoir.

And here it is: with my special thanks to Eileen Huestis for not only taking the time to write to me in the first place but for volunteering her time to help her fellow countrymen and women understand 'Lisa' speak. Also thanks to Mike Cavanagh in Australia and Susan Jackson in the US, and to my good friend Leo here in Galicia (though we will never agree on the true meaning of the word pancake).

Allotment – A remote piece of land for growing vegetables. Also called a *huerta* in Spain
Aubergine – eggplant
B&Q – a DIY store in the UK
Bap – burger bun
Barrowed/barrowful – wheelbarrowed/wheelbarrowful
Beetroot – beets

TOMATO, FIG & PUMPKIN JELLY

Biscuit – a biscuit is a hard sweet cookie
Blot your copybook – harm one's reputation (literally to make an ink blot in your notebook)
Boiled eggs and soldiers – soft boiled eggs in their shells with toast fingers (soldiers) to dip in... thus Eggy soldiers are toast fingers dripping with egg (nicer than it sounds!)
Butties/butty –a sandwich, or bread and butter
Candyfloss – cotton candy
Car boot sale – garage sale
Chuntering – muttering
Chawl – pressed pigs' head meat pate. Very tasty,
Chips – fries, hot chips
Chuffed – very pleased
Colliery – coal mine
Cool box – cooler or ice chest
Courgette – zucchini
Cuppa – a cup of (usually) very British tea. Or in our case normally a large mug
Duff – useless, not fit for purpose... in this case eggs unlikely to hatch
Elevenses – a snack eaten at eleven am or mid-morning
Faggots – English faggots are highly spiced pork and liver meatballs... definitely not the American term!
Flat - apartment
Gas hob – gas burner
Hen do – bachelorette party (hens and stags are female and male turkeys though what relevance that has to a pre-wedding party I have no idea!)
Hosepipe – garden hose
Jumper - sweater
Kiwi vines – Chinese gooseberries
Knickers – underpants or underwear
Loo - toilet
Lorry – semi-trailer
Marmite – a wonderful savoury spread full of B vitamins and totally addictive. A brewery by-product made very near to where I was born in England

A GLOSSARY OF ENGLISH WORDS

Marrow - a vegetable marrow. A type of pumpkin or gourd, usually long, green and striped.
Mash - mashed potatoes
Mizzly - a combination of misty and drizzly, fine rain
Mortaring - to push mortar into the joints of a brick or stone built house
Nosey - being a busybody
Petrol - gasoline
Pinny - apron
Postie - postman or mailman
Potty - traditionally a ceramic chamber pot kept under the bed for night time use
Prom - promenade, a walkway along the seafront
Prick out - to transplant the first tiny seedlings
Pudding - a sweet or sometimes savoury dish In Britain we have a sweet plum pudding or Christmas pudding but also a savoury Yorkshire pudding. The explanation for this term, in my Collins English Dictionary, covers half a page!
Roasties - roast potatoes or other root vegetables
Scrummy - delicious, yummy
Scrumping - stealing fruit from an orchard or garden
Secateurs - pruning shears for one-handed use)
Sloppy - a Midlands term for slushily sentimental
Stag do - bachelor party (see above)
Strim - to cut grass with a motor trimmer, weed eat
Swimming baths - swimming pool
The big smoke - London
Tatty - worn out or shabby
Tombola wheel –A large drum which is turned and tickets are picked out for prizes. A type of lottery wheel
Water butt - a large container for collecting rainwater
Wellies - rubber boots
Wilkos - a UK homeware store
Windscreen - windshield

Spanish/Galician words used throughout this book

Augardente (*aguardiente* in Spanish) – a Galician firewater, or moonshine, of varying quality and strength!

A Casa do Campo – the country house. The original name given to our stone farmhouse

Casa nosotros – our house

Churrasco – a huge Galician mixed grill of sausages, pork ribs and beef steak, often including seconds, thirds or even fourths should you manage it.

Cocina – a wood-fired range cooker

Empadronamiento – proof of residency in a particular council area

Fe de vida – certificate of life. The Spanish equivalent of a birth certificate and the cause of a lot of trouble for us

Horno – a wood-fired stone-built oven, usually outside and used for baking bread

Hórreo – grainstore. In central Galicia these are usually stone-built with wooden slatted sides and a stone overhang at the base to prevent mice and other pests spoiling the grain

Huerta – a vegetable garden (as opposed to *Jardín*, a flower garden)

Galego/a – a person from Galicia, a Galician male/female

Jefe/jefa – the boss (man/woman) often used in a light hearted way

Jamón/jamones – Spanish cured ham(s)

Vida dulce – sweet life or good life, my definition of our life here in Galicia

Xulgado – registry of births, deaths and marriages in Galicia

ACKNOWLEDGEMENTS

An Indie author can never succeed alone so here's my chance to say a great big thank you to all those wonderful people who have helped this book come to fruition.

To my beta readers, Julie Haigh, Val Poore, and Alyson Sheldrake. Thank you for daring to read the first draft and for your helpful comments. I hope this final version meets all your approvals!

To my US and Antipodean beta readers Mike Cavanagh, Eileen Huestis, and Susan Jackson for help compiling the glossary to foster Australian-US-British relations. I have learnt much of our common language!

To Maayan Atias (spacecadetstudio@yahoo.com) for her wonderful cover artwork once more. This series could not have been the success it is without her vision.

To the friendliest group on Facebook, We Love Memoirs, for support, and for lots of fun-filled hours when I should have been working but was instead online. If you love reading memoirs (or writing them), enjoy competitions and chatting with like-minded people, then I highly recommend this wonderful group. We can be found at http://www.facebook.com/groups/welovememoirs

To Mum for keeping eight years' worth of letters home (and there are still more!) As ever, without you this book would not have been possible – even though transporting boxes of said letters back to Galicia with you was… interesting!

To S, my blue-eyed husband, for alpha, beta and omega reading, and for actually saying 'I do'.

And to my readers – without you this book would just be another dream.

ABOUT THE AUTHOR:

In 2007 Lisa left a promising career as an ecologist catching protected reptiles and amphibians, and kissing frogs, to move to beautiful green Galicia with her blue-eyed prince (now blue-eyed husband).

She divides her time equally between growing her own food, helping to renovate a semi-derelict house (or actually two... but that's another story) and getting out and about to discover more of the stunningly beautiful area she calls home.

Lisa is happiest outside in her *huerta* weeding; watching the antics of her chickens; or in her kitchen cooking interesting recipes on her wood-burning range.

Tomato, Fig & Pumpkin Jelly is the second in the *Writing Home* trilogy. The series is available in paperback, eBook and free with Kindle Unlimited at Amazon stores worldwide.

For more details about Lisa, her life in Galicia, and her writing, go to her website at
http://www.lisarosewright.wixsite.com/author
or follow her on
Facebook
http://www.facebook.com/lisarosewright.author
or Twitter
http://www.twitter.com/lisarosewright.author

Printed in Great Britain
by Amazon